ISBN 978-1-250-08076-9

St. Martin's Griffin books may be purchased for educational,
business, or promotional use. For information on bulk purchases,
please contact the Macmillan Corporate and Premium
Sales Department at 1-800-221-7945, extension 5442,
or write to specialmarkets@macmillan.com.

First Edition: October 2015

10 9 8 7 6 5 4 3 2 1

The New York Times

CROSSWORDS ON THE ROCKS

Edited by Will Shortz

ST MARTIN'S GRIFFIN 🐝 NEW YORK

DIFFICULTY KEY

Easy:

Medium:

Hard:

ACROSS

1 PC connection means: Abbr.
4 Downloads for mobile devices
8 Floats through the air
13 Greenish blue
15 Country located in what was once the Inca Empire
16 Stan's partner in comedy
17 Instruments played at theaters during silent films
20 Tehran's land
21 Shrek, e.g.
22 Clock-setting standard: Abbr.
23 Singer with the 1963 hit "If I Had a Hammer"
26 Françoise, to François, maybe
27 Quantity: Abbr.
28 Guy's rental for a gala
29 Inactive, as a volcano
31 Drinker's party instruction, for short
33 Lay eyes on
35 Needle and cone producers
36 First president to live in the White House
40 Welles of "Citizen Kane"
43 Large coffee server
44 Sword handle
48 Understand speech without hearing
51 Letters on a wanted poster
53 Atlas page
54 "Micro" and "macro" subject, for short
55 Ha-ha producer in a sitcom
58 Sun. follower
59 "___ She Lovely"

60 Shakespeare character who says "I hate the Moor"
61 Why this puzzle is like "Seinfeld"?
66 Hurricane or blizzard
67 Hit on the noggin
68 Peeved state
69 Dresses in Delhi
70 Therefore
71 Earth-friendly prefix

DOWN

1 Detroit-based labor org.
2 Having ants in one's pants
3 Hand-held Mexican food
4 Likely (to)
5 Dispenser candy
6 Before surgery, informally
7 Increased rapidly, as troop numbers
8 Had on
9 "Solve for x" subj.
10 Traffic signaler near highway construction
11 Source of a metal once used for foil
12 Ensembles for six
14 Political commentator Colmes
18 Monogram letter: Abbr.
19 Ricelike pasta
23 File folder feature
24 Drunkard
25 Yoked animals
26 Pennsylvania Dutch speakers
30 45 or 78: Abbr.
32 Tennis's Borg
34 ___ Claire, Wis.
37 Area code lead-in
38 Tow
39 Egyptian symbol of life
40 Dixie school, affectionately
41 Cheese stuffed in stuffed shells

42 "And now a word from our ___"
45 Lennon song with the lyric "You may say I'm a dreamer . . ."
46 Terse
47 Toll road: Abbr.
49 The first "A" of 51-Across
50 Vienna's river
52 Going ___ (bickering)
56 Say
57 Pep rally cries
59 Many early PCs
62 Onassis who married Jackie
63 Complain, complain, complain
64 Yoko who co-produced 45-Down
65 Old Pontiac muscle car

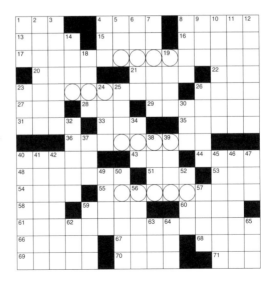

by Lynn Lempel

ACROSS

1 Wii ancestor, briefly
4 Barely bite, as heels
9 Stratagem
13 "Hooray!," to José
14 First rapper to win an Oscar for Best Original Song
16 Investment firm T. ___ Price
17 Up to, informally
18 Having the trajectory of a pop-up hit
19 Time on end
20 Player of a summer lilt
23 -
24 "Uh-huh"
25 Place to get a blowout
28 And others: Abbr.
29 Shows rudeness at checkout
31 Hearty steak
33 Went without
34 Tire meas.
37 Fury
38 Roman 155
39 Twisty road curve
40 Absorption
42 ___ breath (flower)
44 Jeopardy! or Facts in Five
46 Samoan capital
50 Big name in chicken
51 ___-de-France
52 Opponents of "shirts"
53 Cocktail stirrers
56 Pad see ew cuisine
58 Chevrolet model beginning in 1958
59 Holder of first-aid supplies
60 Score before deuce, maybe
61 Staple of Agatha Christie mysteries
62 German connector
63 Edifice: Abbr.
64 Eye problems
65 BlackBerry, e.g., for short

DOWN

1 "Gotta fly, sorry!"
2 Bring out
3 Pop star portrayed by J.Lo
4 Approaches
5 Hungarian patriot Nagy
6 Paltry
7 Bring to life
8 Kind of a place to the right of a decimal
9 Advanced algebra class, informally
10 Resemble
11 Not lease, say
12 "You bet!"
15 Sched. maker
21 Kind of movie
22 Org. with the song "Anchors Aweigh"
26 Kind of a place to the left of a decimal
27 Oscar nominee Beatty and others
29 Chick of jazz
30 "You don't say!"
32 Pageant wear, at times
34 Tap in, perhaps
35 Full of life for one's age
36 "So the story goes . . ."
38 Was a snap
41 Promising
42 Colorful play area for kids
43 H. H. Munro pseudonym
45 Thingies
47 Learn . . . or a word that can precede the ends of 20-, 29-, 44- and 53-Across
48 How some nonmonetary payments are made
49 Helper in preparing the govt.'s legal case
52 "South Park" kid and others
54 Pep
55 ___ gin fizz
56 Web browser feature
57 Cholesterol abbr.

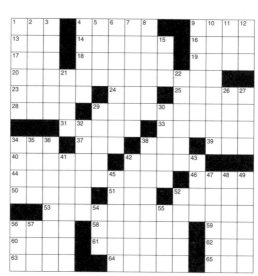

by Alex Bajcz

ACROSS

1 Secret stash
6 Doorframe's vertical part
10 Water, in Latin
14 Buenos ___
15 Dial button sharing the "0"
16 Big oafs
17 Samsung Galaxy or BlackBerry
19 1953 Leslie Caron musical
20 Number after Big or top
21 Two cents' worth
22 CBS police drama that debuted in 2003
23 Be hot under the collar
26 Green ogre of film
28 Carriage puller
31 Where oysters and clams are served
34 It's beneficial
37 Beneath
39 "___ your head!"
40 "That's rich!"
41 Devious trick
43 When repeated, a Latin dance
44 Turkish official
45 Jimmy who works with Lois Lane
46 Worker with an apron and a white hat
48 Go carousing with a drinker, say
50 Archaeologist's find
52 Trails
54 "Sic 'em!"
58 Makes a pick
60 Book of the world
63 Guy's date
64 It's beneficial
65 What an optimist always looks on
68 ___ of Sandwich
69 Comfort
70 Witty Oscar
71 Unit of force

72 "___ the night before Christmas . . ."
73 Does as told

DOWN

1 Selects for a role
2 'Til Tuesday singer Mann
3 Machine at a construction site
4 "Tell Laura I Love ___" (1960 hit)
5 Suffix with winning
6 Chief Justice Roberts
7 Individually
8 Hostess's handouts
9 Fellow members of a congregation
10 Never-before-seen
11 Easily made profit
12 Hybrid citrus fruit
13 In its existing state
18 Dockside platform
24 Start of many band names
25 Hurry, with "it"

27 Melted cheese on toast
29 Figure (out)
30 Go in
32 Tennis legend Arthur
33 Backside
34 Vengeful captain
35 Long, involved story
36 Abrupt left or right
38 All over
42 Kindergarten learning
47 Statute
49 Give a hard time
51 Mascara target
53 Something to stick in a milk shake
55 Able to move well
56 G.M. luxury car, informally
57 Some German/Swiss artworks in MoMA
58 Newspaper think piece
59 ___ on words
61 Bart's intelligent sister
62 Years on end

66 Number of points scored by a safety
67 Bro or sis

by Gary Cee

4

ACROSS

1 Big shindig
5 Plaid-clad miss
9 Southpaw
14 Arab chieftain: Var.
15 BP sale of 2013
16 Required reading for a classics major
17 1987 Buster Poindexter hit
19 You might pick up good ones from people
20 Tattoos, informally
21 Vegetarian's no-no
22 Wall St. watchdog
23 1980 Bob Seger hit
28 It may be picked by the picky
29 Delete, as from an article or video
31 Times before eves
34 Agricultural apparatus
36 Italian monk's title
37 Local news feature suggested by the answers to 17-, 23-, 48- and 60-Across
41 Animal that bugles
42 Burp
43 Lead-in to boy or girl
44 Go way past one's usual wake-up time
46 Defense grp. founded in Bogotá
48 1971 Bill Withers hit
54 15-Across product
55 Patella's place
56 Fist bump
57 Bit of mistletoe
60 1977 Foreigner hit
62 Steinway or Baldwin
63 Not a facsimile: Abbr.
64 Went like hell
65 Guitar players in rock bands, slangily
66 Novel conclusion?
67 Sport-___ (vehicles)

DOWN

1 Brazilian state northeast of São Paulo
2 Honor ___ thieves
3 Alaskan panhandle city
4 Title for a princess: Abbr.
5 Newest news
6 Enlightened Buddhist
7 Writer Turow
8 Bar habitué
9 Firecracker
10 Draw out
11 Little lie
12 ___ Bo
13 QB's stat.
18 Upscale hotel company
22 Passover feast
24 Part of M.I.T.: Abbr.
25 Spartan serf
26 Jack Sprat's dietary restriction
27 Limp Bizkit vocalist Fred
30 "See ya!"
31 Bowls over
32 Gal's guy
33 George who played Sulu on "Star Trek"
34 2009 Sacha Baron Cohen comedy
35 Patriots' grp.
38 Shape of the British 50-pence piece
39 CNN's Burnett and others
40 A.T.M. supply
45 V-8, e.g.
46 Keyed up
47 Cruising
49 Cousin of culottes
50 Dark
51 Numbskull
52 Mother-of-pearl
53 Modern pentathlon equipment
57 Place for sweaters?
58 Fotos
59 Aries animal
60 Cedar Rapids college
61 Early Beatle Sutcliffe

by Tracy Gray

ACROSS

1 "___ all she wrote"
6 Poe bird that quoth "Nevermore"
11 "Disgusting!"
14 Opulent
15 Without company
16 Playfully shy
17 "To recap . . ."
18 Sound familiar
20 Suffix with orange or lemon
21 "See ya!"
23 Timber wolf
24 "Stop being such a pompous jerk!"
29 Russian city on the Ural
31 Grassy cover
32 Aye's opposite
33 Get out of bed
34 Represent
37 "Zoinks!"
39 Actress Sandra of "A Summer Place"
40 "Will you please hurry?"
44 Physically strong
45 Multigenerational story
46 Sonnets and haikus
47 Some: Fr.
49 Gunderson on "The Simpsons"
50 One whose work is taxing, for short?
51 Meadow bird
52 Extremely cool, in slang
57 Begin to come out of sleep
59 Play it by ___
60 Hurry
61 Do a job with minimal effort
65 Daybreaks
67 Hooey
68 Dodge
69 Came out of sleep
70 Special ___
71 Train station
72 Full of the latest

DOWN

1 Group of three
2 Language of Delhi
3 Adrift, say
4 Lao-___
5 Relationship between barnacles and whales, e.g.
6 Stood on hind legs, with "up"
7 Boxer known as "The Greatest"
8 ___ Trapp family of "The Sound of Music"
9 The "E" of E.S.L.: Abbr.
10 Best Actress Oscar winner Patricia
11 Frozen structure that facilitates animal migration
12 World's largest amphitheater
13 Former Senate minority whip Jon
19 Lout
22 Since Jan. 1
25 Aspiring atty.'s exam
26 50%
27 Hourly compensation
28 When repeated, a child's taunt
30 Play for ___
34 Horrible
35 What may have a "no bull" policy?
36 Cylindrical alternative to French fries
38 Sharply dressed guy
41 Kind of palm
42 End-of-week cry
43 2014 biblical title role for Russell Crowe
48 "Canvas" for tattoos
50 "___-ching!"
53 Basic belief
54 "That's amazing!"
55 Pig sounds
56 Ken who wrote "One Flew Over the Cuckoo's Nest"
58 ___ instrument
61 Expert
62 "Nobody Knows the Trouble ___ Seen"
63 Faucet
64 Words of commitment
66 Amazement

by Michael Hawkins

6

ACROSS

1 Walked into the shallow end of a pool
6 Univ. V.I.P.
10 Meat stamp
14 Make giggle
15 Cassino cash, once
16 Close
17 Informal eateries with Mexican fare
19 Meat-and-potatoes dish
20 "Naughty, naughty!"
21 Corn cake
22 50 minutes past the hour
23 Blue-turfed home for Boise State football
27 Dunces
29 The Rolling Stones' "Get ___ Ya-Ya's Out!"
30 King Kong, for one
31 The Big Easy
32 "MMMBop" band
35 Beef cuts named for a New York restaurateur
41 Napped noisily
42 The "A" of N.A. or S.A.: Abbr.
43 Inits. in a military address
46 Percent add-on?
47 Ontario's second-largest city
49 Service site with a star
53 Peter of "Everybody Loves Raymond"
54 Unwrinkler
55 Alternative to a spinner in a board game
58 Ship in the search for the Golden Fleece
59 Unexpected expense . . . or a feature of 17-, 23-, 35- and 49-Across?
62 Rackful in a closet

63 "A Death in the Family" novelist
64 1933 Physics Nobelist Schrödinger
65 Avec's opposite
66 Cap'n's underling
67 "Parks and Recreation" woman

DOWN

1 Unit often preceded by kilo-
2 Amo, ___, amat . . .
3 Platypus feature
4 That, to Tomás
5 Ruler who rules by force
6 White, as vin
7 Sal of "Giant"
8 Former fort on Monterey Bay
9 These: Fr.
10 Saw to a seat, informally
11 Country music's Twain
12 Minor melee

13 Opposite of away
18 Cargo measures
22 Medium deck?
24 Wanders
25 Church council
26 Hardy heroine
27 Oh./Ill. separator
28 Buck's mate
32 Puts on the payroll
33 Part of a soft hand in blackjack
34 "Nifty!"
36 Cooling, as champagne
37 ___ contender
38 Short playerwise, as in hockey
39 London's ___ Gardens
40 Sp. Lady
43 Times up
44 Illinois home of Caterpillar
45 Network co-founded by Oprah Winfrey
47 Plains tribe
48 Plated, in a way

50 Thrown for ___
51 They rise and fall periodically
52 "As You Like It" forest
56 "The devil ___ the details"
57 Sicilian rumbler
59 Montreal Canadien, familiarly
60 "___ Blind" (Hootie & the Blowfish hit)
61 ___-Magnon man

by Peter A. Collins

ACROSS

1 Afternoon TV's Dr. ___
5 Deep-sea diver's equipment
10 Little trickster
13 No longer in the closet, say
15 Grandmothers, affectionately
16 Mother of a fawn
17 "Hip-hop" song of 1967
19 Prospector's find
20 When a cock crows
21 Cock
23 Shocked reaction
25 "Pay ___ mind"
27 Super-duper
28 Pilot's announcement, briefly
29 "Rap" song of 1966
32 Mennonite group
34 Race with batons
35 Workers with lots of baggage
38 "No, No" woman of Broadway
42 Residents of the Sooner State, informally
44 Belief system
45 "Country" song of 1971
50 Young fellow
51 Main part of a church
52 Winter coat material
53 Friend in war
54 Brewed drink often served with lemon
57 Prefix with -hedron
59 Ending with Wolf, Bat or Super
60 "Metal" song of 1950
64 Thunderstruck feeling
65 "Stormy Weather" composer
66 Role for which 11-Down won her Oscar

67 It was dropped at Woodstock
68 "Start over" button
69 Prefix with dynamic

DOWN

1 "Wham!"
2 "What's that?"
3 "According to some . . ."
4 Abate
5 Suddenly become alert
6 Taxi
7 Intact, as a chain
8 Scott of "Charles in Charge"
9 Concerning
10 "Same here"
11 Rita who won an Oscar for "West Side Story"
12 Looked hard
14 Home for a bear
18 Destroy
22 Fictional Tom or real-life Diane
23 Equipment
24 "Look ___!"
26 Big maker of A.T.M.'s
29 Military uniform material
30 Suffix with pay or schnozz
31 F.D.R. veep John ___ Garner
33 Crossed home plate, say
36 Photo
37 Coastal defenses against flooding
39 Fib
40 Blue-green
41 Water whirl
43 ___-Caps (candy)
45 Neither vegetable nor mineral
46 Easily tamed tropical birds
47 Made level
48 Packing a wallop

49 Robert of "The Sopranos"
53 Madison Square Garden, e.g.
55 Ivan or Nicholas
56 Dublin's land
58 TV schedule abbr.
61 Peace sign, for one
62 Piece of mail: Abbr.
63 ___ Paulo, Brazil

by Dan Margolis

8

ACROSS

1 Centers
5 Greetings from Oahu
11 Carrier in the Star Alliance
14 Amo, amas, ___ . . .
15 Actor Radcliffe
16 The Cowboys of the Big 12 Conf.
17 Kemo ___
18 *Like software that can be freely used and altered
20 One with whom your safe is not safe
22 Veiled vow?
23 Wineglass feature
24 Walk about
26 *Samsung or LG product
28 Aleve alternative
30 Flew the coop
31 Museum docent's offering
32 F.B.I. file, e.g.
36 Prez on a fiver
37 Shelf prop . . . or a hint to both parts of the answers to the six starred clues
38 ___-toothed
41 More cheerful around the holidays, say
42 Ask, as a question
43 Bog fuel
45 Tiger's home
47 *Tournament competition
51 Fanta and Sprite
52 One of a pair in a fast-food logo
53 Suffix with bass
54 Nimble
55 *Class assignments
58 Many, many moons
61 Go out with
62 Cinco de Mayo celebration
63 Get under control
64 Windy City transports
65 "Bambi" setting
66 Start of a conclusion

DOWN

1 Owns
2 Thurman of "Kill Bill"
3 *Like many a heartthrob's eyes
4 Pittsburgh pro
5 Sick as ___
6 Drink like 5-Down
7 Baseball great Buck
8 Language that gave us "guru" and "pundit"
9 "The Tortoise and the Hare" storyteller
10 ___-mo
11 A bit
12 Mountain climber's climb
13 "Guys and Dolls" song whose title follows "Call a lawyer and . . ."
19 One who walks down the aisle
21 Brig. ___
24 Lead-in to girl
25 Rebuke to an eavesdropper, for short
26 Speed away, with "it"
27 Made a case
29 Skunk's defense
33 Word with bunny or bum
34 Run-down
35 About
37 "Little Women" woman
38 *Company whose logo includes the winged foot of Mercury
39 Home to the Himalayas
40 Strokes . . . or ones getting stroked
41 Full of swagger, say
42 Divide appropriately
43 Mail carrier's charge
44 Makes a lasting impression?
46 Dosage amt.
47 Shot for those who have mastered English?
48 Vaccine target
49 Let down
50 Win by ___
54 32-card game
56 On leave
57 Some football linemen: Abbr.
59 "Wow!," in textspeak
60 Prefix with colonial

by James Tuttle

ACROSS

1 Quick second
5 Push
10 ___ law (physics formulation)
14 One who Googles, e.g.
15 "Yippee!"
16 "Go ahead!"
17 Total misery
19 Capital of Norway
20 Forbidding words?
21 Odd
22 $20 bill dispenser, briefly
25 Sleep extender
28 "Beats me!"
30 Horse feed
31 ___ uncertain terms
32 Cubs slugger Sammy
33 Long-distance inits.
36 2000 Olympics site
41 Suffix with lion
42 Hair job at a salon
43 Wild guess
44 Prefix with pad or port
45 Top-notch
47 Founding father who had a beer named after him
52 Bit of sunshine
53 Midterms, e.g.
54 Piano exercise
56 ___ mater
57 Wisenheimer
62 Bar mitzvah boy, barely
63 Divide 50–50
64 Flowing hair
65 Concordes, in brief
66 Kind of test . . . or a phonetic hint to 17-, 25-, 36-, 47- and 57-Across
67 Like carols at Christmas

DOWN

1 Roast beef au ___
2 Relative of -esque
3 Doctor's charge
4 Wilma's hubby on "The Flintstones"
5 "All ___ Do" (Sheryl Crow hit)
6 Nearsighted Mr. ___ of cartoons
7 Snapshot
8 Long, long time
9 Myrna of "The Thin Man"
10 Nonalcoholic beer brand
11 Book between Daniel and Joel
12 Middle-distance runner
13 Blizzard or hurricane
18 Valentine's Day flower
21 Persian Gulf emirate
22 Absinthe flavor
23 Stage statuettes
24 Keeps an eye on
26 Crazy places
27 3:00, on a compass
29 ___ Juan (ladies' man)
32 1 + 2 + 3, e.g.
33 Tweak, say
34 Pageant crown
35 Striped cat
37 Fencing weapons
38 Holler
39 Prima donna's delivery
40 Cleopatra's killer
44 Earthlings
45 Raunchy
46 Fed. food inspector
47 Goals for musical chairs players
48 Ones keeping the wheels turning?
49 Playwright David who wrote "Glengarry Glen Ross"
50 Mergers and buyouts
51 Skylit courtyards
55 Street-lining trees
57 U-turn from NNW
58 Hunters of AWOLs
59 Water, in Waterloo
60 Wolf Blitzer's channel
61 Big beer order

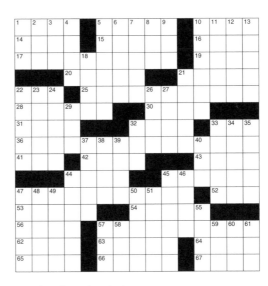

by Andrea Carla Michaels

10.

ACROSS

1 Big A.T.M. maker
4 Part of TWA
9 One turning to enter?
14 "Now I get it!"
15 One of Santa's reindeer
16 Serengeti scavenger
17 Brand with the tagline "Established in Milwaukee 1844"
20 Glowing coal
21 Roi's wife
22 Part of the back
25 They precede sigmas
29 Vote of support
30 Garden of Eden creature
32 Prez on a penny
35 ___-mo
37 Big and cumbersome
38 Extremist group
42 Best friend of Thomas the Tank Engine
43 Election day: Abbr.
44 Mary ___ cosmetics
45 Local's counterpart
48 Triangular sail
50 Hardly brow-furrowing
51 Deli counter cheese brand
57 Hero of New Orleans
59 Aquafina competitor
60 What Thanksgiving turkey may come with . . . as suggested by parts of 17-, 22-, 38- and 51-Across?
65 Tricks
66 Therefore
67 Nat ___ (cable channel)
68 Bub
69 Relatively cool red giant
70 Mess up

DOWN

1 Pickup sites?
2 Titleholder
3 Temple teacher
4 Couch potato's table
5 Josh
6 Rock's ___ Rose
7 Prefix with surgeon
8 Dirty looks
9 A guard may protect it
10 Science fiction subgenre
11 Yank's foe
12 Brian who pioneered in ambient music
13 Lacking color
18 D.C. V.I.P.
19 Hitchhiker's need
23 In case that
24 Colombian city
26 Wyeth subject
27 Pleasant to the ear, say
28 Pig's place

31 M.L.B. stat
32 Vega of "Spy Kids"
33 Pats on the back, maybe
34 Unreadable without a key
36 Big campaign mo.
39 Vote of support
40 Honshu peak
41 Derby strap
42 Second of April?
46 Kemo ___
47 Sluggish creatures
49 3 or 5 Series car, in slang
52 Combustible heaps
53 Early year in Nero's reign
54 Former Celtic Danny
55 54-Down was one
56 Belgian painter James
58 Very
60 Ship in a 2014 Russell Crowe film

61 Him: Fr.
62 Acid
63 Acct. earnings
64 Longtime record label

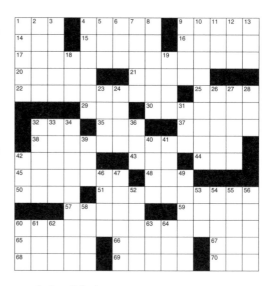

by Susan Gelfand

ACROSS

1 Covered Greek walkway
5 Go the way of snowmen
9 Rapidness
14 "Phooey!"
15 Operatic solo
16 ___ vortex (winter weather phenomenon)
17 Curse
18 Curse
19 High, as expectations
20 Telephone handset
23 Sounds from a sound sleeper?
24 Morn's counterpart
25 Cigarette dropping
28 Corset part
32 Perform in a play
35 Vote in favor
36 South Dakota's capital
37 Teaser
40 High's opposite
42 Condescend (to)
43 Former secretary of state Colin
45 Deface
47 Split ___ soup
48 Army unit
52 Nav. rank
53 ___ Francisco
54 Trail for Hansel and Gretel
58 Three strikes . . . or a description of the theme clues
61 Rome's home
64 Codger
65 "The Naked Maja" artist
66 End of an Aesop fable
67 Cabbagelike vegetable
68 Revise, as copy
69 Tick off
70 Hollywood Walk of Fame feature
71 Unit of force

DOWN

1 Garbage boats
2 Amtrak service
3 One-up
4 Cling (to)
5 Your ___ (way to address a queen)
6 Singer Clapton
7 Queue
8 Went along the tarmac
9 "Delightful!"
10 "You ___ thing!"
11 Keebler figure
12 "Please, have some!"
13 Like deserts
21 "Oedipus ___"
22 #2 exec
25 Take ___ down memory lane
26 Beetle's boss, in the comics
27 "Laughing" animal
29 Fish that can give you a shock
30 Actress Watts
31 "What did I tell you?"
32 Golden Delicious, e.g.
33 Sing like Bing Crosby
34 Villages
38 Ryan of "When Harry Met Sally . . ."
39 Antiquated
41 Used to be
44 Perjurer
46 ___ scale (earthquake measurer)
49 Features of some daring sweaters
50 Mined metal
51 Gently elbowed
55 Subject to emotional swings
56 Poker entry fee
57 Misery or Missouri
58 Serb or Pole
59 Perfectly
60 Pepsi-___
61 Mischievous kid
62 It may be tapped when you listen to music
63 "Come as you ___"

by Tom McCoy

12

ACROSS

1 Alexander Graham Bell, for one
5 Places to go fishing
10 Asteroid ___
14 Cay
15 Harden (to)
16 Region
17 One way to ride a horse
19 Vegas hotel transport
20 Brief 1831 headline?
22 Museum's ends?
25 Golf ball's position
26 Mends, as socks
27 Brief 1727 headline?
32 Goes fishing in go fish?
33 "I am woman, hear me ___"
34 Jet that once made a boom, in brief
37 Prefix with -genarian
38 Alternative if things don't work out
40 Home of Waikiki Beach
41 Badger's home: Abbr.
42 Castle protection
43 Employee of TV's Sterling Cooper & Partners
44 Brief 1931 headline?
47 Take advantage (of)
50 Switch positions
51 ___ lingus
52 Secretive classroom activity . . . or what 20-, 27- and 44-Across are anagrammatic examples of?
57 Rickman of the Harry Potter films
58 Where the Carpenters "long to be" in a 1970 #1 hit
62 Ill-mannered
63 "Funeral Blues" poet
64 Beaver projects
65 Drop of melodrama?
66 Historic event on Bikini atoll, briefly
67 View from a pew, maybe

DOWN

1 Beyoncé, to Solange, or vice versa
2 CBS drama with multiple spinoffs
3 Superannuated
4 Be overflowing
5 2013 Sheryl Sandberg best seller
6 Steel magnate Carnegie
7 Bit of praise, in modern usage
8 Writer ___ Stanley Gardner
9 Witnessed
10 Gotham City V.I.P.
11 Bobble or fumble
12 Get smart
13 Busts, as broncos
18 Arias, e.g.
21 Disinfectant target
22 Set up, as a chair
23 Word of thanks overseas
24 Hits a fly, say
28 "Terrible" age
29 Clio : history :: ___ : lyric poetry
30 Fictional opening?
31 You might pick one up in a bar
34 Girl Scout cookie with toasted coconut
35 "The L Word" role for Katherine Moennig
36 Piano man, maybe
38 Luau dish
39 Part of U.N.L.V.
40 Not even
42 The year 1551
43 It's a plus
44 Onetime Disney chief
45 Old West "neckties"
46 Something to be proven in a criminal case
47 In different places
48 Pawnshop estimate
49 Carne ___ (Mexican dish)
53 Org. with eligibility rules
54 Fill to excess
55 Lymph ___
56 Root beer, e.g.
59 Chihuahua sound
60 Meditation syllables
61 Find a purpose for

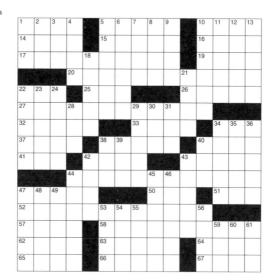

by Pamela Klawitter

ACROSS

1 *Replaceable part of a lamp
5 "Immediately!"
9 *Rum-soaked cakes
14 Dr. Frankenstein's assistant
15 *___ Ruth
16 The "U" of UHF
17 *Villainous noble of a classic French tale
19 Dweebish
20 Cousin of a mandolin
21 *Dodo
23 Kardashian who married Kanye
25 Pouty look
26 6 on a telephone
27 *Bench-pressing equipment
31 Shakespeare's fairy queen
33 Love personified
34 *Neighborhood financial institution
40 Peeve
41 Rooster's mate
42 "Goodbye, Guido!"
43 *Hungarian composer whose only opera is about 17-Across
47 Something a mini leaves exposed
48 Made a ditch, say
49 *The Tommy Dorsey Orchestra, e.g.
51 Tally (up)
54 Maple syrup sources
57 Boxer played by Will Smith in a 2001 biopic
58 *Base of many gravies
61 "Them's fightin' words!"
65 Eskimo's home
66 *Physical attribute of Homer Simpson
68 What vegans don't eat besides meat

69 Roman poet who wrote about 33-Across
70 Blood-boiling state
71 Road curves
72 Gen ___
73 Sultan of ___ (nickname for 15-Across)

DOWN

1 *Things to drool over?
2 Not-so-cute fruit
3 Boorish sort
4 *Have a meal
5 16th president, familiarly
6 Car from the same country as Volvo
7 Nearly overflowing
8 Director Almodóvar
9 *Bogeyman
10 Twin or Tiger, informally

11 Subs . . . or a feature of the answers to the 17 asterisked clues?
12 Alan of "Argo"
13 Refuse an offer
18 Gooey cheese
22 Boneheaded
24 Diamond org.
27 *Part of a fishhook
28 French girlfriend
29 Item often served with a pat of butter
30 Bert of "The Wizard of Oz"
32 *Ones who criticize others in their absence
35 Badminton barrier
36 Radio tuner
37 Ship of 1492
38 Normandy city where William the Conqueror is buried
39 Weeded, in a way
44 *Restaurant staffers
45 Food thickener

46 Car from Korea
50 Smooth-talking
51 Put up with
52 Impressionist Edgar who painted ballerinas
53 Sub builders?
55 Part of many a bus. address
56 Actor McQueen
59 Golfer's cry
60 ___ to the throne
62 BBQ side dish
63 Gymnast Korbut
64 Veto from Vladimir
67 Hwys.

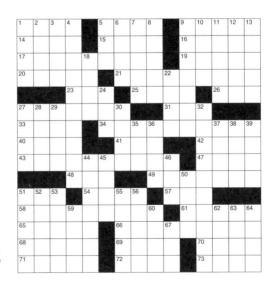

by Bruce Haight

ACROSS

1 Easy mark
4 Air Force One honcho
8 1960 Alfred Hitchcock thriller
14 Overseer of corp. accounts
15 Start all over
16 Start of a rumor
17 "In what way?"
18 Gulf State leader
19 Despise
20 2012 John C. Reilly animated film
23 Prefix with 28-Across
24 N.Y.C. home to works of Picasso
25 Musical improv
28 Jet
31 Pop the question
34 Kabayaki fish
36 Main part of a monocle
38 Conductor Zubin ___
39 2012 Quentin Tarantino western
43 Columbus's hometown
44 Student aid
45 Its score is reported on some univ. applications
46 Demi or Julianne Moore
49 Colleague of Roberts and Scalia
51 Gridiron positions: Abbr.
52 Historical
54 Ages and ages
57 2010 James Mangold action comedy
61 Popular sleep aid
64 River through Florence
65 Space station until 2001
66 Knitted item for a baby
67 Gambling mecca
68 Arabic name meaning "high"

69 ___ movies (8-, 20-, 39- and 57-Across, in a way)
70 Sharp
71 Org. named in WikiLeaks documents

DOWN

1 Beginning or end of "Athena"
2 Prior to, in poetry
3 Electricity producers
4 Like school for toddlers, in brief
5 Notes after do
6 It has Cut, Copy and Paste commands
7 Swordsman of book and film
8 Notable one in a community
9 Butchery or bakery
10 "You betcha"

11 Subject of many a viral video
12 Letters for a prince
13 William Collins's "___ to Evening"
21 ___ Mustard (Clue character)
22 Roadie's tote
25 "The Big Lebowski" co-star
26 Autumn bloom
27 General at Gettysburg
29 Pond growth
30 Prefix with conservative
32 Muscat native
33 Bank of China Tower designer
34 Mystery award
35 Kick out
37 Comedy/variety show since '75
40 Fish ___ fowl
41 Front hallway item
42 Prince with 21 Tonys
47 Small piano

48 Droop
50 Kennedy aide Sorensen
53 Jet fighter?
55 Finalizes, with "down"
56 Gulf War ally
57 Toy with a tail
58 "Forget it, Friedrich!"
59 Rice on a shelf
60 Lunch time, maybe
61 Things that exercisers crunch
62 "You mean me?"
63 La Paz's land: Abbr.

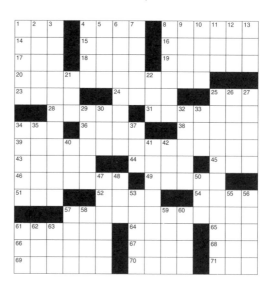

by Zhouqin Burnikel

15

ACROSS

1 College concentration
6 Craze
9 Ladies' service org. since the 1850s
13 ___ acid (building block of biology)
14 Flub
15 Newborn horses
16 The fourth (but not the first) letter of "cancel"
17 It has lions and tigers and bears (oh my!)
18 Real corkers
19 Green-lighted, as a project
21 "Nothing ___ sleeve"
23 Baseball's ___ Griffey Jr.
24 Cairo native
28 Weight-loss programs
30 London bathroom
31 What a card player is dealt
32 Ruler unit
33 Perhaps
35 And so on: Abbr.
37 Van Susteren of Fox News
40 Unflinching in the face of pain, say
41 "Guess ___!"
42 Architectural style named after a British royal family
43 "Gone With the Wind" plantation
45 Dubai ruler
47 What three strikes make
48 Paris's Musée d'___
49 Saw red
51 When most movies open: Abbr.
52 Art ___ (1920s–'30s architectural style)
54 Gorilla, e.g.
55 Train that makes all stops
57 Get under the skin of

59 English racetrack site
63 Joint sometimes twisted when running
64 ___ G (Sacha Baron Cohen persona)
65 Musician Frank with the Mothers of Invention
66 Blog entry
67 Not even
68 Thrill

DOWN

1 Pas' mates
2 ___, amas, amat
3 Rival of Peter Pan or Skippy
4 Winning
5 MTV competitive reality show featuring children of pop stars
6 Hat with a tassel
7 Where Phileas Fogg traveled "in 80 days"
8 Plummet

9 "___ wanna take this outside?"
10 Do a chore with a pet
11 Things hidden in treasure hunts
12 The "A" of 9-Across: Abbr.
15 Circus act above a net
20 Day: Sp.
22 The year 1501
24 O'Neill's "Desire Under the ___"
25 Animal that butts
26 What 5-, 7-, 10- and 15-Down all are
27 All over again
29 Neutral color
34 Editorial slant
36 Senseless state
38 What some bands and just-published authors do
39 Affectedly cultured
44 Matey's yes
46 "Yes, there ___ God!"

48 Maine town bordering Bangor
50 Katmandu's nation
51 Envelope part
53 Italian goodbye
56 Ctrl-___-Delete
58 25-Down offspring
60 Baden-Baden, for one
61 Make a decision
62 West who wrote "Goodness Had Nothing to Do With It"

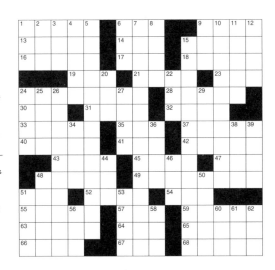

by Brendan Emmett Quigley

16

ACROSS

1 "Oh, so that's it!"
4 Impetuous
9 Norwegian tourist attraction
14 Tease
15 Author of Gothic short stories, in short
16 Slave away
17 Music producer Brian
18 Sleep state for an electronic device
20 Fesses up
22 Ruckus
23 Tidbit for a bird
24 Outsource, as part of a job
27 Still-life subject
28 SXSW festival setting
33 Blossom support
36 Really cool, in slang
39 Hooch
40 Secret military mission . . . or a hint to the circled letters in this puzzle?
43 Oscar winner for "Skyfall"
44 Yemen's capital
45 Ye ___ Shoppe
46 What covers many blocks?
48 Gremlins and Pacers
50 Like World of Warcraft and other fare for 66-Acrosses
56 Coin whose front varies by country
60 Stable diet?
61 Mopey donkey of children's literature
62 It's on the left in the U.S. and the right in the U.K.
65 Boy
66 See 50-Across
67 Doughnut's shape
68 Wildcats of the N.C.A.A.

69 Kagan of the Supreme Court
70 Potter's potions professor
71 Simone de Beauvoir's "The Second ___"

DOWN

1 Fields
2 One who believes in karma
3 Weapon of mass destruction in '45 headlines
4 Confer (upon)
5 Tangle
6 Therapists' org.
7 Submarine sensor
8 ___ Gabler, Ibsen heroine
9 Really cool, in slang
10 Copier malfunctions
11 Instrument that tunes an orchestra
12 Cycled, say
13 Great Scott?

19 ___ Raton, Fla.
21 Magnesium chloride, e.g.
25 Nirvana and Destiny's Child
26 Big horn
29 In a manner of speaking
30 Slave away
31 Preppy clothing brand
32 Protected bird in Hawaii
33 Grift, e.g.
34 ___ list
35 Of all time
37 One working overtime in Apr., maybe
38 Alaskan peninsula
41 20 quires of paper
42 Increased, as production
47 German coal region
49 "Monty Python" actor John

51 Persists
52 Astrophysicist Neil deGrasse ___
53 They provide richness in batter
54 Wipe away
55 Brought back
56 Sharp part
57 Eurasia's ___ Mountains
58 Frost
59 Place for a roast
63 Historical interval
64 Flatow or Glass of public radio

by Heather Valadez

ACROSS
1 Airline to the Holy Land
5 Finishes
9 Baseball gloves
14 N.Y.C. institution with works of Warhol and Dalí
15 Italian currency before the euro
16 Sound muffled by a handkerchief
17 Celebrity chef and host of the Food Network's "Boy Meets Grill"
19 Crooks, to cops
20 Licorice flavoring
21 For what reason?
23 AOL or EarthLink: Abbr.
24 Tell tall tales
25 Theme music for TV's "The Dating Game"
30 Majority of the contestants on "The Dating Game"
31 Equivalent of a Roman X
32 Pacified
33 Bygone jets, informally
35 Like a wet noodle
38 Byways
39 Insect that causes sleeping sickness
42 Actor Davis
45 "The Thin Man" pooch
46 ___ tape
50 Proverbial place for bats
52 Biblical boat
54 "___ hear"
55 It's typically slow during rush hour
58 Hosp. triage areas
59 Stimpy's TV pal
60 One who plays for pay
61 Jackson 5 hairstyles
63 Disentangled

66 Dismissive term for chronic fatigue syndrome
69 Judges to be
70 Grand ___ (auto race)
71 Remove, to an editor
72 Dashing Flynn of old films
73 Sugar amts.
74 Adriatic and others

DOWN
1 Mummifies, e.g.
2 Fruitcakes
3 Surrounding, as sound
4 Experiment sites
5 Santa's little helper
6 Nothing
7 Sketched
8 Give an informal greeting
9 Poster with a "You are here" label
10 Rink surface
11 ___ in Manila (Ali/Frazier fight)
12 Favorite entrant in a tournament
13 Kitchen scourers
18 Tues. vis-à-vis Wed.
22 Handbag monogram
26 Brazilian soccer legend
27 Singer Baker with the 1988 hit "Giving You the Best That I Got"
28 Throw
29 "Pretty Boy" of crime
34 Completely unlike a wet noodle
36 Author's submissions: Abbr.
37 Flower part
40 Feudal peasant
41 Casino card game
42 Stick out
43 More calm
44 Spoken slur

47 Charge for entering a park, e.g.
48 Flower part
49 Kleenexes
51 Pup's cry
53 "The Bridge on the River ___"
56 Burial vault
57 On all ___ (crawling, say)
62 G-men
64 "If you ask me," in chat rooms
65 Internet connection inits.
67 "Great Expectations" boy
68 Stores for G.I.'s

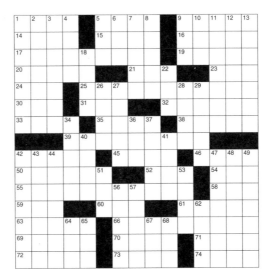

by Ed Sessa

18

ACROSS

1 Dead as a doornail
6 Listings in a daily planner: Abbr.
11 Marble ___ (London landmark)
15 Justice Kagan
16 Book leaf
17 Oscar winner Sorvino
18 Appeal from Elvis, 1956
20 Burden of proof
21 Prom attendee, typically
22 Mine vehicle
24 Clock-setting std.
25 Reassurance from the Beach Boys, 1964
29 "If you haven't seen ___, you haven't seen New York" (old ad slogan)
32 Tennis star Mandlikova
33 Rapper ___ Wayne
34 Financial adviser's recommendation, in brief
35 ___ Paul (classic guitar)
36 Start liking
39 Encouragement from Journey, 1981
44 Impoverished
45 "Modern Family" network
46 Business monthly
47 Bob Marley's "___ Love"
48 Movie that introduced the line "Bond, James Bond"
50 Went up
52 Plea from the Human League, 1982
56 Decline
57 ___ mater
58 Young travelers' crash site
62 Ray of light
64 Reproach from the Buckinghams, 1967
67 Capri or Wight
68 Art house film, often

69 Ward attendant
70 Relate
71 Divisions politiques
72 Quizzes

DOWN

1 Sneaker brand
2 Sunburn relief
3 School founded by Ben Franklin
4 Not neat
5 Iconoclasts break them
6 Jaguars' grp.
7 ___ favor
8 Mass of crystallized magma
9 ___ del Fuego
10 Certain renewable
11 "I love," in Latin
12 Game similar to hide-and-seek
13 Part of a path left by Hansel and Gretel
14 Done in a rush
19 Seaside eagle
23 Vietnam War locale
26 Kojak's first name

27 Insect with a stinger
28 Ten-speed, e.g.
29 Skirt hemmed at the calf
30 Elvis's middle name
31 Dive done with the arms around the knees
35 Classic Ford
36 Doting affection, briefly
37 Quaint food containers
38 Formerly
40 Collapsible shelter
41 "It's been real!"
42 Eric who played Nero in 2009's "Star Trek"
43 Black, to poets
48 Groucho foil Margaret ___
49 African country known as the Land of a Thousand Hills
50 Bill line
51 Save from danger
52 ___ card

53 Very heavy
54 Almost any doo-wop song
55 However, for short
59 Sailors
60 Formerly, in the past
61 Some jeans
63 Brooks who has won an Oscar, Emmy, Grammy and Tony
65 Small bird
66 "I'm game"

by Gary Cee

ACROSS

1 Toot one's own horn
5 Terrytoons' Deputy ___
9 Kitchen and garden vessels
13 Having X and Y chromosomes
14 Sooner State resident, informally
15 Wood-shaping tool
16 Tom Sawyer's bucketful
18 French ___ soup
19 Draft org.
20 Lure for bargain hunters
22 Like birthday greetings sent after the fact
26 "What time ___?"
27 Privileged few
28 Physicists' work units
30 Aid for catching a mouse
34 Prepare to shoot
35 Olympics sword
37 Patriotic chant at the Olympics
39 Mac or PC hookup
40 General way of thinking
42 "All Things Considered" network
43 Believer in God
45 "Star Wars" sage
46 Mideast export
47 What a knitter might have a ball with?
48 Covered in frosting
50 Beach town that's home to Cape Cod's oldest lighthouse
52 Pet's teensy tormentor
54 Knitter's creation
56 Like some champagne
60 Chicago trains
61 Wilt
62 Sweet spot in a hive
67 Takes in, as at the box office
68 Was in the red
69 Carpet layer's calculation
70 Vladimir's veto
71 Stratagem
72 Obscene

DOWN

1 Parent company of Rolls-Royce
2 When tripled, pep rally cheer
3 Louisville's Muhammad ___ Center
4 Insinuates
5 Use a divining rod
6 Letters before an alias
7 Bit of smoke or hair
8 Yankee who was the first major-leaguer to have his number retired
9 Leon who was Obama's first C.I.A. director
10 Suffix with psych-
11 "All hail, Macbeth, ___ shalt be king hereafter!"
12 Transmitted
15 Centers of activity
17 Holds in high regard
21 Published
22 With 33-Down, where to go for the ends of 16-, 20-, 40-, 56- and 62-Across
23 Actress Cuthbert of "24"
24 Flexible, as a gymnast
25 Celebrity chef Paula known for Southern cuisine
29 Change back to brunet, say
31 Expire, as a subscription
32 Have as a goal, with "to"
33 See 22-Down
36 Felt sorry for
38 Dignified
41 Puts down roots?
44 Close to the stage, say
49 Server at a drive-in restaurant
51 Mischief-maker
53 Swimmers' back-and-forths
55 Like an untended garden
56 Biblical garden
57 Cavity detector
58 Ripped
59 Pained cry
63 Prefix with conservative
64 Lucky rockhound's find
65 Kitten's cry
66 Crummy

by Lynn Lempel

ACROSS

1 Safe havens
5 Start of some French street names
10 1974 C.I.A. spoof
14 Israel's Golda
15 Spanish rice
16 Warning on a highway
17 Calligraphers' supplies
18 Like much snack food for hikers
20 "___ have to?"
21 Is for more than one?
22 Bit of gaucho gear
23 Small order of greens
27 Reads rapidly
29 Detective's coat, informally
30 Some savings plans, for short
32 Lion or tiger
33 Shot contents
34 Nerve-racking test, for some
35 Goes to pot
36 Clearing
39 Flowerless plant
42 Pine (for)
43 Corn covering
46 End of a school email address
47 Fashion designer Gernreich
48 Rubberneckers
50 Japanese assassin
52 Season ticket holder for baseball, basketball and football, say
54 Hoity-___
56 Ones "over there"
57 The "H" of H.M.S.
58 Glazed dessert
61 Special seating section
62 Back talk
63 ___-gazing
64 Metal containers?
65 Tiny, to a tot
66 Club alternative
67 Signs of cell service . . . or a word that can follow both parts of 18-, 23-, 36-, 52- and 58-Across

DOWN

1 Surrounded by
2 Some Impressionist paintings
3 Duettist with Elton John on 1976's "Don't Go Breaking My Heart"
4 Sophs., two years later
5 Openly enthusiastic
6 One of the archangels
7 Fraction of a joule
8 Outburst from Homer
9 Former Israeli president Weizman
10 Meat sometimes served au poivre
11 Colonnaded entrance
12 You might sit cross-legged on one
13 Squalid digs
19 Loch ___
21 Music-licensing org.
24 Bankrupted company led by Kenneth Lay
25 Blimp
26 Curtain
28 N.Y.C.'s Bleecker and Canal
31 In the style of
34 Obsolescent way to store music
35 Does another stint
37 ___ de toilette
38 F.D.R.'s fireside addresses
39 Swampland
40 Delete
41 Postelection elections
44 Lady of Brazil
45 Freddy of Elm Street
47 Miles per gallon, e.g.
48 Car part that may have a decorative design
49 Accentuate
51 Second
53 Eyed
55 Longings
58 Special effects graphics, briefly
59 Grammy category
60 Egg cells
61 Smashable shot

by Bruce Venzke and Gail Grabowski

ACROSS

1. ___, crackle, pop
5. Shapely shade trees
9. Beer mug
14. Mani-___ (nail job)
15. Breakfast or lunch
16. Drink often served with marshmallows
17. Stairway safety feature
18. Web designer's concern
20. "Relax, soldier!"
22. Milky gems
23. Annoyed "Hel-LO!"
25. 65 on a hwy., maybe
28. Tit ___ tat
29. Complete
31. Japanese compact S.U.V.
36. In addition
37. Disposable lighter
38. 2012 Ben Affleck film set in Iran
39. Sandwich cookie with abundant filling
44. Kind of fin
45. Mauna ___
46. James Bond, for one
47. Eerie encounter . . . or a hint to 23-, 31- and 39-Across
54. Stop on ___
55. "Yay, we did it!"
56. Locked up in
60. Secretary, say
61. Like some Peruvian ruins
62. First, second or reverse
63. "The check ___ the mail"
64. Conductor Solti
65. Elvis's middle name
66. "Don't give me ___!"

DOWN

1. Hose setting
2. "Cool beans!"
3. Mademoiselle's goodbye
4. Rice ___ (dish)
5. Caesar or Charlemagne
6. Meadow
7. Myopic Mr. ___
8. Snoozed
9. Like a triangle with sides of different lengths
10. Yo-yo and Etch A Sketch
11. Prefix with friendly
12. Note of indebtedness
13. Singer ___ King Cole
19. Less funny, as a joke
21. Davenport
24. Roots (around)
25. Anglican bishop's hat
26. Pasta sauce brand
27. Foot-long sandwich
30. Old Russian ruler
31. Small sailboat
32. Exorbitant interest charge
33. Goes up and down, as a buoy
34. Physically strong
35. Round windows
36. Opposite of subtracts
40. Singing the praises of
41. Fairylike
42. Blast from a lighthouse
43. Honolulu's home
48. What follows phi, chi, psi
49. Passover feast
50. Hazel eyes or curly hair
51. Dubliners, e.g.
52. Gold-medal gymnast Comaneci
53. Treaty of ___, pact ending the War of 1812
54. From a distance
56. Marlboro or Camel, informally
57. 21st word of the Pledge of Allegiance
58. Sgt., e.g.
59. "___ Te Ching" (old Chinese text)

by MaryEllen Uthlaut

ACROSS

1 Test runners
5 Many a carnival game
9 Lower California, informally
13 "Splendor in the Grass" director Kazan
14 "Changed my mind" computer command
15 "Entertainment Tonight" host Nancy
17 Founder of 6-Down
19 Loads and loads
20 Relief on a hot day
21 Stuffed
23 Near eternity
24 Pre-A.D.
26 Hit back?
27 Precious
28 Old name for Tokyo
29 Aliens, for short
32 "That's not news to me"
36 World's largest online retailer
38 Macy's symbol
39 Word after Dead or Red
41 Seat with cushions
42 Get tangled
45 Splits, as a couple
48 Uncooked
49 Where to find a soft drink's promotional code
51 End-of-season honorees, for short
52 Hawk's home
54 Soak up, as gravy
55 Pub draught
58 World's biggest private employer
60 Andean ruminants
62 Winning
63 Founder of 47-Down
66 Cybermemo
67 Skye of "Say Anything . . ."
68 Domain

69 Many bills in tip jars
70 Pre-K enrollees
71 Fall back (on)

DOWN

1 Ignored
2 Olds of old
3 Obama's veep
4 Fill to the gills
5 "No prob"
6 World's most widely distributed syndicated news service
7 Suffix with lemon
8 Down in the mouth
9 Cause of yawning
10 On ___ (how some pranks are done)
11 Founder of 36-Across
12 Old one, in German
16 One may trip on it
18 Turkic tongue
22 "Livin' La ___ Loca"
25 Lover of Psyche

27 Critical
30 Pretty tasteless food
31 Lose it
32 River through Flanders
33 Italian hothead?
34 Founder of 58-Across
35 Fly trap
37 Pops, as the question
40 Combat supplies
43 Just gets (by)
44 Eyelash, e.g.
46 Slowly changes
47 "World's most admired company," per Fortune
50 Look after a neighbor's dog, say
53 Ham it up
55 Love, to Valentino
56 Valentino, e.g.
57 Op-ed piece
58 "___ unto him . . ."
59 A.D. part

61 Slightly open
64 Overly
65 M.D. specialty

by Zhouqin Burnikel

ACROSS

1 Counterparts of sirs
7 ___ number on
10 $2.50 per ⅕ mile, e.g.
14 Street
15 "Ich bin ___ Berliner"
16 Khrushchev's land, for short
17 Louisiana language
18 New England cookout
20 Big name in ranch dressing
22 "So what ___ is new?"
23 Dumb ox
24 Unit of work, in physics
27 Classic of English children's literature, with "The"
31 When a plane is due to take off: Abbr.
34 Narrow inlets
35 Mystical glow
36 Diary
38 Military hairstyle
41 The Emerald Isle
42 California ballot measure, informally
43 Nav. rank
44 Small paid item in the back of a newspaper
49 Start of many a countdown
50 Running shoe brand
51 24 bottles of beer
55 What unmentionables cover . . . or what 20-, 27- and 44-Across all begin with?
58 YouTube and Yahoo!
61 Go from pub to pub
62 With warts and all

63 "No ___!" (Spanish surrender)
64 Like the eyes just after waking
65 "See ___ run"
66 Punk rock subgenre
67 Schedules

DOWN

1 Papier-___
2 "Sk8er Boi" singer Lavigne
3 Real estate documents
4 Battery ends
5 Stubborn animal
6 "As ___ on TV"
7 Divisions of a century
8 Like many old lanterns
9 Not digital, as a clock
10 Color of Dorothy's slippers
11 Flat ___ pancake
12 "Naughty, naughty!"
13 Before, to poets
19 Prefix with physics

21 Like the "Gangnam Style" video
24 Bring out
25 Many a showing on TV Land
26 Flying pests
28 Suffix with east or west
29 Spy org.
30 Like most sushi
31 Emergency function on a fighter plane
32 Decorative cotton fabric
33 When doubled, "Hungry Like the Wolf" band
37 ___ ipsa loquitur
38 Top of a wave
39 Fishing stick
40 Org. tasked with enforcing the Clean Air Act
42 Painter with a Blue Period
45 Delhi dress
46 Self-conscious question

47 When some morning news programs begin
48 Bethesda, Md., is in it
52 Enlightened Buddhist
53 Boutique
54 Annual awards for athletes
55 [Hey, buddy!]
56 ___ and flows
57 Funeral drape
58 Used to be
59 Mind reading, for short
60 Prefix with physics

by Matt Fuchs

ACROSS

1 Knee-ankle connector
6 With 8-Down, lime shade
11 Texter's "Holy cow!"
14 "Sorry, already have plans"
15 Screenwriter Sorkin
16 With 12-Down, not natural
17 Harmonize
18 Refine, as ore
19 Nabokov's longest novel
20 One in service to the queen?
22 Rapper's posse
23 Bottom-of-the-ninth pitcher
24 Like Michelangelo's "David"
26 Ponder, with "on"
27 Philadelphia summer hrs.
29 "Survivor" host Jeff
33 With 23-Down, deli product
34 Was incredibly embarrassed, in slang
36 Be of ___
37 20-volume ref.
38 With 38-Down, place to drop a coin
40 With 31-Down, jazz legend
41 Rhone tributary
43 Michael of "Arrested Development"
44 Ancient Greek colonnade
45 Try to improve a Yahtzee turn
47 LAX listing
48 Items in pocket protectors
49 Oodles
51 Making a bundle
53 Get-rich-quick offer, typically
56 Like gas tanks and many prescriptions, again and again
58 With 54-Down, waffle alternative

59 With 57-Down, part of a morning routine
60 Unpopular baby name
63 ___ out a living
64 Dentist's directive
65 Lawn tool
66 Drops on the ground?
67 Takes a breather
68 Bug

DOWN

1 "My country" follower
2 Standoffish
3 Count Basie, e.g.
4 Exclusive group
5 One of the Three Musketeers
6 Bygone video format
7 Foot used to keep rhythm?
8 With 6-Across, approve
9 Go into hiding
10 "Falling Skies" airer
11 Sharif of "Doctor Zhivago"
12 With 16-Across, mob inductee
13 Act like a beaver
21 "___ say more?"
22 Board hirees
23 With 33-Across, fan of the N.F.L.'s Packers
25 Narcotize
26 It often functions with the help of an organ
28 Little laugh
30 Demoralized
31 With 40-Across, coerce
32 Spanish inquisitor ___ de Torquemada
35 Off-road two-wheelers
38 With 38-Across, desiring happiness for someone
39 Winner of the most French Open singles titles

42 Drift
44 Watched through binoculars, say
46 Moore who wrote "Birds of America"
50 Many Snapchat users
52 Fleeced beast
53 Hightailed it
54 With 58-Across, bakery container
55 Over again
57 With 59-Across, basketball tactic
59 "It's so-o-o cold!"
61 Fierce, loyal sort, it's said
62 Cook, as bacon

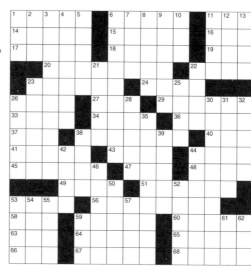

by Joel Fagliano

ACROSS

1 Squander
6 Like a cat in need of a firefighter, stereotypically
11 N.Y.C. alternative to J.F.K.
14 Notions
15 Mandel of "America's Got Talent"
16 Galley propeller
17 Chance of an impossibility
19 666, for the numbers on a roulette wheel
20 In the manner of
21 Fraidy-cat
22 Portent
24 Cutters that cut with the grain
27 Innocent's opposite
29 Watery abysses
30 Nickelodeon show whose protagonist has a football-shaped head
33 From ___ Z
35 Note between fa and la
36 Functions
37 Classical music group . . . or what the four sets of circled letters make up?
41 Yank
42 ___ de Cologne
43 ___ the pants off
44 For even a second more
47 Insipid
51 Observed
52 Nineveh's land
54 Indian dress
55 ___ mater
57 Critical hosp. department
58 A.T.M. co.
59 Component of a language class, informally
63 Mattress's place
64 Weasley family owl

65 Prepared to be knighted
66 Coupon bearers, often
67 Baseball's Pee Wee
68 Somebody ___ problem

DOWN

1 ___ of Menlo Park (Thomas Edison)
2 Penguin variety
3 Mexican wrap
4 "___ Te Ching" (classic Chinese text)
5 Psychic's "gift," briefly
6 Plump songbird
7 Birds in the "Arabian Nights"
8 Rams' mates
9 German article
10 Roundabout route
11 Like a catch-22 situation
12 Knight's glove

13 One of eight on an octopus
18 "Gross!"
23 With great attention to detail
25 Hand-held Fourth of July firework
26 ___ Spumante
27 Black-tie parties
28 N.F.L. lengths: Abbr.
31 Suffix with Kafka
32 Word pronounced the same when its first two letters are removed
34 Upright, as a box
37 Grew old
38 Those who put a lot of effort into social climbing, in modern lingo
39 Joke
40 Chafes
41 Short boxing punch
45 Dickens's "___ Twist"

46 Talk on and on and on
48 Comes up
49 Kidman who is neither a kid nor a man
50 Intimidates
53 Mule on a canal, in song
55 Unit of farmland
56 Thailand/Vietnam separator
58 Org. for LeBron James
60 Rock with gold or silver, say
61 Squeeze (out)
62 Sketch comedy TV series since '75

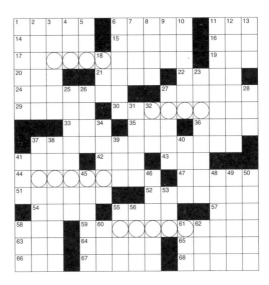

by Tom McCoy

26

ACROSS

1 Willy of "Free Willy," e.g.
5 Kind of breath
10 Transportation for Mary Poppins or E.T.
14 Bit of office greenery
15 Forge a deal, say
16 How a sale item may be sold
17 United Nations headquarters decoration
18 *Nursery worker's suggestion for a backstabber?*
20 Gets more clearheaded
22 Pontius ___
23 Part of a place setting
24 Killer bees and others
25 Shrew
27 Ones cutting in line, e.g.
28 Tennis's Ivanovic
29 Former New York governor Spitzer
31 Deuces
35 Peaks: Abbr.
36 *. . . for a scoundrel?*
39 Physicist Georg
40 Ask, as a riddle
42 Run away (with)
43 The Tigers of the S.E.C.
44 Responds hotly?
47 Atmospheric phenomenon during low temperatures
49 Mujer of mixed race
52 Noted filmmaker with a dog named Indiana
53 Milanese fashion house
54 Overly devoted son
57 *. . . for a fall guy?*
59 Connecticut Ivy

60 Away from a chat program, say
61 It's debatable
62 From the top
63 Cartoon collectibles
64 Wheelbarrow or thimble, in Monopoly
65 Line parts: Abbr.

DOWN

1 Does a mob hit on
2 Move, to a Realtor
3 *. . . for a grouch?*
4 German chancellor Merkel
5 Extended piece by John Paul Jones of Led Zeppelin or John Entwistle of the Who
6 ___ Dei
7 Snare
8 Cry at a horror house
9 Like the diving end of a pool vis-à-vis the other end

10 Gas balloon supply
11 "Shaft" composer Hayes
12 Kunta ___ of "Roots"
13 ___ Park, Colo.
19 Rosy
21 Was fierce, as a storm
24 "I second that"
25 Improvise musically
26 "What's gotten ___ you?"
27 Features of a droopy face
30 Sinatra's "___ Kick Out of You"
32 *. . . for a lothario?*
33 Extremely
34 Self-satisfied
37 Old-time drug hangout
38 Bing Crosby's record label
41 Millionaires' properties
45 One in Munich

46 Rapper who hosted MTV's "Pimp My Ride"
48 Light courses?
49 Illusions
50 Wear away, as a bank
51 Picayune
52 Lash ___ of old westerns
54 Purchase for Halloween
55 Designer Cassini
56 Trees for making longbows
58 Spanish "that"

by Timothy Polin

ACROSS

1 Marathon or sprint
5 Toots one's own horn
10 "___ out of your league, man!"
14 Shah's land
15 Des Moines native
16 Vehicle with a hatch on top
17 Venus de ___
18 Muppet with a long bluish nose
19 ___ in a blue moon
20 Lets some air in, say
23 Any graduate from a women's college
25 Becomes an Elvis impersonator?
26 Compromised, as two parties
30 Actor Damon
31 German state whose capital is Dresden
32 "Sounds good!"
33 Cacophony
34 Jane Austen classic
38 Hypes
41 Lab container
42 Get hitched
46 Start watching a TV show, say
47 Parts of a moral code
48 What the ends of the answers to 20-, 26- and 42-Across are
52 Narrow opening
53 Mideast's ___ Heights
54 Close, in a guessing game
57 Make an engraving
58 Illuminated from below
59 Horror film assistant with a Russian name
60 Salon tints
61 Down-and-out
62 Word that's only coincidentally made up of the four main compass points

DOWN

1 Wheel's edge
2 "Exodus" hero
3 India's capital before New Delhi
4 Sheer awfulness
5 Lions and tigers, but not bears
6 Corner chess piece
7 Plant bristles
8 Mideast's ___ Strip
9 Strands at a chalet, say
10 High as a kite
11 "Messiah" composer
12 Shout after the band leaves the stage
13 Distorts, as data
21 ___ Taylor, women's clothing chain
22 ___ 500
23 BBs and bullets
24 Plumbing problem
27 Wore
28 Be
29 Calendar page
34 Facetious fall guy for one's wrongdoings, maybe
35 Malapropism
36 ♂
37 Pub orders
38 Be hot, hot, hot
39 Exercise one's right under the Second Amendment
40 Common highway speed limit
42 Opposite of innocent
43 How chop suey is often served
44 Ocean bottoms
45 Baseball designation one step below Major League
46 Zapped, as during an arrest
49 Slangy dissent
50 Woman's name that sounds like a letter
51 Uttered
55 Pull an oar
56 ___ Fields cookies

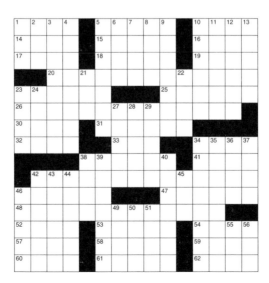

by Joel Fagliano

ACROSS

1 Corn throwaways
5 Emcee
9 Swampy tract
14 Common sunscreen additive
15 Sufficiently skilled
16 ___ State (Hawaii)
17 "That makes three strikes for O'Toole!"
19 Japanese model
20 "That's plain wrong!"
21 Miscalculates
23 Monopoly acquisition
24 Shish kebab meat
26 "Uh-oh, Sajak has fallen in the field!"
28 Spot for some local suds
31 Ring king, once
32 Lummoxes
33 Basic training grads
35 Christmas glitter
39 Cincinnati-to-Detroit dir.
40 "Now we have Nicklaus at bat"
42 Good Grips kitchen brand
43 Handyman's assignment
45 Thus far
46 Chocolaty nibble
47 In the past
48 Shakespearean storm
50 "There goes Zuckerberg, trying for a steal!"
55 Bellow in a bookstore
56 Inkling
57 Margarita option
59 Luster for the lips
62 Dishonest types
64 "Fisher made it to first base!"
66 Word with Sea or Star
67 Lake in an old railroad name
68 Classic soda brand
69 College applicant's composition
70 Office sub, perhaps
71 Non-Derby pace

DOWN

1 Title for Horatio Magellan Crunch, on cereal boxes
2 Promise product
3 Like some motherless calves and foals
4 Vacillates
5 Contains
6 Double-reed woodwind
7 Eat noisily
8 Neon ___
9 Bub
10 Magic lamp rubber of lore
11 The "thou" in "Wherefore art thou?"
12 Headstrong woman, as in Shakespeare
13 Joseph who wrote the "Surprise" Symphony
18 Cavort
22 Things passed on the way to the White House?
25 Persistent problems
27 Freudian mistake
28 Knighted U2 singer
29 Name on many a road map
30 Pen name?
34 Wild blue yonder
36 One moaning and groaning after a defeat
37 Custody sharers, often
38 Plunder
40 Goes once or twice around the track, maybe
41 Encyclopedia from A to Z, e.g.
44 Indonesia's capital
46 Splendidly luxurious
49 New Testament gift bearers
50 "Now We Are Six" writer
51 "Hasta mañana"
52 Brings up
53 Aspect
54 Signal light
58 Cut back a bit
60 Gallery-filled Manhattan neighborhood
61 State of vexation
63 Like a shrinking v iolet
65 One of 435 in D.C.

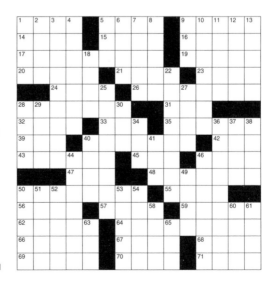

by Lynn Lempel

ACROSS
1 Give for free, as a ticket
5 Quite a ways off
9 Off-the-cuff remark
14 French girlfriend
15 "Buy two, get one free" event
16 Bowling score component
17 Top scores in Olympic diving
18 "Thank God Almighty!"
20 Dress
22 With ice cream
23 Of an ancient Greek period
26 Meadow
27 Mammal with webbed paws
28 Scheduled to arrive
29 Skidded
30 Phone-tapping org.
31 Gas in advertising lights
33 Food fight sounds
35 Jed Clampett, e.g.
37 Difficult experience
40 Cajun cooking pod
41 Cambridge sch. from which I. M. Pei graduated
44 Apt rhyme of "crude"
45 Feeling of reverence
46 Nonsensical
48 Dr. ___, Eminem mentor
49 Sauce made with butter, egg yolks and lemon juice
52 Comedy Central's "The ___ Report"
54 Stage whispers
55 Uproar
58 Polish hero Walesa
59 Swallowed a loss
60 500 sheets of paper
61 "Do ___ others as . . ."

62 Mug shot subjects, informally
63 iPhone assistant who says that "42" is the meaning of life
64 Test cheater's sound

DOWN
1 Grow in popularity
2 Folded breakfast dishes
3 Longtime Nikon competitor
4 Mortar's partner
5 Pale-faced
6 Air traffic watchdog, for short
7 The whole shebang
8 Give an account of
9 Insurance company with a "spokesduck"
10 Snare or tom-tom
11 Home of U.C. San Diego

12 Cry after reaching the summit
13 Guillotines
19 Wallach of "The Magnificent Seven"
21 Result of overstrain, maybe
24 Fox's "American ___"
25 Annual El Paso football event
29 Cagey
32 Building addition
33 Camera letters
34 Patterns used for kilts
35 "___ give you the shirt off his back"
36 Company said to use about 1% of the world's wood supply
37 British buddy
38 Change the direction of, as traffic
39 Inhabitant
41 Cinderella and Rapunzel
42 Bees and butterflies
43 Start of a hole

45 Places to say "I do"
47 Seal, as a shipping crate
49 Sticks in the oven
50 Space ball
51 Supermodel Campbell
53 Radar screen point
56 Hawaiian gift
57 Regatta implement

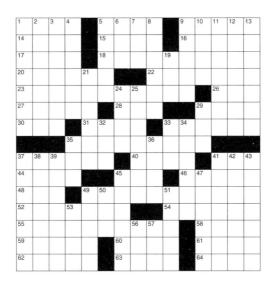

by David Steinberg and Bernice Gordon

ACROSS

1 Cry after an epiphany
4 Butt
7 Toy in a crib
13 *"Grey's Anatomy" actor Patrick
15 *Actress Jane who was a "Medicine Woman"
16 Short opera piece
17 "No kidding!"
18 Three-card hustle
19 "Where ___ go wrong?"
21 Wall St. initials
22 Annoyed one's bedmate, perhaps
24 Hawaii's state bird
26 With 40- and 48-Across, much-mocked ad phrase that could have been said by the answers to the four starred clues
32 Wood shaper
35 Sheet music abbr.
36 Brown beagle?
37 Whip . . . or something that can be whipped
40 See 26-Across
42 Said with one's hand on a stack of Bibles
43 Sparkly headwear
45 Follow closely
47 Fleur-de-___
48 See 26-Across
52 ___ close to schedule
53 Attends to hair and makeup, say
57 A long way off
61 And
63 Bonehead
64 Offshore race
66 Chocolaty spread since 1964
68 *Actor Jack who was "Quincy"
69 *"ER" actor George
70 Equilibrium
71 Lair
72 Publishers' hirees, for short

DOWN

1 Douglas who wrote "The Hitchhiker's Guide to the Galaxy"
2 Long-legged bird
3 Acid in proteins, informally
4 Look up to
5 Fishbowl accessory
6 Set of two
7 Jogs, in a way
8 Yes
9 Counterfeiter fighter
10 U.S. equivalent to the U.K.'s Laurence Olivier Award
11 San ___ Obispo, Calif.
12 Art Deco icon
14 ___ dish
15 "I Want to Hold Your Hand" through "All My Loving," on "Meet the Beatles!"
20 Crashers, e.g.
23 ___ lab
25 A seeming eternity
27 Celestial sphere
28 Milk dispenser
29 Handyman's belt item
30 Nashville site, familiarly
31 Bartender's stock
32 Prologue follower
33 Reason to call a plumber
34 Gusto
38 Coach Parseghian
39 Potato salad ingredient, informally
41 And
44 32 Beethoven pieces
46 Econ. indicator
49 Hall-of-Fame pitcher Ryan
50 King in "The Little Mermaid"
51 Single accompanier
54 Kanga and Roo creator
55 Propelled, as a raft
56 Remains behind
57 Temple receptacles
58 Arts and crafts material
59 Rain, in Spain
60 Cleaning cloths
62 How much 1990s music was issued
65 "Eww, I don't want to hear about it," in a text
67 Diminutive ending

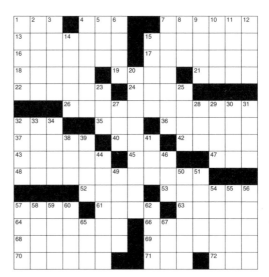

by Robyn Weintraub

ACROSS

1 Rude dude
4 Trash-hauling boat
8 Rigid
13 "___ wide" (dentist's directive)
15 Skye of "Say Anything . . ."
16 English Channel port town
17 Film designed to attract Academy Awards consideration
19 BMW and VW
20 "Orange" tea
21 Like most TV shows starting in the 1960s
23 War-torn part of Russia
25 Ninny
26 Fireplace residue
28 Go out, as a fire
29 Cable TV's Heartland, formerly
31 Relative of a frog
33 "Now!," on an order
36 Liability's opposite
40 Misfit . . . or what you get after the sequence described by the ends of 17-, 21-, 57- and 63-Across?
43 Pub game
44 ___ Grant (college financial aid)
45 Like him but not her
46 Colorado tribe
48 "___ so-o-o-o sleepy!"
50 "For shame!"
51 Feeling blue
53 Shiner
57 Problem with teeth alignment
59 Jobs to do
62 River flowing beneath Paris's Pont Neuf
63 Projection room item
65 Swimming competitions
66 Country whose name sounds like a Jamaican's cry
67 Hamlet, for one
68 Pizza part often eaten last
69 I.R.S. IDs
70 Quiet fan setting

DOWN

1 Home for hens
2 Vaulted church area
3 Piece of patio furniture
4 Brother or sister, for short
5 Instructs, informally
6 Chopping one might bring a tear to your eye
7 How sloppy kisses are given
8 Practice boxing
9 Avian Froot Loops mascot
10 Specks
11 Dental string
12 Suffix with Oktober or Ozz
14 Chemical formula for sodium hydroxide
18 Bassoon, e.g.
22 Quaker cereal grain
24 Informal goodbye
26 Only minimally
27 Furniture item that might seat three
30 Opposite of "Yep!"
32 Pupils who score in the 60s
34 Chowed down
35 Paddy wagon
37 Louisiana's has a nesting pelican with three chicks
38 Morays, e.g.
39 Long, long hike
41 D.D.E.'s predecessor
42 ___ jacket (protective wear)
47 Recede, as the tide
49 Pass (out)
51 Villain's look
52 Formal goodbye
54 Wheels for big wheels
55 Molecular bits
56 One of 10 in a series of football downs
57 "Semper Fi" org.
58 A little shuteye
60 Gambling game whose name spells a gambling town when the first letter is changed
61 Killed, as a dragon
64 Tie-___ (commercial promotions)

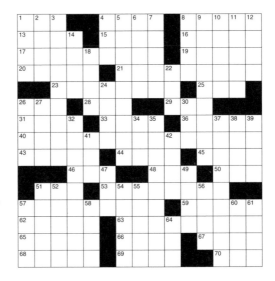

by Ian and Katie Livengood

ACROSS

1 Olympics awards
7 Nabs
15 Actress Mayim of "The Big Bang Theory"
16 Deals buyable via a tap on an app
17 IBM's Watson, essentially
19 "What did I tell you?"
20 "___ Carter III" (Lil Wayne 3× platinum album)
21 Finishes
22 Put down, as an uprising
24 Smooching on the street, e.g., briefly
26 Embolden oneself
33 Cookie ingredient in dirt cake
34 Tin Man's worry
35 Corn Pops competitor
36 "Leaving ___ Vegas"
37 23-Down of a classic L. Frank Baum novel
40 "So ___ heard"
41 Communication used at Gallaudet University, for short
42 Yours, in Tours
43 Declare
44 Dear
49 Take advantage of
50 Key key on a keyboard
51 Stick with a knife
54 Actor Efron of "Neighbors"
55 Beats by ___ (popular headphone brand)
58 Path taken by 37-Across to find the ends of 17-, 26- and 44-Across in [circled letters]
64 Unaided vision, with "the"
65 Ham-handed

66 Charge of the 1% against Occupy Wall Street
67 Feels

DOWN

1 Degs. held by Romney and Bush
2 The Emerald Isle
3 Possible outcome of an eHarmony match
4 2001 Will Smith biopic
5 Boost
6 Top of a mountain?
7 Film special FX
8 Southern constellation
9 David Axelrod or Karl Rove, for short
10 Rubber ducky locale
11 Erect
12 Horse hue
13 City west of Tulsa

14 Figs. with two hyphens
18 "Cold, hard" money
22 Quid pro ___
23 See 37-Across
24 Fancy-schmancy
25 Responsibility
26 Israel's ___ Heights
27 Clear
28 Electric car company
29 Abbreviate
30 ___ Goldsman, Oscar-winning screenwriter of "A Beautiful Mind"
31 Donor
32 Apply, as force
37 "___ what I'm talkin' 'bout!"
38 Plains tribe
39 Friend of Pooh
43 ___ Lingus
45 What Stolichnaya is sold in
46 Wyoming senator Mike
47 Library area

48 Jeer
51 Match up
52 Green-blue
53 ___-Seltzer
55 i's and j's have them
56 Bulldoze
57 Ben & Jerry's alternative
59 Some serious hosp. cases
60 Fifth-century Chinese dynasty
61 Fly-___ (close passes by plane)
62 "Losing My Religion" band
63 Jog

by Sam Buchbinder

ACROSS

1 Flower stalk
5 Secy., e.g.
9 Blue Ribbon brewer
14 Pledge drive bag
15 Sport with mallets
16 Mail carrier's rounds
17 Baja's opposite
18 Univ. instructor
19 St. ___ fire
20 Muzzle-loading firearm
23 Sandwich with toasted bread, for short
24 Surgical instrument holders
25 Lipton alternative
27 Lemon-peeling utensil
30 All wound up
31 Following behind, as a trailer
32 Rec room feature
36 Sch. in Lower Manhattan
37 "Oops!"
38 "All you can ___"
39 TV news employee
42 Topple
44 Smiles proudly
45 New moon and full moon
46 Self-confidence
48 All-American Soap Box Derby city
50 "The dog ate my homework," probably
51 Promotional ballpark giveaways
56 Site for washing instructions
58 Burden
59 Roof problem
60 Occupied, as a restroom
61 Riga resident
62 The "E" in HOMES
63 Wanderer
64 Rice-shaped pasta
65 Medicinal amount

DOWN

1 Knife wound
2 Ring, as a bell in a steeple
3 "___, Brute?"
4 Had it in mind
5 Show up
6 "Oops!"
7 Unpopular roommates
8 Bean curd
9 Birthday party staple
10 "You've got mail!" company
11 Big pollinators
12 Embezzled, e.g.
13 Short-tempered
21 Took from a card deck
22 Jouster's mount
26 Screener's org.
27 ___ oxide (beachgoer's protection)
28 New Age star from Ireland
29 Second-rate prizefighter
30 Federal tax enforcer, informally
32 "Y" facilities
33 Litigator's org.
34 Lois at the Daily Planet
35 Gate expectations, for short?
37 Sensual ballroom dance
40 Fair-hiring inits.
41 Talked pointlessly
42 "I'm in trouble now!"
43 Like the walls of many dens
45 Magician's cry
46 How a daring poker player goes
47 Instrument for Lady Gaga
48 Doubleday of baseball lore
49 One who might cry "Oops!"
52 Shoestring necktie
53 Prefix with dynamic
54 Locale for a speaker and honorees
55 ___-Ball
57 Spanish "that"

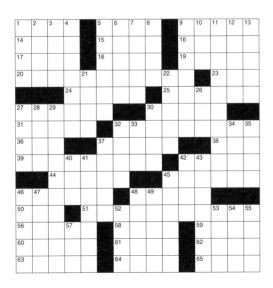

by Greg Johnson

34

ACROSS

1 Light bender
6 Hole to be dug out of?
10 Robbers' take
14 In verse, "His cheeks were like roses, his nose like a cherry!"
15 Vicinity
16 Mean sort
17 "It was ___ and stormy night . . ."
18 *Traveler on the Silk Road
20 Flora seen around Lent
22 "Watch your ___, young man!"
23 *Eggnog relative
26 Wing it
30 Anglers after morays
31 "O.K., have it your way"
32 Vietnamese holiday
35 ___ extra cost
36 Thing seen on a lab slide
38 70 yards square, approximately
40 "Hmm, can't remember"
41 Department store founder James Cash ___
42 Height: Prefix
43 Correctional workers, for short?
44 Comment immediately following a stage cue
45 What rain and paper towels may come in
47 Billy Ray or Miley
49 *Lover of Kermit
53 Cut with a ray
55 Novelist ___ de Balzac
56 *Edison lab site
61 International powerhouse in cricket
62 Window part

63 Canadian Plains tribe
64 Eggheaded sorts
65 Like patent infringers, often
66 Part of P.G.A.: Abbr.
67 Secret rendezvous

DOWN

1 Sacred hymn of praise
2 Many lines on pie charts
3 Taken together
4 X, in bowling
5 *Sign a treaty, say
6 Hoover ___
7 Disco '70s, e.g.
8 Playoff spots
9 ___ Bell
10 Desired
11 In times past
12 Clickable address, briefly
13 Guitarist Kottke

19 Bon Jovi's "Livin' ___ Prayer"
21 Torrid
24 50th state's state bird
25 ___-Magnon
27 For whom a vassal worked
28 Sleeping, say
29 Local politics and high school sports, for news reporters
32 Item under discussion
33 Foe
34 Kind of sax
36 Over again
37 *It's not worth arguing
39 Legally voided
40 Treats for swelling, as a joint
42 Tuna type, on menus
45 Slings mud at
46 One making a confession
48 ___ Paulo

50 Stop producing water, as a well
51 Crossword needs
52 Baker's supply
54 Pet care specialists, for short
56 AWOL chasers . . . or a hint to the answers to the six starred clues
57 Perrier, par exemple
58 Little Rock-to-Chicago dir.
59 Hi-___ monitor
60 Kesey or Follett

by Victor Fleming

ACROSS

1 Pyramid city close to Cairo
5 Mocking remarks
10 "Yikes!"
14 Achieved a perfect score on
15 Obstinate reply
16 African country bordering 12-Down
17 Socialite who inspired 1950's "Call Me Madam"
19 Texts, e.g.: Abbr.
20 Fossil fuel
21 Sulu and Uhura, e.g., on the Enterprise
23 1957 hit covered by Creedence Clearwater Revival in 1968
25 First word in many newspaper names
26 "___ you for real?"
27 ___ Dhabi
28 Stale-smelling
31 Like Old Norse writing
33 Workplace communication
35 Letters before an alias
36 Not eat eagerly
37 Pastrami and salami
40 Vietnam War weapon
43 Make a goof
44 Sea of Tranquility, for the Apollo 11 astronauts
48 Car fuel additive
49 Army NCOs
51 Site of a church kneeler
52 ___-la-la
53 McKellen who played Magneto in the "X-Men" films
55 One of a 1980s demographic
57 Run out of energy
61 Martinique et Guadeloupe
62 Many a car on the autobahn
63 Groups hired for high-profile cases

66 Carpentry spacer
67 Sky-blue
68 Where Vietnam is
69 Roget's listings: Abbr.
70 Theater reservations
71 1930s art style, informally

DOWN

1 Clothing chain with a "Baby" division
2 Drink cooler
3 Like a game with equal winners and losers
4 Old politico Stevenson
5 "Garfield" cartoonist Davis
6 Leaves dumbstruck
7 Deluxe
8 It's really something
9 ___ infection
10 Jane Austen heroine
11 What's filled up in a fill-up

12 African country bordering 16-Across
13 Cut up, as a frog
18 Kind of school after nursery school: Abbr.
22 Boy Scout ___ badge
23 Uncle ___
24 Hesitation about something
29 Slalom, say
30 Breaks . . . or an anagram of the ends of five Across answers in this puzzle
32 Golden State school up the coast from L.A.
34 Old jazz icon Anita
36 The "P" of G.O.P.
38 Perry of fashion
39 Part of a joule
40 Business setback recorded on Schedule C
41 Wither away
42 Add by degrees

45 Mollify
46 Earth-shaking
47 Animal whose name sounds like a pronoun
49 It goes "Ah-h-h-choo!"
50 Zoot ___
54 Mythical strong man
56 Beg
58 State trees of North Dakota and Massachusetts
59 Spanish water
60 Many a service station adjunct
64 "___ Misérables"
65 ___ Paulo

by Allan E. Parrish

ACROSS

1 "Oh, hell!"
5 Blood component
10 Bandmate of Crosby, Stills and Young
14 Dog bullied by Garfield
15 Snoop Dogg, for one, since 2012
16 "Let me think . . . yeah, that's stupid"
17 Perfect illustration
20 Fishhook attachment
21 Utterly wear out, in slang
22 Unfulfilled potential
29 Do one's best
30 Record company
31 Something horrible, with "the"
34 Battlefield food, for short
35 Honeydews, e.g.
36 Big Apple airport code
37 Pub tidbit
39 Letters in a help wanted ad
40 With the concession that
42 Palais ___ Sports (Paris arena)
43 Belief systems
44 Christopher who directed three Batman films
45 John who directed "The Maltese Falcon"
47 Gatherings in which C.E.O.'s are chosen
50 With 24-Down, blowout result
51 Stop
54 What tuition and the starts of 17-, 22-, 37-(?) and 47-Across are
60 Length × width, for a rectangle
61 Got the goat of
62 Functions
63 Slightest of complaints
64 Female students, condescendingly
65 Literary Jane

DOWN

1 Parts of an ellipsis
2 Yemeni port
3 First-week-of-school social event
4 Unfortunate bottom line on an earnings report
5 Old hand
6 China's ___-tzu
7 Invite
8 "Family Guy" baby
9 "It takes money to make money," e.g.
10 What's required in some passwords
11 Bit of sound equipment
12 Show on which Lennon and McCartney considered reuniting, for short
13 Hard row to ___
18 Rorschach test image
19 Small computer program
23 Citi Field mascot
24 See 50-Across
25 Late, as a video store rental
26 Wind instruments
27 Snake poison
28 Someone ___ (not mine or yours)
31 Contingency arrangement
32 Place where one can come home and chill?
33 Indian drum
35 "Can you give me any alternative?"
37 Hobo's accessory
38 Home located in the sticks?
41 Batting helmet feature
43 Naive young woman
45 Not homo-
46 "___ upon a time . . ."
48 Card tricks, e.g.
49 Smart-alecky
52 Fortuneteller
53 "To be," in Latin
54 Headgear often worn backward
55 Miner's find
56 Appomattox surrenderer
57 Barely manage, with "out"
58 Crossed (out)
59 Groups of cops: Abbr.

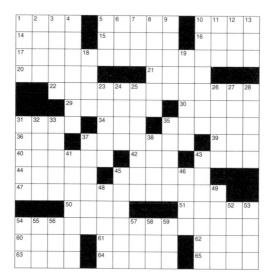

by Ethan Cooper

ACROSS

1 Glasgow natives
6 Horse's feedbox fill
10 Spill the beans
14 "Yippee!"
15 Get-out-of-jail money
16 Toy construction piece
17 Ann ___, Mich.
18 Long-distance callers' necessities
20 2011 Tony-winning religious satire, with "The"
22 Cunning
23 Speckled horse
24 "___ Bovary"
28 A toddler might throw one
29 Wager
30 Hip, in the '60s
31 Hyperlocal way to campaign
36 Barbecue fare
37 Hall-of-Fame Broncos QB John
38 Charged particle
39 Skater Sonja who won three Olympic gold medals
40 Slight coloring
41 Black magic item
43 Mother of Cain and Abel
44 ___ Lingus (Irish carrier)
45 London lav
46 Edit
48 Cutlet meat
50 European peak
53 Milestone birthday, informally . . . with a hint to 20-, 31- and 41-Across
56 Uncle Ben's offering
59 Actress Greta who famously said "I want to be alone"
60 Boingo service at airports
61 Pub potables
62 Flying saucer occupant

63 Computer that runs OS X
64 Where to get eggs
65 Destitute

DOWN

1 Q-tips, e.g.
2 Christmas song
3 "Goody!"
4 Conned
5 Campus sisterhood
6 First president born outside the continental U.S.
7 Boy's name that's almost always first alphabetically
8 Cake layer
9 Jail, slangily
10 Golden-haired
11 Was ahead
12 "Act your ___!"
13 2013 World Series winner, on scoreboards
19 Paint layer

21 Pic
25 ___ acid (protein building block)
26 Exxon merger partner
27 Famous auto flop
28 Campus brotherhood, briefly
29 007
31 Discourage
32 ___ Oyl
33 Had possession of
34 Christian of couture
35 Tic-tac-toe winner
36 Start all over
39 Rowdy soccer fan, for one
41 Purple Heart recipient, e.g.
42 Scandinavian saint
44 Heartsickness, e.g.
47 Place for a ghost
48 Drinking and gambling
49 Discharge
50 Eagle's perch

51 Like oak leaves and brains
52 Insincere type
54 Ill temper
55 Hollow between hills
56 1910s conflict: Abbr.
57 That guy
58 ". . . woodchuck chuck, ___ woodchuck could chuck wood?"

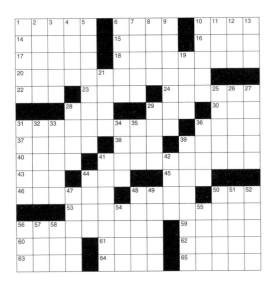

by Dan Schoenholz

ACROSS

1 Easy toss
4 Country getaways, in Russia
10 Cliff feature
14 Start of a Latin trio
15 Support, as a principle
16 Subject of Dante's "Inferno"
17 Behavioral quirks
19 Together, in France
20 Oven button
21 These, to Thérèse
22 Addis ___, Ethiopia
23 Sub commander of fiction
25 Home to James Joyce
26 Bow (to)
29 Smartly attired
31 See 39-Across
32 Electricity source
37 Thin as ___
39 With 31-Across, natural flavor enhancer
40 Noted performing whale
41 Electricity source
44 Environmental activist Brockovich
45 Many babysitters
46 Pepsi competitor
48 Round a certain corner in Monopoly
51 Brought (along)
52 "No" voters
53 Number often given to a maître d'
55 Brown-toned photo
59 River to 16-Across
60 Class outings
62 Pinball infraction
63 Open, as a letter
64 Pond fish
65 ___-deucey
66 Noisy like a clunker
67 Hollywood's Harris and Helms

DOWN

1 Very soft fleece source
2 Poet Khayyám
3 Cher's son Chaz
4 Crossed swords
5 Mo. when Shakespeare was born
6 TV's "___ and the Man"
7 Cheat, in slang
8 Old-fashioned charity
9 Onetime New Left org.
10 Starter of a dance craze in 18-Down
11 Kidney-related
12 "I was home watching TV," e.g.
13 Gather bit by bit
18 See 10-Down
22 BMWs, but not BMXs
24 Kitten call
25 The shakes, with "the"
26 Rush order
27 Dear one, Italian-style
28 Discovery in a British mystery
29 Reds and Pirates, for short
30 Jai ___
33 Dog of 1930s–'40s mysteries
34 Corn syrup brand
35 Jannings who won the first Best Actor Oscar
36 ___ roll (sushi offering)
38 Proceeds like a boring meeting
42 ___-Caps (movie candy)
43 For, in a debate
47 Like a mistake that's going to hurt you
48 Lasagna or linguine
49 Three Stooges bit
50 Fashion sense
51 Apartment rental sign
53 Turner who sang "The Best," 1989
54 Last part of the country to report election returns, usually, with "the"
56 Highway
57 "Mini" music player
58 How used goods are often sold
60 Lab's coat
61 The Cowboys, on a scoreboard

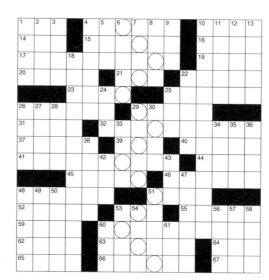

by Ed Sessa

ACROSS

1. ___ and Clark expedition
6. "Romeo and Juliet" has five of them
10. Stomach muscles, for short
13. Juneau's home
15. Season to be jolly
16. Singer Reed or Rawls
17. Performer who may have a navel decoration
19. Color, as Easter eggs
20. Eye amorously
21. Souped-up engine sound
22. Bebop, e.g.
23. Bread for a ham sandwich
24. Drunk's interjection
25. Wine: Prefix
27. Some British pub food
32. Diana Rigg's role on "The Avengers"
35. With precise timing
36. ___ Cong
37. Junk, from Yiddish
40. Precursor to a game of chicken
41. Hall-of-Fame QB John
43. Jailbird
45. Risk, figuratively
48. Doozy
49. TV show created by Lorne Michaels, for short
50. Car item that speaks, in brief
53. Jetty
56. "Don't Cry for Me Argentina" musical
58. Eins, zwei, ___
59. Web address
60. Common stir-fry ingredients
62. Suffix with expert
63. Bruins of the N.C.A.A.
64. Command used when creating a new file name
65. April payment
66. ___ ex machina
67. What quivering legs feel like . . . or a word that can precede the starts of 17-, 27-, 45- and 60-Across

DOWN

1. Childbirth
2. Funeral song
3. Hit 2008 Pixar film with a robot
4. Getaway spot in the sea
5. Clouds' locale
6. The "A" of A.D.
7. What a butterfly emerges from
8. Overflowed (with)
9. Camera type, in brief
10. Alan of "M*A*S*H"
11. ___ II Men (R&B group)
12. Canal to the Red Sea
14. Counseled
18. Zodiac symbol for Sagittarius
22. Mr. X
24. Au courant
26. Cpl. or sgt.
27. How Hamlet stabs Polonius
28. Hebrew "A"
29. "Not if ___ help it!"
30. 100%
31. Crystal ball gazer
32. "Be it ___ so humble . . ."
33. Venus de ___
34. Whimper
38. Colorful parts of many birds
39. Takes for ransom
42. Word that completes the song titles "___ Baby" and "Baby It's ___"
44. The "S" in R.S.V.P.
46. Lamb's coat
47. Polynesian land whose Internet suffix is .tv
50. Dish that Oliver Twist asked for more of
51. "He loves me, he loves me not" flower part
52. Spacek of "Carrie"
53. Leave work for good
54. ___ Major
55. "Jeopardy!" host Trebek
57. Bring ___ a third party
58. Peace symbol
60. Blossom-to-be
61. Old British rule in India

by Andrea Carla Michaels

ACROSS

1 Horse race's starting point
5 Lovers' quarrel
9 Bracelet location
14 Rows
15 Novelist ___ Stanley Gardner
16 Lena of stage and screen
17 Golf course hazard
18 Use friendly persuasion
19 Territory east of Alaska
20 1990s R&B group with a repetitive-sounding name
23 Some doorways
24 Sinus specialist, briefly
25 Genre of Walter Isaacson's "Steve Jobs," for short
26 ___ pedal (guitar accessory)
29 City midway between Detroit and Toronto
33 Throws a tantrum
35 Thumb-to-forefinger signal
36 Hats, informally
37 What Velcro may substitute for
38 Commercial ending with Water
39 Curriculum ___
40 Looked at
41 Early Mets manager Hodges
42 Ophthalmologist's concern
43 June to September, in India
46 Bank acct. earnings
47 Whiskey variety
48 ___-roaring
49 "Today" rival, for short
52 How a motormouth talks . . . or what 20-, 29- and 43-Across literally have in common
55 Last word of "The Star-Spangled Banner"
58 "Topaz" author Leon
59 Penny
60 Psyched
61 Dish you might sprinkle cheese on
62 "Get it?" response
63 File material
64 Ugly Duckling, eventually
65 "The ___ the limit!"

DOWN

1 The family in the 2009 best seller "This Family of Mine"
2 Hank who hit 755 homers
3 Like sheer fabric or sautéed onions
4 Catch sight of
5 Another round at the buffet, say
6 Immediately
7 Jai ___
8 Required school purchase, maybe
9 "Oh, what the heck?"
10 Philanderer
11 Grate on
12 ___-cone
13 Important number on Downing Street
21 Camp sights
22 Porker's sound
26 Secretary
27 Actor Quinn
28 Old Testament book
30 Maureen Dowd pieces
31 They can take a pounding
32 Samuel on the Supreme Court
33 Resin used in incense
34 Synthetic fabric
38 Ingredients in pesto
39 Italian motor scooter
41 Francisco who painted frescoes
42 Dampens, as a parade
44 Stubborn
45 Beethoven's Third
50 $$$
51 Gets the pot started
52 Choice on a gambling line
53 Stalemate
54 TV drama set in the D.C. area
55 Busy one
56 Crash into
57 Store in a cask, say

by Gary Cee

ACROSS

1 Noggin
5 Handout to a party guest
10 Almost any "Get rich quick!" offer
14 House overhang
15 Jong who wrote "Fear of Flying"
16 Frat house party wear
17 Bank heist group
19 Visa or MasterCard rival, informally
20 Conversed
21 Tiny type size
23 The "S" in 36-Across
24 Sweet rum component
28 Relatives by marriage
30 Rome's ___ Fountain
31 Appurtenance for Santa or Sherlock Holmes
34 Cheer for a torero
35 Morgue identification
36 Sch. in Baton Rouge
37 Indy 500 leader
39 Russian jet
40 Changes
42 Hamburger holder
43 Hair goops
44 Kind of question with only two answers
45 South-of-the-border nap
47 Company downsizings
49 Signed, as a contract
53 "A pity!"
54 Coastal land south of Congo
55 Couple
57 British rocker with the 1979 #1 hit "Da Ya Think I'm Sexy?"
60 Electrical adapter letters

61 Japanese dog breed
62 ___ vera (skin soother)
63 Cry on a roller coaster
64 Adjusted the pitch of, as an instrument
65 Sunbeams

DOWN

1 Opposite (or synonym) of worsts
2 Really bother
3 St. Teresa of ___
4 Item not worn on casual Fridays
5 Fight between late-night hosts, e.g.
6 Dadaist artist Jean
7 Pep
8 Atlantic and Pacific
9 Stove
10 Height
11 "I'm stranded and need a ride"
12 Grow older

13 Reach the limit, with "out"
18 Astute
22 Fur trader John Jacob ___
24 Telephone
25 Not very much
26 To no ___ (in vain)
27 Bobby who lost 1973's Battle of the Sexes tennis match
29 Eton johns
31 "Hamlet" and "Macbeth"
32 Speck of land in the sea
33 Takes off the front burner
35 Gets color at the beach
37 Univ. lecturers
38 Stage prompts
41 Carry out, as a law
43 Fight over turf
45 Numerical puzzle with a 9 x 9 grid

46 Fork prong
48 Gem weight
50 Down Under "bear"
51 Jetson boy of 1960s TV
52 Results of using eHarmony
54 Not very much
55 Animal foot
56 German's "Oh my!"
58 Loud noise
59 Sault ___ Marie, Ont.

by Ian Livengood

ACROSS

1 Drink with a lizard logo
5 Big balls
10 W.W. I's Battle of the ___
14 Winter truck attachment
15 Lagoon surrounder
16 Brand of shoes or handbags
17 Advantage
18 One of the Gabor sisters
19 Exercise on a mat
20 Reds and Braves, for short
22 Rodeo rope
24 Swiss river
25 Like some home improvement projects, briefly
26 Actor Claude of "B. J. and the Bear"
28 Jazz great named after an Egyptian god
30 Riddle
32 "Trust me!"
33 Home of the University of Nevada
34 Cooks gently
38 Valuable finds suggested by the circled letters
41 Rascal
42 Snowman in Disney's "Frozen"
45 Scattered
48 Like the snow in a shaken snow globe
50 Rub out
51 Makes a harsh sound
54 Mahmoud Abbas's grp.
55 "Ugh, German sausage is the wurst," e.g.
56 Think optimistically
58 Settles (into)
60 Nothing doing?
62 Poet Nash

64 Advanced law degs.
65 Stravinsky ballet
66 Cheddarlike cheese
67 Pricey seating option
68 Darns, e.g.
69 What comes out of an angry person's ears in cartoons
70 Sprinted

DOWN

1 Big ___ (person who takes a date to a fast-food restaurant, jocularly)
2 Well-established
3 Barely missing par
4 Pitcher
5 Group of whales
6 Maker of Asteroids and Missile Command
7 Access a private account
8 Actors Alan and Robert
9 Blind part
10 "We did it!"
11 Everett ___, player of Mr. Bernstein in "Citizen Kane"
12 Mystery prizes
13 Greet with loud laughter
21 Spade of "The Maltese Falcon"
23 Hit ___ spot
27 Lawrence who co-wrote two of the "Star Wars" films
29 Take out of an overhead bin, say
31 Stimulates, informally
32 Billy
35 Red Roof ___
36 Nasty political accusations
37 Old British sports cars
39 Gave a cattle call?
40 Twaddle

43 Roone who created "Nightline" and "20/20"
44 Obeyed a dentist's directive
45 Brown-toned photos
46 Plod
47 Almost had no stock left
49 NNW's opposite
51 Sired
52 Soup server
53 Itsy-bitsy creature
57 Fabulous birds
59 "___ well"
61 U.S.N.A. grad: Abbr.
63 Citi Field team, on scoreboards

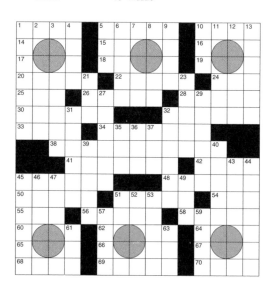

by Gerry Wildenberg

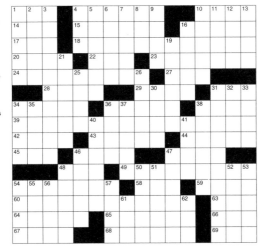

43

ACROSS

1 Hwy. speed
4 Shocked . . . SHOCKED!
10 Brothers and sisters, for short
14 Sun. talk
15 Hang around a public place
16 Actor/stand-up comic Foxx
17 Opposite of yeah
18 Words to a local success story
20 Unexciting
22 Org. on a toothpaste tube
23 After everything's been said and done
24 What a local success story achieves
27 Italian "god"
28 "Darn it!"
29 Salinger girl
31 Catch in the act
34 Longtime Pittsburgh product
36 Dispute
38 Mud
39 What a local success story comes from
42 Website with a "Buy It Now" button
43 Not in the ___
44 Cookies that can be twisted apart
45 Zero-star review
46 "___ have to wait"
47 Pacific island "where America's day begins"
48 Sign of a sellout
49 What a local success story does
54 Copy-and-paste illustrations
58 Year, in Mexico
59 Automaker Ferrari
60 Local success story
63 Dance often done with top hat and cane
64 With speed
65 Hit 2002 film with talking sloths
66 Charlemagne's domain: Abbr.
67 1/4 bushel
68 O.K.'d silently
69 Wild blue yonder

DOWN

1 Rachel Maddow's channel
2 Norman Vincent ___, author of "The Power of Positive Thinking"
3 Nixon White House chief of staff
4 Foreman opponent
5 Racing vehicle on a small track
6 Delhi language
7 Greatly bothered
8 Use needle and thread
9 "___ Little Tenderness" (1960s hit)
10 Dealt with
11 Start of a web address?
12 Actress Jessica
13 Bad thing to hit if one didn't mean to "reply all"
16 Andrews of "Mary Poppins"
19 Geezers
21 As a result, in formal language
25 Event attended by Cinderella
26 Safecrackers
30 Hearts or clubs
31 Pregnant pause?
32 2012 Best Picture with Ben Affleck
33 Mrs. Truman
34 Herding dog, informally
35 Big instrument in a marching band
36 Brother of Cain
37 Kingdom
38 Vision of a distant oasis, maybe
40 Six Flags coaster whose name is Spanish for "The Bull"
41 Entre ___
46 Livid
47 First name of three U.S. presidents
48 Bit of dust
50 Oohed and ___
51 Work, as dough
52 Arkansas's ___ Mountains
53 Idiotic
54 Fellow
55 Horse's run
56 Computer whose second letter is capitalized
57 Romulus or Remus
61 Sgt., for one
62 Word ref. started in 1857

by Eric Sydney Phillips

ACROSS

1 Friend of Gandalf
6 Put ___ disadvantage
9 Microwaves, informally
14 Like a whole lot
15 ___ Chemical (Fortune 500 company)
16 NATO alphabet letter between Alfa and Charlie
17 Mars explorer
18 Modern host of 35-Across
20 Erupted
21 Aplomb
22 "Peter Pan" dog
23 Proctor's command
25 Touches
27 King with a golden touch
28 Reliever's stat
30 Air Force One occupant, acronymically
31 Shopping ___
32 Ad Council output, for short
35 Long-running game show with a feature spelled out clockwise by this puzzle's circled letters
38 Dummkopf
39 Its chips aren't for eating
40 Device read with a laser
41 How some home videos are stored
42 Food that gets tossed?
43 ___ Madness (Snapple flavor)
45 Principle
46 Father-___
47 Exudes
50 Crumble under pressure
53 Longtime host of 35-Across
55 Sal of "Exodus"
56 "O, I am ___!" (Polonius's last words)
57 ___ fly (R.B.I. producer)
58 ___ Marbles (British Museum display)
59 Unhealthily pale-skinned
60 Flamenco shout
61 "In my opinion . . ."

DOWN

1 Zinger
2 Winner of a popular TV talent show
3 Red marks of affection
4 Fomented, as trouble
5 Anthem preposition
6 Append
7 Doughnut shapes
8 Leaves slack-jawed
9 Jimmy Fallon's home
10 Planet with 27 moons
11 One of 14 in a gold chain
12 18 of 38 roulette numbers
13 ___ bean
19 Drives recklessly
21 Rho preceders
24 Blue circle on a range
26 Fraternity party detritus
27 Mineralogist for whom a scale is named
28 Drive recklessly, maybe
29 Seed coat
30 Bake sale grp., perhaps
31 Canadian comedy show of the 1970s–'80s
32 They may be given for rude humor
33 Like many horses' feet
34 Banking convenience, for short
36 Like many rainy-day activities
37 Original name for J.F.K. Airport
41 At all
42 Parisian possessive
43 Dinero
44 Palestinian leader Mahmoud ___
45 Canonical hour before sext
46 Recipe amt.
48 "Your point being . . . ?"
49 Enthusiasm
51 Luke Skywalker's twin
52 Broadway honor
54 "___ questions?"
55 "Don't tell ___ can't!"

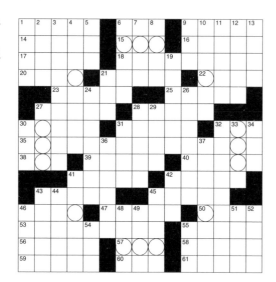

by Kyle T. Dolan

ACROSS

1. Org. with merit badges
4. Cousin of a clarinet
8. Sir ___ Newton
13. Western Hemisphere treaty grp.
14. Earns in the end
15. Gradually changes (into)
17. 1975 Eagles hit about a woman having an affair
19. Push
20. Bangkok native
21. Mined rocks
23. Pleasantly warm
24. Title hit of a 1952 Gene Kelly musical
27. When an airplane is due to take off, for short
28. Rubbish
29. Manipulate
30. "___ goes nothing!"
32. On ___ with (equal to)
34. Drunk's condition, for short
35. Tyrannosaurus ___
36. Lost . . . or, in two words, an apt description of 17-, 24-, 47- and 59-Across
39. Hectic hosp. areas
40. Circle section
41. Tiniest amount
42. Small whirlpool
44. Old AT&T rival
45. Figured out, as a joke
46. Lady of la casa: Abbr.
47. 1930 Harry Richman hit whose title describes ostentatious living
54. Feature of a clock radio
55. Singer/song-writer Laura
56. Memo heading
57. Antigovernment force

59. 1978 Billy Joel hit that gave its name to a 2002 Broadway musical
61. Yammerer
62. ". . . lived happily ___ after"
63. "___ changed man!"
64. Where chicks hang out?
65. "Bill & ___ Excellent Adventure"
66. Forerunners of CDs

DOWN

1. Heavy door locks
2. Give an informal greeting
3. Chinese or 20-Across
4. Start of almost every ZIP code in New York
5. Farther past
6. Cheri formerly of "S.N.L."
7. German industrial city
8. Unruly child
9. Ice cream alternative
10. Loud, as a crowd
11. Clapped
12. Element-ary school subject?
16. Guile
18. French-speaking African nation
22. Narrow marine passageway
25. List component
26. Part of a rhinoceros
30. Almost impossible, as a task
31. Easily enthused
32. Kutcher of "Two and a Half Men"
33. Letter before omega
35. Defensive embankment
37. Victor's cry
38. Richard of "American Gigolo"
43. Bobby of 1950s–'60s pop
45. Lime-flavored cocktail

46. Pushed hard
48. Arduous journeys
49. Citi Field player, for short
50. Treasure cache
51. How much food is fried
52. Card that tops all others
53. Some sorority women
58. Class older than jrs.
60. Apr. 15 payment recipient

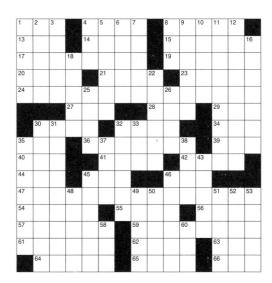

by Robyn Weintraub

46

ACROSS

1 Fix, as an election
4 Mountaineer's undertaking
9 Oktoberfest exclamation
14 Swiss river
15 Fisher with a pot
16 Show one's sorry (for)
17 Lt.'s inferior
18 Hoist
19 Out-and-out
20 Oktoberfest exclamation
23 Opening of a play
24 Amped
28 Oktoberfest exclamation
31 Metro stop: Abbr.
32 Vegetarian's protein source
33 ___ Vegas
34 Joe of "Casino"
36 Access the Internet, say
37 Oktoberfest exclamation
39 Mother hen's charges
42 Zones
43 Size of an idiot's brain, jokingly
46 Flight-related prefix
47 TV channel often on in airports
48 Oktoberfest exclamation
50 Loses one's grip?
52 Lose one's grip
53 Oktoberfest exclamation
58 Martian, e.g.
61 The "U" of E.U.
62 Time in history
63 Sci-fi or romance
64 Hedren of Hitchcock's "The Birds"
65 ___ Aviv
66 9-, 20-, 28-, 37-, 48- or 53-Across
67 Knight's ride
68 Used a tuffet, e.g.

DOWN

1 Klugman's co-star on "The Odd Couple"
2 Lee who led Chrysler, 1978–'92
3 Warts and such
4 ___ denied (Supreme Court phrase)
5 One of Jacob's wives
6 "Would ___ to you?"
7 See-through stocking material
8 Recess
9 Impertinent
10 With nowhere to go but down
11 Auction grouping
12 Arles article
13 German magazine ___ Spiegel
21 Actress Vardalos
22 ___ cozy
25 Follow relentlessly
26 Martian's craft, say
27 Many a "?" clue in a crossword
29 Apple music player
30 Encountered
31 Derision
35 All-stars
36 Sot
37 Enthusiastic supporters
38 Cul-de-___
39 Prada product
40 Old car that's an anagram of 41-Down
41 Refinery input
43 Some rabbit food
44 Land on the Red Sea
45 Paver's supply
47 Low isle
49 That: Sp.
51 Claude who painted "Water Lilies"
54 The "U" of C.P.U.
55 Offensive-smelling
56 Bill Clinton's Arkansas birthplace
57 Sooner city
58 Insurance worker: Abbr.
59 Fierce sort, astrologically
60 ___ pickle

by Matt Skoczen and Victor Fleming

ACROSS

1 German auto whose logo depicts a rearing horse
8 ___ Sprockets, George Jetson's employer
15 It's played with mallets and wickets . . .
16 . . . with 108 cards
17 Fastened
18 Six years, in the U.S. Senate
19 Reply ___ (email option)
20 Chews like a beaver
21 Exams for H.S. juniors
24 Frilly, as lingerie
25 Autos
29 No ifs, ___ or buts
30 "Here, boy!"
31 One whose job is to park 25-Across
32 Silent "yes"
33 Japanese rice wine
34 Swiss watch city
35 ___ and don'ts
36 . . . with a mat with colored circles
38 Like one after work?: Abbr.
39 Cousins of giraffes
41 Slippery
42 Prefix with cycle
43 "Don't worry about it!"
44 Infomercial, e.g.
45 Additionally
46 ___ and sciences
47 Chaz Bono's mom
48 Enter, as data
49 Place to get a perm
51 Counterpart of his
52 Test taker going "Psst!," say
55 Brave deeds
59 . . . with dashes on paper
60 . . . with steelies and aggies
61 Plays the market
62 Watches secretly

DOWN

1 Dell and HP products
2 Mined rocks
3 Bird in "Arabian Nights"
4 Leg-building exercises
5 Biceps-building exercises
6 Achilles' weak spot
7 When to expect takeoff, for short
8 Ornamental light fixture
9 Philippine island in W.W. II fighting
10 From square one
11 X-ray type
12 WNW's opposite
13 8½" × 11" paper size: Abbr.
14 Candied Thanksgiving food
20 Playoff series finale . . . or an apt title for this puzzle considering the number and length of its theme entries
21 Box opener of myth
22 . . . with cues and 22 balls
23 Season to taste, in a certain way
24 Trickster of myth
26 With attentiveness
27 . . . with black-and-white disks
28 Depot
30 Crows' cries
31 Extremely
33 Pixy ___ (candy)
34 Neuter, as a male horse
37 Rip
40 Book excerpt
44 Roses' defenses
45 Oxygen-needing bacteria
47 Baseball shoe feature
48 ___ Walsh, three-time Olympic beach volleyball gold medalist
50 Convenience store conveniences
51 Pile
52 White Sox home, for short
53 ___ Solo of "Star Wars"
54 It's stamped at the P.O.
55 "___ Pinafore"
56 They, in Paris
57 Corp. bigwig
58 Fig. in the form XXX-XX-XXXX

by Greg Johnson

ACROSS

1 Sign of healing
5 Place to put a stethoscope
10 With 16-Across, donate
14 Doctor Zhivago's love
15 Pry bar
16 See 10-Across
17 Candid
18 Midwest air hub
19 Rib, e.g.
20 What gossip columnists do?
23 Headache
24 One ___ time
25 Peep from a sheep
28 "Sucks to be you!"
31 Earth tones
33 Slow flow
36 What mathematicians do?
38 Big name in appliances
40 Producer of a tirade
41 Missouri city, familiarly
42 What bouncers do?
45 Madre's brothers
46 Strands in December?
47 Squeeze, informally
49 ___ trice
50 Hi-___
52 Starr of old comics
56 What literary critics do?
59 Thomas ___ Edison
62 "The Gentleman Is ___" (Rodgers and Hammerstein song)
63 Soul singer Redding
64 With 67-Across, coastal Maine
65 Bygone communication
66 SeaWorld attraction
67 See 64-Across
68 Put up
69 Twitter ___ (news source)

DOWN

1 It's a sin
2 Frank who directed "It Happened One Night"
3 Fields
4 Outdoor concert sites
5 Tight shot
6 Gleeful giggle
7 Rescue mission, briefly
8 Missionary Junípero ___
9 "Rock-a-bye, baby" location
10 Yaks
11 ___ Jima
12 Vehicle for a news team
13 Needle feature
21 "Evil Woman" band, for short
22 Food items that can be messy to eat
25 Cinema canine
26 "Star Wars" droid, informally
27 Total idiots
29 Smooth-tongued
30 Dances around a lifted chair, maybe
32 Go ballistic
33 Christine of "Chicago Hope"
34 How the Titanic was going before it struck an iceberg
35 Woman who has a way with words?
37 Semester, e.g.
39 Old Olds
43 Take to another level
44 What lies between the lines
48 Hit sign
51 Meal that often includes matzo ball soup
53 Saltpetre
54 Clear for takeoff?
55 Syrian strongman
56 "I ___ blame you"
57 Something to audition for
58 Architect's detail, for short
59 Citrus drink suffix
60 Mauna ___
61 Golfs, e.g., informally

by Adam G. Perl

ACROSS

1 Travel aimlessly, with "about"
4 Sis's sibling
7 Studio with a lion mascot
10 Standard sugar measure: Abbr.
13 King Kong, e.g.
14 Permit
15 Answer to "Paris est-il la capitale de la France?"
16 Indian immigrant on "The Simpsons"
17 Instant
20 Gen ___ (member of the MTV Generation)
21 Nutritional supplement brand
22 Lo-cal beers
24 Attire for Caesar
26 Product that competes with Uncle Ben's
29 John who won the 1964 Heisman Trophy
31 High-ranking angels
32 Apt anagram of COSTAR – S
33 Bridge
35 Midnight
42 Bald person's lack
43 Expire, as a subscription
44 ___ illusion
49 What a medical examiner examines
50 1965 Beatles hit that begins "Got a good reason for taking the easy way out"
53 Almighty
54 Judy's brother on "The Jetsons"
55 It's north of California
57 ___ of Tranquillity
58 Time leading up to Easter
63 555-55-5555, e.g.: Abbr.
64 Apex
65 Gulager of "McQ"
66 TV scientist Bill
67 Courtroom figure: Abbr.
68 Cloud's locale
69 "For ___ a jolly good fellow"
70 Number of years in a decade

DOWN

1 Exxon product
2 Smartphone purchase
3 Political conventiongoer
4 Nonkosher sandwiches
5 Sheet that might list one's college degree and work experience
6 Cheri of old "S.N.L."
7 Oink : pig :: ___ : cow
8 Revolver, e.g.
9 Bette of "Beaches"
10 Piece of advice from H&R Block
11 Oration
12 Pocketbooks
18 How pawns are arranged, at first
19 100 yrs.
23 Lyricist Gershwin
24 "___ is so you!"
25 Response to an insult
27 Southwest alternative, for short
28 Home to Dollywood and Graceland: Abbr.
30 Prefix with glyceride
33 Resell, as concert tickets
34 Letter after upsilon
36 From Bangkok
37 Shine, in some brand names
38 Jean of "Bombshell"
39 Foe
40 Lenin's land, for short
41 Critic Rex
44 Texas city named after a Ukrainian city
45 Least tanned
46 Despot
47 "Who am ___ argue?"
48 Underground tombs
49 Louisiana style of cooking
51 Opposite of neg.
52 Psychologist Fromm
56 Wildebeests
59 "All systems go"
60 007, for one
61 Cyclops or cyclone feature
62 Range of knowledge

by Patrick Blindauer

50

ACROSS

1 Alternative version of a song
6 Is into
10 Karl, Richard or Harpo
14 Actress Donovan of "Clueless"
15 Something spinach has
16 Switchboard attendant: Abbr.
17 Dramatic note in Verdi's "Di quella pira"
18 Grandma, familiarly
19 Story with many chapters
20 TIME
23 Baseball family of note
24 Not optional: Abbr.
25 ___ Miss
26 Part of 31-Down: Abbr.
28 Force = ___ × acceleration
30 Single
32 "Much ___ About Nothing"
33 Egg cell
34 Mo. that seems like it should be seventh
35 TIME
41 Mined material
42 Arduous hike
43 Palindromic woman's name
44 Rho-tau linkup
47 Senator Harry of Nevada
48 Kristoff's reindeer in "Frozen"
49 "Much ___ About Nothing" ("The Simpsons" episode)
50 Speedometer letters
52 Pier
54 TIME
59 Days of ___
60 Uptight, informally
61 Preoccupy

62 Brings to a close
63 Giant in the fruit and vegetable market
64 Avoid
65 Word before home and room
66 ___ for it (invites trouble)
67 Two-time U.S. Open winner Monica

DOWN

1 Talk show host Diane of 31-Down
2 "On the Waterfront" director Kazan
3 Seasonal traveler
4 Promising beginning?
5 Craft knife brand
6 Natural history museum display
7 Dry country whose name is an anagram of wet weather
8 They're doomed . . . doomed!
9 Trap

10 Swamp stuff
11 Judd who wrote and directed "Knocked Up"
12 Delight
13 Like "Midnight Cowboy," originally
21 Gulf War vehicle
22 Tiny complaint
26 Few Z's
27 Org. with an oral fixation?
29 Struck, old-style
31 "Fresh Air" airer
33 Cloverleaf part
34 Home of Pippi Longstocking
36 With 44-Down, fictional prankster
37 Beans in a burrito
38 Elite fighter
39 Palindromic woman's name
40 Vied for office
44 See 36-Down
45 What Apple's Project Purple became

46 Two of five in basketball
47 Big chargers in Africa
48 Endeavor
51 Luxury label
53 French heads
55 Word repeated by a roadie into a microphone
56 Bacteriologist Jonas
57 "My man!"
58 Unlocks, in verse

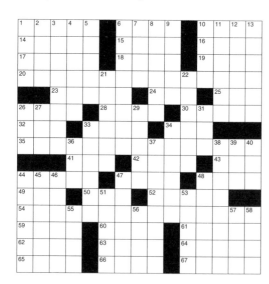

by Patrick Blindauer

ACROSS

1 Topmost points
6 Tennis champ Kournikova
10 Scribbles (down)
14 Target number to hit
15 Jetty
16 Southern vegetable that's often deep-fried
17 Opposite of rural
18 1/640 of a square mile
19 Banister, e.g.
20 Muscles that are crunched
21 Eponymous star of a 1960s sitcom, the only American TV star with his three initials
24 Author Gay
25 Desert rest stops
26 Subsequent prescription order
29 Abel's brother
31 "Top Chef" appliance
32 ___ Corner (Westminster Abbey locale)
34 Gasoline additive brand
37 Long-running western anthology, the only American TV series with its three initials
41 Make a misstep
42 Urge to act
43 Downloadable programs
44 Any "Salome" solo
45 Very beginning
47 Gettysburg general George
50 New Hampshire senator Shaheen
53 TV hookup option . . . or what you are by solving this puzzle?
55 TV host Dobbs
58 Chocolate ___ cake (dessert with a molten center)
59 River that starts at Pittsburgh
60 Amherst school, in brief

62 "What's ___ for me?"
63 Peeling potatoes in a mess hall, say
64 Stew-serving utensil
65 Maui or Kauai
66 Standardized H.S. exam
67 Toys on strings

DOWN

1 Pastel blue
2 Street's edge
3 Angry crowds
4 Pilot's in-flight announcement, for short
5 Beach footwear
6 Speedily
7 Shaving mishaps
8 Place for an axon
9 Field of expertise
10 Amman's land
11 Approves
12 Tot's three-wheeler, informally
13 They're rung up on cash registers
22 Sick
23 Raucous
24 Slight coloration
26 Went in a vehicle
27 Ceaselessly
28 Haunted house feeling
30 Corroded
32 Rival of Domino's
33 Hispanic hurray
34 Drains, as one's energy
35 Ilk
36 "Hey, I've got a secret . . ."
38 New person on staff
39 Sch. known as the West Point of the South
40 Social engagement
44 Charge for a commercial
45 Result of dividing any number by itself
46 Hard to control
47 1552, on a cornerstone

48 Bob ___, restaurant chain
49 Aleve alternative
51 Eleniak of "Baywatch"
52 Get a pet from the pound, say
54 Chicken house
55 Lord's partner
56 Norway's capital
57 Applications
61 His portrait is at the entrance to Beijing's Forbidden City

by Stanley Newman

ACROSS

1 Edie of "Nurse Jackie"
6 Not quite right
11 Prime meridian std.
14 Hipbone-related
15 "Holy cow!"
16 Waikiki wear
17 Related add-ons, informally
19 "___ long gone daddy in the U.S.A." (Springsteen lyric)
20 Golden Horde members
21 Suffix with sucr- and lact-
22 Brouhaha
23 Tennis umpire's call
24 "Straight ___ Compton" (seminal rap album)
25 Tom Cruise/Nicole Kidman racing film
31 Things confessed at confession
32 Bad things from sharks?
33 Dodgers great Campanella
35 It's attention-getting
36 Figure skater Harding
37 Scotch ___
38 Whiz
39 Place for a kiddie hawk?
40 Elevator innovator
41 "That" something in an Arlen/Mercer standard
45 Exotic jelly fruit
46 "No thanks, I already ___"
47 The Beatles' "___ Love Her"
48 Org. whose only members with nonplural names appear at the ends of 17-, 25-, 41- and 56-Across
51 "Fiddler on the Roof" setting
55 Old-time actress Hagen
56 Keep cool in summer

58 Obama or Clinton, informally
59 Add-on
60 So unhip as to be hip, maybe
61 Gridiron gains: Abbr.
62 One of the Coen brothers
63 Din-making

DOWN

1 Company that owns Ferrari
2 Milan's Teatro ___ Scala
3 Gentle rise and fall of the voice
4 It makes things happen
5 Earthy tones
6 First anti-AIDS drug
7 Luck that's workin' for ya
8 "___ a Teenage Werewolf"
9 Jumbo, for one
10 "Oh yeah? ___ who?"
11 Fashionable celebs
12 Like the climate of Miami or Rio
13 Princess topper
18 Concerning
22 South of France
24 Follower of clip or slip
25 Not full-price
26 Famous Yosemite photographer
27 Fauna's counterpart
28 Elixir
29 "Frida" star Salma
30 Acapulco article
31 Hot spot?
34 "You betcha!"
36 Business card abbr.
37 With it
39 Lawyers' org.
42 Roman 506
43 Turn to pulp
44 Subject of a massive statue in the ancient Parthenon

45 Tastelessly showy
48 Call at a deli counter
49 "Splish Splash" spot
50 Gillette brand
52 Architect Saarinen
53 Cry made with a curtsy, maybe
54 Astronomical meas.
56 Honey Nut Cheerios mascot
57 Catch some rays

by Andrea Carla Michaels

ACROSS

1 Ancient Briton
5 Bulgarian or Croat
9 Writing surface for chalk
14 One ___ (vitamin brand)
15 Something a surfer catches
16 Was sick
17 Next-to-last chemical element alphabetically, before zirconium
18 Iowa State's city
19 Raises, as young
20 Ship heading
23 The Bible's Queen of ___
25 Still, in poetry
26 ___ Blanc, the so-called "Man of 1,000 Voices"
27 Liberal arts school in Waterville, Me.
32 Everyone
33 7UP or Pepsi
34 Reads quickly
38 Unwelcome look
40 Prevent
43 Insect in a summer swarm
44 Did sum work?
46 Cookie sometimes dunked in milk
48 Genetic info carrier
49 Service at Staples or FedEx Office
53 ___ Jima
56 To the ___ degree
57 Ancient Roman robes
58 Person in overalls sucking a piece of straw, stereotypically
63 Ancient 71-Across land in modern-day Turkey
64 Pieces with 90-degree bends
65 Taxis
68 Long guitar parts
69 Assistant
70 It may be slapped after a joke
71 Like Zeus and Hera
72 Did some weeding
73 Meat-and-vegetables dish

DOWN

1 La ___, Bolivia
2 Dictator Amin
3 No longer on the air
4 Baseball great known as "The Georgia Peach"
5 Exchange
6 Tibetan priest
7 Birds, scientifically speaking
8 Bowl or boat
9 Polynesian wraps
10 In ___ of (as a replacement for)
11 Frighten
12 Like one-word answers
13 '50s Ford failure
21 Baseball great Willie
22 Major component of the euro symbol
23 Milan's La ___ opera house
24 Sank, as a putt
28 How some packages arrive, for short
29 Praiseful poem
30 Process leading up to childbirth
31 Heart diagnostic, in brief
35 Highly offended
36 Food from heaven
37 Male-only parties
39 Tape machine button abbr.
41 ___ de Triomphe
42 1920s car that had its inventor's initials
45 Exasperated response to "How was your day?"
47 Makes a choice
50 8½" × 11" page size: Abbr.
51 "Definitely!"
52 Bygone cry of high spirits
53 Cake topper
54 Beau with roses, say
55 1/16 of a pound
59 Brand with a swoosh
60 Muse of history
61 Ye ___ Antique Shoppe
62 Secondhand
66 Hive dweller
67 Do needlework

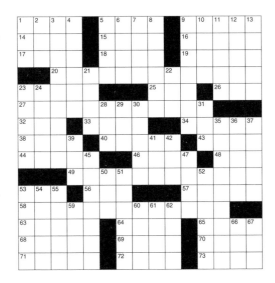

by Janet R. Bender

54

ACROSS

1 Stops
6 Stoned
10 Genre for N.W.A. or T.I.
13 Honolulu hello
14 Everglades bird
16 "Yes, there ___ God!"
17 Gave in
18 Critic's positive review of drummer Keith of the Who?
20 Had down pat
21 Its national animal is the vicuña
22 Small matter?
23 Powerful industrialist
25 Please, quaintly
27 Whine tearfully
29 Thick-skinned one
30 Tribal symbol
31 With 40-Across, critic's positive review of a Fox medical drama?
32 Male turkey
35 Nonhuman sign language learner
36 Posted an opinion, maybe
38 "___ had it up to here!"
39 "Agreed"
40 See 31-Across
41 Chair designer Charles
43 Mythical man-goat
44 First family of the 1840s
45 Galaxy competitors
48 They're hard to run in
49 Incessantly
50 "___ be surprised"
52 Homer Simpson's favorite beer
55 Critic's negative review of a 1988 Hanks film?
57 Word before range or cord
58 "___ with caution"
59 Everglades bird

60 Place for a court-ordered monitor
61 ___ Taco (fast-food chain)
62 Decisive time
63 Car introduced by Elon Musk

DOWN

1 Unrespected writer
2 Mathematician Turing
3 Critic's negative review of singer Courtney?
4 Stand-up routine?
5 Down
6 Macho dudes
7 Dr. Frankenstein's helper
8 Many "Family Feud" celebrations
9 Mama bird
10 Digital camera brand
11 Help desk sign
12 Old-hat

15 Asset for an umpire or editor
19 ___ the Orange (Syracuse mascot)
21 Typical "Meet the Press" guest, for short
24 Band that sang the "Friends" theme song "I'll Be There For You," with "the"
26 React to yeast
27 Certain court order
28 "Uh-uh"
29 "___ that" ("Understood")
31 Eastern Catholic ruling body
32 Critic's negative review of a newsmagazine?
33 More than
34 Predicament
37 Minstrel's instrument
42 "Finished!"
43 Mamas' boys
44 Sen. Cruz
45 About to bloom

46 Asset in a beauty pageant
47 "Science of Logic" philosopher
48 Iditarod dog
51 Plant also known as ladies' fingers
53 When many network shows debut
54 Pet pest
56 "___ be my pleasure!"
57 Winery fixture

by Joel Fagliano

ACROSS

1 The "joe" of a cup of joe
5 Knight's pursuit
10 Leftover part of a ticket
14 Declare
15 Excessive
16 Poi plant
17 "No way!"
20 Finish
21 Similar (to)
22 Say
23 Tied
24 Like a couch potato
26 "No way!"
32 Popular satirical news source, with "The"
33 Maui mementos
34 Gear tooth
36 Makes cool, in a way, as jeans
37 Between, poetically
39 Gyro bread
40 Sternward
41 Suddenly get the attention of
42 Winnie-the-Pooh's favorite food
43 "No way!"
47 Big name in sneakers
48 Telephoned
49 Undress
52 The Eagles or the Byrds
53 "Just a heads-up," on a memo
56 "No way!"
60 Move like sludge
61 Foolish
62 Russia's ___ Mountains
63 Air Force One passenger: Abbr.
64 Bottomless pit
65 Heredity unit

DOWN

1 Green stone
2 Stratford-upon-___
3 Sell
4 The "A" of MoMA
5 Trembled, as with fear
6 Grinchlike
7 Idyllic garden
8 15, for any row, column or diagonal of a 3 x 3 magic square
9 Golf ball elevator
10 Said
11 Stretched tight
12 Hankering
13 Physics Nobelist Niels
18 Expert
19 Doozies
23 Swelled heads
24 Wild Alpine goat
25 "Just ___" (47-Across slogan)
26 ___ song (cheaply)
27 Bring together
28 Savvy about
29 "I couldn't have done it because . . . ," e.g.
30 Sweetest part of a cake, often
31 ___ pole
35 Marvin of Motown
37 Long hike
38 What might give a water-skier trouble
39 Video game with a paddle
41 Handlebar features
42 Gandhi, for one
44 Marries
45 Empties, as a bathtub
46 School functions with chaperones
49 What a red light signifies
50 Norse god of war
51 Level, as with a wrecking ball
52 Time to blow out the candles, for short
53 "Look out!," to a golfer
54 Chinese money
55 Archipelago component
57 Narrow coastal inlet
58 Schubert's Symphony ___ Minor ("Unfinished Symphony")
59 Haul

by Bruce Haight

ACROSS

1 And so forth: Abbr.
4 Halfway decent
8 Home of Plato's Academy
14 "Your point being . . . ?"
15 Ancient South American
16 Complete mess
17 Powdered lunch product from Lipton
19 Moon of Neptune
20 Digital device used to access Hulu and Netflix
21 Bird bill
22 Fishing device
23 Just marvelous
28 Birdcage swing, e.g.
30 Skip, as a sound
31 Poet's "before"
32 Former Time Warner partner
34 Commercial suffix with Tropic
35 Mouth, slangily
36 Alcoholics Anonymous and others
40 Seamen
41 Contend (for)
42 When repeated, a popular puzzle
43 Acid
44 "The Hangover" setting
46 Hollywood director Sam
50 Confectionery brand with a logo designed by Salvador Dalí
53 "Chestnuts roasting ___ open fire"
54 Eight, to Dieter
55 Stand-up comedian with multiple Emmys
57 Drink that gets its name from the Tahitian word for "good"
60 Share a single bed . . . or a hidden feature of 17-, 23-, 36- and 50-Across
61 Town with Yiddish speakers
62 In ___ (actually)
63 In the style of
64 Pooped
65 Blacken on a grill
66 "Spy vs. Spy" magazine

DOWN

1 Steep slope around a rampart
2 "Rug"
3 Statue of Liberty material
4 River to the Seine
5 Units of nautical speed
6 Contact lens brand
7 Annoying bark
8 Under the cloak of night
9 Angry rant
10 Three-line verse
11 N.H. winter setting
12 Sarge, e.g.
13 Junior
18 WHAT THIS IS IN
21 Existence
24 Stop getting any higher
25 One chased in a car chase, for short
26 Parts of history
27 John Boehner, e.g., in two ways: Abbr.
29 Use a pogo stick
33 1968 #1 hit for Diana Ross & the Supremes
35 Good source of omega-3 fatty acids
36 Where a Brownie's merit badges are attached
37 Language of Pakistan
38 "I know, ___ ?"
39 "___ the land of the free . . ."
40 Nurse's focus, in brief
44 Move out
45 Quiet sound of water on the side of a pail, say
47 Clothes line?
48 Eye part subject to degeneration
49 What gets rubber-stamped?
51 Hors d'oeuvres toppings
52 "Minnesota March" composer
56 Modern cab service alternative
57 Asian food additive
58 "Got it!"
59 "___ your call"
60 Kwanzaa time: Abbr.

by James Mulhern

57

ACROSS

1 Pocketbook part
6 Waiter's last word after serving food
11 Place ___ (part of a table setting)
14 Hunt illegally
15 France's longest river
16 Award bestowed by a queen: Abbr.
17 Busybody
18 Ban Ki-moon's predecessor at the U.N.
20 Jeopardize
22 Colon, in analogies
23 Classic video game with ghosts
27 Mosey
30 "Two and a Half Men" co-star starting in 2011
33 Femur's locale
34 Two Romanov czars
35 Photo ___ (campaign events)
38 Gumshoes, in old crime fiction
39 Grand feather
40 ___ of Capri
41 Annoy
42 Country singer Steve
43 Trojan king during the Trojan War
44 Sporting champion with a drive for success?
47 Descriptive language
49 "Of course you're right"
50 Anger
51 Not commissioned, after "on"
53 "The Fast and the Furious" co-star
57 What "E" means on a gas gauge
62 Verb-forming suffix
63 Witch
64 Brainteaser
65 Court divider
66 Crimean conference site
67 Minnesota baseball team . . . or what 18-, 30-, 44- and 53-Across all are

DOWN

1 James Bond, for one
2 Little piggy, in a children's rhyme
3 Sprinted
4 Play a role
5 Pyramid schemer?
6 ___ Club (civic group)
7 Reading place . . . or reading device
8 Competitor of Skippy and Peter Pan
9 "Either he goes ___ go!"
10 Word before "verily" in the Bible
11 Freak of nature
12 Lessen
13 Kind of sax
19 Number of heads of the Hydra, in myth
21 Bed-and-breakfast, e.g.
23 Rocker Smith
24 "My Name Is ___ Lev"
25 Sexy guy
26 Boardroom events: Abbr.
27 Flower's pollen holder
28 Teenager's bane
29 Sounds of hesitation
31 "___ was here" (W.W. II catchphrase)
32 Throat dangler
36 Part of a table setting
37 Round after the quarters
39 10-10 or Q-Q
40 Angers
42 Before, poetically
43 General rule
45 Elderly
46 Easter egg need
47 Football Hall-of-Famer Michael
48 Indian corn
51 Mailed
52 Entreaty
54 Treacherous, as winter roads
55 Long presidential term, perhaps
56 The sun
58 Cut, as grass
59 Trident-shaped letter
60 Number of Canadian provinces
61 Soph. and jr.

by Tom McCoy

58

ACROSS
1 ___-retentive
5 Plane, on a radar screen
9 Sarcasm
14 "Swans Reflecting Elephants" painter
15 ___ Club (pilot's group)
16 Kind of butter
17 Luminary among luminaries
19 Like many rural roads
20 Cigarette residue
21 Whom "unto us" is given, in Isaiah
22 What dogs' tails do
23 Hear about
25 Competent
29 Stand an artist might take
30 Flat out
32 Champagne opening sound
34 Novelist Anaïs
35 Half of an umlaut
36 Beyoncé and Jay Z, e.g. . . . or a hint to 17-, 30-, 44- and 61-Across
40 Partner of shock
42 Hawaii's Mauna ___
43 Link
44 Snooty attitude
48 Low pair?
52 "Piece of cake!"
53 Accidentally say
55 CBS forensic series
56 There's one in this cleu
57 ___ Khan
58 Wackos
61 Bodybuilder, for one
63 Pastoral composition
64 ___ cheesecake (black-and-white dessert)
65 Show petulance
66 Brawl

67 PBS station behind "Live From Lincoln Center"
68 Certain Protestant: Abbr.

DOWN
1 Magazine agent's success
2 Feeling after a roller coaster ride
3 Top dogs
4 Perjurious statement
5 Voice in the role of Mefistofele, e.g.
6 Excuse from responsibility
7 Country bordering three "-stans"
8 "___ favor" (Spanish "please")
9 Leftovers
10 Candy bar filling
11 One may be hard to follow
12 "Hogwash!"
13 ___ Jewelers
18 Became depleted
22 Waldorf salad morsel
24 Seized car, for short
25 Muse sometimes pictured with a book or scroll
26 "Venerable" scholar of old England
27 Vientiane native
28 First responder, for short
31 Last of the Mohicans in "The Last of the Mohicans"
33 First female speaker of the House
36 Cribbage score keepers
37 Actor Calhoun
38 Energetic sort
39 Many August births
40 Yellowfin tuna
41 Tina Fey display
45 Shout "Ref, are you blind?!," e.g.
46 Pain in the neck
47 Parisian palace

49 Stop talking
50 Capital of Rwanda
51 Hits bottom?
54 Florida tourist attraction
56 Spin of the dial or roll of the dice
58 Most common Korean surname
59 Poet's dedication
60 Olive of the comics
61 Cut (down)
62 Ending for Nepal

by Jacob McDermott

ACROSS

1 Lawyer's charge
4 Shopaholic's indulgence
9 Cursor controller
14 Lenient
15 Was nosy
16 Deceive
17 Turkish title
18 Items for flattening dough
20 Bad reputation
22 Blackens, as a reputation
23 Unleash
24 Alpha, ___, gamma . . .
25 Choose
28 Secretly
31 901, in old Rome
34 Dropped a bit, as the stock market
35 Doing nothing
36 Texter's expression spelled out by the starts of 18-, 28-, 46- and 59-Across
38 Affirmatives
41 Toll road
42 Bang-up
43 Boat in "Jaws"
45 "Dig in!"
46 Some dressing room conveniences
51 Tit for ___
52 Longest river wholly in Switzerland
53 Mess up, as hair
57 Norway's capital
58 College reunion attendee
59 Nitrous oxide
63 Columbus Day mo.
64 Shake hands (on)
65 Absurd
66 Beaver State: Abbr.
67 Dog treats
68 Whey's partner in a nursery rhyme
69 The "p" in m.p.g.

DOWN

1 Thrash
2 Two under par
3 Glorify
4 Ankle woes
5 Right away
6 Agitate
7 Conger, e.g.
8 Not raw, as text
9 Country singer Tim
10 "My bad!"
11 Arm of Israel
12 Schumer or Shaheen: Abbr.
13 U.S.N.A. grad
19 What 26 countries in Eur. belong to
21 To and ___
24 Long-term hospital patient's problem
25 Blast from the past
26 ___ dot
27 Message that might include an "@" and a "#"
29 Get a move on
30 Frostiness
31 Beermaking or knitting
32 Cold hard cash
33 Otherwise
37 Only three-letter zodiac sign
39 "To ___ is human . . ."
40 Site of a 2014 vote for independence
44 Shakes from a slumber
47 Symptoms of poison ivy
48 French Sudan, today
49 Like a firehouse burning down?
50 2+2=4, e.g.
54 Buttinsky
55 "Filthy" riches
56 Banana oil, e.g.
57 Arch type
58 Culture medium in a 59-Down
59 See 58-Down
60 "Give it ___!"
61 Ashes holder
62 African antelope

by Robert Seminara

ACROSS

1 Sights in marinas
6 Conventioneer's ID
11 Emergency signal
14 Computer screen array
15 Bottled water with three mountain peaks in its logo
16 Granite State sch.
17 Position of 62-Across
19 "Masters of Sex" channel, in TV listings
20 ___ loss
21 Castle defense
22 Savory gelatin-based dish
24 With 27-Across, record-setting achievement of 62-Across
27 See 24-Across
28 "Am I my brother's keeper?" speaker
29 Morton product
32 Prefix with bellum
33 In good physical shape
35 Avoid work
37 California's Big ___
38 Duration of 62-Across's 24-/27-Across
42 Necessity for a doctor or taxi driver: Abbr.
43 Bridge
44 Before, to the Bard
45 Med. school course
47 Ovine mothers
49 Figure (out)
52 & 54 Moniker of 62-Across
57 ___ Brown, host of "Iron Chef America"
58 Pink-slip
60 Texter's "Here's what I think"
61 Take the gold
62 American athlete born 11/25/1914

66 ___ dye
67 In first place
68 Carrots and turnips, basically
69 Conifer with toxic seeds
70 Baker's supply
71 Sacred choral composition

DOWN

1 Bible book after Jonah
2 ___ acid
3 Hyundai model with a musical name
4 Explosive stuff
5 Seattle-to-Phoenix dir.
6 Enshrouds in a mist
7 Sports shoe brand
8 Insects and seeds, for many birds
9 Guy's partner
10 Have as a terminus
11 Mood suffusing "Psycho"

12 Temporarily not airing, as a TV show
13 The shower scene in "Psycho," e.g.
18 D.D.E.'s running mate
23 Paris : Mme. :: Madrid : ___
25 Petty quarrel
26 D.D.E. or J.F.K.
27 The boards, to an actor
30 Dress style introduced by Dior
31 Bagel go-with
34 Melville's first book
36 Language of Iran
38 Complete, as arrangements
39 "Sorry, ask me later"
40 Glimpsed
41 Pick-___ (refreshing drink)
42 Purchasing plan
46 Ruling from a boxing ref
48 Lines to be memorized

50 Faucet
51 Jew or Arab
53 Relish
55 Early moon lander, for short
56 Sleep in a vertical position?
58 Greek salad component
59 Vows made "for better or worse"
63 Single
64 Sleeve
65 Melted chocolate, e.g.

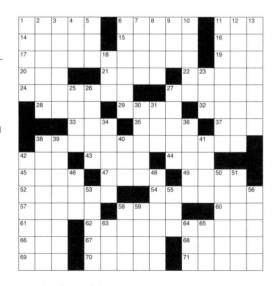

by Jeffrey Wechsler

61

ACROSS

1 & 6 Subject of an eerie rural legend . . . illustrated by connecting nine identically filled squares in this puzzle with a closed line
15 Member of the chordophone family
16 Bisectors pass through them
17 Whizzes
18 Far south?
19 Site of many hangings
21 Some Spanish zoo exhibits
22 Some glass paperweights
24 Tolkien's Prancing Pony, e.g.
26 Texted, say
27 Not believe in spirits?
32 Viscosity symbols
33 Big, big, big
36 Any of the Four Noble Truths
37 Join with
39 Confident, ambitious, loyal sort, supposedly
40 Guillotine targets
41 "Cómo" follower
42 Purchase on delta .com, e.g.
44 M.D. grp.
45 Raising a stink?
47 Focus (on)
50 "I'd rather not"
51 Mother who appeared on two covers of Time
52 Former Saudi king
55 Some runners
56 One feeling warm on the inside?
59 Ethyl acetate, e.g.
63 Push too far

64 Currency worth about 1/36 of a dollar
65 Clean-shaven
66 Fit

DOWN

1 Batting fig.
2 Fiction
3 It's charged
4 Call up
5 Tool used with a hammer
6 Accumulate
7 Intelligence researcher Alfred
8 Chemical restricted by the Stockholm Convention
9 ___ tree
10 Ornamental headpiece
11 Nerves may cause them
12 Loving
13 Mayberry town drunk
14 Foreign policy grp.

20 Polynesian term for an island hopper
22 Some positive reinforcement
23 Flower-shaped decoration
24 "No worries"
25 Wedding announcement word
26 Like Seattle vis-à-vis Phoenix
28 Baseball great who had a career batting 1-Down of .304
29 Gets choppers
30 Weakness
31 Pretends
34 "Mutiny on the Bounty" captain
35 Intl. trade org.
38 Charter ___, symbol on the Connecticut state quarter
42 Noted stratovolcano
43 Heavens
46 "Absolutely!"
48 They may be barked

49 Goof
51 Goods stolen by the Knave of Hearts
52 "Lincoln"
53 An integral can compute it
54 Munich mister
55 Reacts fearfully
56 Waistcoat item
57 Rose in the music world
58 Texas has a big one
60 Not yet on the sked
61 Loop takers
62 Band with the 1991 hit "Shiny Happy People"

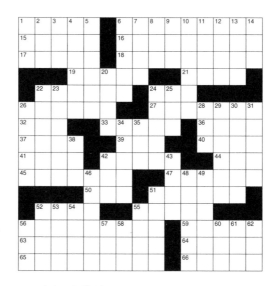

by Brandon Hensley

62

ACROSS

1 None-too-bright sorts
5 Summaries
11 Tippler
14 Drop ___ (start to strip)
15 Lacking in harmony
16 When tripled, a dance move
17 Ed McMahon intro words
19 Have
20 ___ nous
21 French vote
22 Synthesizer pioneer Robert
23 Charles on a piano
24 Lawrence Welk intro words
28 Grub, e.g.
30 Way out of N.Y.C.
31 Italian ballad subject
33 Will ___, "The Realistic Joneses" playwright
35 Setting for many van Gogh paintings
39 Chevy Chase intro words
43 Diamond datum
44 Tidy ___
45 When doubled, a Billy Idol #1 hit
46 ___ Cass
49 Broad valleys
51 Jackie Gleason intro words
55 Summer setting in Mass.
58 Inside dope
59 Teachers' grp.
60 Conger hunter
62 Qt. or gal.
63 Possible title for this puzzle
66 Tattle (on)
67 Pan producer, perhaps
68 In the know about
69 Sample

70 Settings of Delacroix and Ingres paintings
71 Ain't fixed?

DOWN

1 Remaining
2 Where the action is
3 Score just before winning a game, say
4 Litigant
5 British rule in India
6 W.W. II command
7 Small salmon: Var.
8 Like pansies and petunias
9 Bologna sandwiches?
10 Like some winks
11 Get moving
12 "What a surprise!"
13 Letter between sierra and uniform
18 Scorch
22 Proposal words
25 Through with
26 iPod model
27 Command in Uno
29 Hotel handout
31 Gore and Green
32 Cambridge sch.
34 Yoga chants
36 Ship sinkers, in an old saying
37 Suffix with east or west
38 "The daily bread of the eyes," per Ralph Waldo Emerson
40 Hubris, for Icarus
41 Like Rodin's "The Thinker"
42 Slate, e.g.
47 Words to live by
48 Response to captain's orders
50 MGM founder Marcus
51 Spaced out?
52 All-Star shortstop Garciaparra
53 Daft
54 It may be hazardous
56 Speed ___

57 Former Mississippi senator Lott
61 French CD holder
63 I, in Innsbruck
64 "Tell ___," 1962 hit by the Exciters
65 Mil. training site

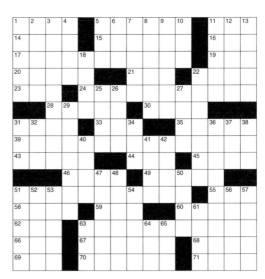

by Kurt Mueller

ACROSS

1 Pink-slips
5 Two- or three-striper, for short
8 Civic bldgs.
12 ___ arms
13 Bud competitor
15 Its first capital was Chillicothe, 1803–'10
16 Casino staple
17 "Yellow Submarine" singer
18 Sandwich style
19 Hit the gym
21 Many figures of "The Last Judgment" in the Sistine Chapel
23 Narrow-brimmed hat
24 Title character played by Sarah Jessica Parker on Broadway
25 Santa Maria is one of them
27 David, when taking on Goliath
30 Use a divining rod
31 Heyward, Stone or Nelson, as each signed the Declaration of Independence
32 Rounded projection
33 Sea bird
34 What 3- and 9-Down are an example of
37 Jon Stewart display
38 Puccini piece
40 Rake
41 Cessation of breath
43 Person without direction
45 What volunteers do
46 Openly disregard
47 Pops
48 Jason of the Harry Potter movies

50 Medium for school announcements
53 Fourth-largest city in Deutschland
54 Hair-raising
56 The Ronettes, e.g.
57 A.L. or N.L. division
58 Whiff
59 Currency with a 20-cent coin
60 Specialty
61 Stratego piece with a monocle
62 Stalk

DOWN

1 Salad veggie
2 Top
3 Statement #1
4 Bad bedfellows, say
5 Like 4-Down
6 Retina feature
7 Assn.
8 Lassoing lass
9 Statement #2
10 Mideast currency

11 Biscuits and rolls, sometimes
13 Places for mobiles
14 Scoundrel
20 Scoundrel
22 Dir. from Providence to Boston
24 Certain terminal
25 "It's ___!"
26 Title role for Antonio Banderas
27 Big name in moving
28 Annual May announcements
29 Suggest
31 Word after lake or sea
35 Piques
36 Familiar axes
39 Martin Luther King Jr.'s birthplace
42 Coat heavily
44 Assn.
45 Stand in a studio
47 ___ Double
48 Big name in furniture

49 Go sky-high
50 Some kitchen work, informally
51 Hibernia
52 It may be happy or grumpy
55 What dialing 911 may bring

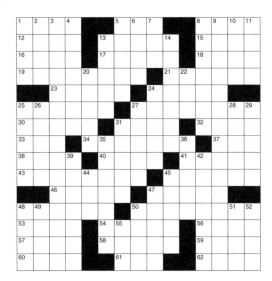

by Matthew Lees

64

ACROSS

1 Does damage to
6 Little handfuls, so to speak
10 Put the whammy on
14 Alternative to U.S.P.S.
15 Securely hide
16 Fig leaf wearer, in some art
17 Words of resignation
20 Son of 16-Across
21 Advisers to players' associations
22 Actor Cariou
23 "Dragnet" broadcast, for short
25 Dick Tracy's girl
27 Barista-operated gadgets
34 Old televangelism org.
35 Food item in quarter-pound sticks
36 "This is looking bad!"
37 "This is looking bad!"
39 Gives kudos
42 Like decalcified water
43 Instrument on the Beatles' "Norwegian Wood"
45 Sushi bar quaff
47 Part of many French surnames
48 Governor elected in a 2003 recall vote
52 Chicken-sized flightless bird
53 "Yay!"
54 Proof-ending letters
57 Bird in the crow family
60 Like poor losers
64 Punny description of the circled letters in 17-, 27- and 48-Across

67 "Pumping ___" (1977 docudrama featuring 48-Across)
68 "Whip It" band
69 What a metronome regulates
70 Historic resignee of 2013
71 Drinks at sidewalk stands
72 "Come on down!" announcer Johnny

DOWN

1 Takes an ax to
2 Friend en français
3 Long broadside
4 Bit of bad luck
5 ___-mo
6 "___ to differ"
7 Drug smuggler's courier
8 "Chop-chop!"
9 Bettor's strategy
10 Pres. Madison or Monroe
11 Golden god, say
12 File directory heading
13 Comics foes of Magneto
18 Old phone company nickname
19 Piece of Bacon or Lamb
24 Tour player
26 Biathlete's needs
27 Set of principles
28 Upside-down sleeper
29 SpongeBob's home
30 W. C. Fields persona
31 Horatian work
32 Send, as to a specialist
33 Old Air France fleet, for short
34 Face, slangily
38 Sharp-eyed sort
40 Brown who wrote "The Da Vinci Code"
41 Lampoon but good
44 "Spider-Man" director Sam
46 ___-surf (Google oneself)

49 Country with a gorilla on its 5,000-franc note
50 Did part of a slalom path
51 Staple Singers genre
54 Commercial swab
55 Two-tone coin
56 Barely enough to wet one's whistle
58 ___ the way
59 N.Y.S.E. debuts
61 Resistance units
62 Towed-away auto, maybe
63 School for Prince Harry
65 180 degrees from SSW
66 Ear-related prefix

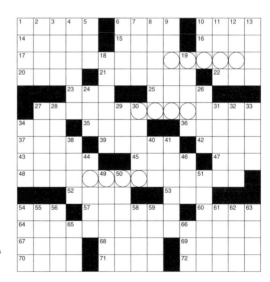

by Victor Barocas

65

ACROSS

1 Ultimate
4 Link
9 Silencer
14 Tulsa sch.
15 ___ planner
16 Soviet spymaster in a John le Carré trilogy
17 Fix
18 What ladies' men tend to have
20 U.S. slalom great Phil
22 Overly flattering
23 Actor whose breakout role was on TV's "21 Jump Street"
24 Very alert
27 Abbr. at the top of a memo
28 Cell in a network
32 Receiver Victor of the Giants' 2011 Super Bowl-winning season
34 Actress Mara of "House of Cards"
38 Classic toothpaste featured in "Grease"
39 Old TV knob: Abbr.
40 Espy
42 Geographic indicator, briefly
43 Out
45 Approaching
46 Some modern viruses and worms
47 Folds
49 Mystery author John Dickson ___
51 1981 #1 Kim Carnes hit
57 Snug
60 Prefix with engine
61 Prefix with biology
62 Misinterpretation of a biblical code . . . or the key to answering 18-, 24-, 40- and 51-Across
65 Going by, for short

66 Genre featured on MTV's "Headbangers Ball"
67 Up
68 Gym unit
69 Hummus, e.g.
70 Scuffle
71 Listen through a door, say

DOWN

1 ___ Desmond, "Sunset Boulevard" diva
2 Setting for much of "My Cousin Vinny"
3 "House" star
4 Most fresh
5 Actress Green of "300: Rise of an Empire"
6 Strobe light element
7 Reversed
8 Inscribed pillar
9 Take to the hills?
10 "Surrender!"
11 Desire
12 Erratum
13 Door securer
19 Role played by Baldwin, Ford, Affleck and Pine
21 Alternative to Premium
25 "Puppy Love" crooner
26 Check
29 High-definition
30 Not dilly-dallying
31 Recharges, in a way
32 Fellow
33 One of three in a Yahtzee turn
35 Objectivist Rand
36 N.F.L. game rarity
37 That, in Toledo
40 Miller product
41 Boat in "Jaws"
44 Some lose it in their teens
46 One from London Town, e.g.
48 Headline
50 Skin-care brand
52 They make tracks

53 Children's character originally voiced by Jim Henson
54 Accomplish, in the Bible
55 Graphic novel artist
56 Joy-filled?
57 Like "The Rocky Horror Picture Show"
58 Eligible to serve
59 Some get them in their teens
63 World Cup cry
64 Notwithstanding

by John Lieb

66

ACROSS

1 Ottoman title
6 Occult cards
11 Beauty
14 Legally impede
15 Say "somethin'," say
16 Wall cover
17 Freestyling pilot?
19 Grand Canyon part
20 Uncommitted?
21 Boot out
22 Comeback
24 STP logo sporter, perhaps
26 Some modern cash registers
28 Music forbidden in Germany?
32 Lavished attention (on)
35 Long, long time
36 Bonanza yield
37 Four-star review
38 Pretentiously showy
40 Google co-founder Sergey
41 Off-road ride, for short
42 ___ cheese
43 Steel giant founded in 1899
44 Top?
48 Long, long stories
49 Honeydew relatives
53 Put locks on?
55 So-so marks
57 Big brass
58 Public house potable
59 Throaty dismissals?
62 Paul McCartney title
63 Sculpted trunks
64 "Sun Valley Serenade" skater
65 Is stricken with
66 Lamé feature
67 Eurasia divider

DOWN

1 "Live for Now" soft drink
2 Narnia lion
3 Orchestra musician's prop
4 Apiary denizen
5 Galoot
6 Samovar, e.g.
7 Albertville's locale
8 Hazards for surfers
9 Ben Jonson wrote one to himself
10 41-Across part
11 Non-coed housing
12 Like some spirits
13 "Land o' Goshen!"
18 Speckled steed
23 Commercial suffix with Power
25 Rotten egg
27 Sneaky tactic
29 Scarf down
30 Cantor of Congress
31 City mentioned in "Folsom Prison Blues"
32 Stud alternative
33 Something sworn
34 Nielsen group
38 Baldwin of "30 Rock"
39 McCarthy-era paranoia
40 Timeout
42 Crop destroyers
43 Friedrich units, for short
45 Campus in Troy, N.Y.
46 Strands, as at a ski lodge
47 Relaxation
50 "___ sera"
51 Bubbling over
52 Ppd. enclosures
53 Party that might get out of hand
54 Director Kazan
56 Language that gave us "smithereens"
60 Response at an unveiling
61 Moo ___ beef

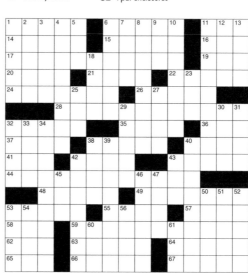

by Mike Buckley

ACROSS

1 Pound
5 Twenty-one words
10 Starbuck's orderer
14 Old station name
15 Youngest Oscar winner in history
16 Part of a pound
17 Caesarean section?
18 Billy's mate
19 Make a long story short, perhaps
20 Brand producers
22 Trail
23 Stood out
24 Plan B, e.g.
27 Wine taster's asset
30 2008 TARP recipient
31 A seemingly endless series
38 One of just 12 in Alaska: Abbr.
39 Pac-12 player
40 Fraternity letter
41 Rule contradicted by science?
48 Little application
49 Does penance
50 Note to a spy, perhaps
55 One with a bag lunch?
56 Part of a krone
57 Waiting, for the impatient, say
61 One acting on impulse?
62 See 13-Down
64 Find the ___ (geometry test instruction)
65 "Open ___"
66 Surmise
67 Knightly wear
68 Start to do well?

69 Name that's a homophone for 13-Down
70 Cosmopolitan competitor

DOWN

1 Role for Helen Mirren, briefly
2 Group of red states, for short?
3 Golfer Aoki
4 Learned perfectly
5 Sugar substitute?
6 Together
7 Break time, perhaps
8 Snapple flavor
9 Ron who played Tarzan
10 Loser to a pair
11 Sported
12 Getting on
13 With 62-Across, dreaded one
21 Jedi foes
23 Pet

25 "Malcolm X" director
26 Actress Charlotte
27 Jardin du Luxembourg, par exemple
28 Against
29 Leopold's partner in crime
32 Whence the word "robot"
33 Taxonomic suffix
34 Formerly
35 Southern hwy.
36 Pickup spot?
37 They may be spilled
42 One of the voices in "Up"
43 Film technique
44 Eastern band
45 Évian, e.g.
46 Bonus, in ads
47 Scam
50 "Chicago" number
51 Undermine

52 Ray Charles hit of 1963
53 Type of scam
54 Green ___
55 "The First Wives Club" co-star, 1996
58 ___-B
59 "Cosmos" host ___ deGrasse Tyson
60 Brown competitor
62 Tip for a writer
63 Long intro?

by Adam G. Perl

68

ACROSS

1 British brew with a red triangle logo
8 Ones dying in a fire?
14 Book version
15 Permanent-press
16 Neighborhood spot to order 1-Across, say
18 "Ergo" preceder
19 "You should know better!"
20 Scale-busting
22 Up to the task
26 Shoots in the foot, maybe
27 Gore who sang "It's My Party," 1963
29 Reason for a road warning
30 Aladdin's monkey pal
33 "Seinfeld" gal pal
34 Singers Green and Jardine
35 Wimpy sort
37 Denier's contraction
38 Some advanced degs.
39 Pregame song opener
40 Like dressage horses
41 ___ good deed
42 George Carlin's "___ With Your Head"
43 The Bulldogs' sch.
44 Yadda, yadda, yadda
45 ___ niçoise
46 Prefix with economic
48 Actor Montand
49 Quite cunning
53 Gibbon, e.g.
56 "Better luck next time"
57 Place to eighty-six things
61 The golden years
62 Rockefeller Center style
63 Armadillo defenses
64 "Sure, why not?!"

DOWN

1 Boxer's trophy
2 Commotions
3 Really ill
4 Stop on the tracks: Abbr.
5 Be 3-Down
6 Cut (off)
7 Sufficient, informally
8 Bivouacs
9 Archie Comics character
10 Humongous
11 Holder of a cabinet position
12 ___-Rooter
13 Monet's "___ Scene at Argenteuil"
17 Like a chrome-dome
21 Half of all flips
23 Unable to see the "E" on the Snellen chart, say
24 Post-Carnival time
25 Batter's asset
27 Watch readouts, briefly
28 Yale or Root
31 Working away
32 Foreign relief org. created by J.F.K.
36 January 1 song title word
38 Decorator's theme
39 Kingly name in Norway
41 The 1980s and '90s, e.g.
42 "Gangnam Style" rapper
47 ___ orange
49 "Freeze!"
50 Veg out
51 Luke Skywalker's mentor
52 Help in finding fractures
54 Ancient Brit
55 Grandson of Adam
58 "Come as you ___"
59 Block boundaries: Abbr.
60 "Good" cholesterol, briefly

by Tim Croce

69

ACROSS

1 Knock silly
5 Some Summer Olympics gear
10 "Spider-Man" girl
14 Stone, e.g.
15 "The Alchemist" novelist ___ Coelho
16 Facetious words of understanding
17 Backdrop for the final scene of Antonioni's "L'Avventura"
18 How some legal proceedings are conducted
19 Apocryphal beast
20 #1
23 Comic ___ (typeface)
24 Seaside bird
25 Revolutionary body?
28 New York City's ___ Galerie
30 Odds, e.g.
33 #2
36 Sleep with, in slang
37 Simpleton
38 Afflictions known technically as hordeola
40 This, to Tomás
41 Comparably sized
43 #3
45 "Not in a million years!"
47 Mode of transportación
48 Shape of a timeout signal
49 Genesis' "man of the field"
50 Symbol of softness
52 #4
58 Waiting room distribution
59 Something that's on the record?
60 Where Macbeth, Malcolm and Duncan are buried
61 Aoki of the P.G.A.
62 Things twins share

63 TV greaser, with "the"
64 FiveThirtyEight owner
65 Complete: Prefix
66 Get out of town

DOWN

1 1965's "I Got You Babe," e.g.
2 "No" voter
3 Brass section?
4 Solide and liquide
5 Condition of being awesome, in modern slang
6 Hillary Clinton wardrobe staples
7 Start to pop?
8 Gen. Robert ___
9 Like many works in minor keys
10 "It's Raining Men," for one
11 The place to be
12 Abbr. on a historic building
13 "___ insist!"
21 ___ E (TV channel)
22 "___ my dad would say . . ."
25 Media icon with an eponymous Starbucks beverage
26 Shake, maybe
27 It might pop in the post office
29 Memphis's home
31 More than quirky
32 Held forth
34 Writer with the most combined Tony and Oscar nominations
35 Littoral
39 Sequence of events
42 Tiny irritant
44 Genesis grandson
46 Yield
51 Swing and miss
52 Chuck
53 Romain de Tirtoff's pseudonym
54 Cambodian currency
55 One being used
56 ___ Bradstreet, America's first published poet
57 The Sphinx's is "blank and pitiless as the sun," per Yeats
58 Outdated cry

by Anna Shechtman

ACROSS

1 Pronoun repeated in "America"
5 Weapon with a warhead, in brief
9 "Thriller" singer, in tabloids
14 "Let sleeping dogs lie" and others
15 Board's partner
16 Subject of a donor card
17 Dust, vacuum, do windows, etc.
19 Done to death
20 See circled letters
21 Come ___ price
22 Crucifixion symbol
23 One from column A, one from column B, etc.
27 Go to the dogs
29 See circled letters
31 Big do
32 Tend to another spill
34 How knights roam
36 Take habitually
37 See circled letters
40 ". . . in excelsis ___"
41 What to do when dealt a flush
43 Fast-food utensil
45 Prefix with zone and skeptic
46 See circled letters
49 Adams of "Junebug"
50 Decked out in sequins
52 Vet school subj.
54 Still owing
55 See circled letters
59 Speed skater ___ Anton Ohno
62 "I did bad!"
63 "Quo ___?"
64 Place to place your bets
65 St. Petersburg's river
66 Showing mastery
67 Stickup man on "The Wire"
68 Triathlon start

DOWN

1 Relatives of tuts
2 Hic, ___, hoc
3 Still-life pitcher
4 Grass for cordage
5 Asimov classic
6 Part of an "if only . . ." lament
7 Big name in audio equipment
8 Marie Curie, e.g.: Abbr.
9 See circled letters
10 Bring up on charges
11 Special FX technology
12 Kit ___ Club ("Cabaret" setting)
13 ___-hit wonder
18 "Veep" channel
21 Now, in Nogales
23 Bulblike plant part
24 Realm of Garfield
25 Queen of fiction
26 Voice one's approval
27 Recharge one's batteries
28 Mark who won the 1998 Masters
30 ___ differ (object)
32 Artful dodges
33 Deg. held by Woodrow Wilson
35 Quiz response: Abbr.
38 Fill out the necessary forms, say
39 ___ a soul
42 Like a shower mat, ideally
44 Clientele
47 Daiquiri flavor
48 Win the heart of
51 See circled letters
53 What liver spots may be a sign of
55 "Um, excuse me"
56 From the start
57 Year of Super Bowl XL
58 Line of jeans?
59 "___: My Story" (Tinseltown autobiography)
60 Inflate, as a bill
61 "___ to Joy"
62 Full house indicator

by Jim Hilger

ACROSS

1 Presenter of "The Borgias," in brief
4 Burning
10 Arizona's ___ Canyon Dam
14 Owner of Moviefone
15 Jackie who played Uncle Fester
16 Italian beach resort
17 The "American Moses"
19 Hot spot in "Hansel and Gretel"
20 Four stars, say
21 Critical elements
22 "Attendance is mandatory"
23 Brewed refresher
26 TV great who said "I live to laugh, and I laugh to live"
27 Modern beginning?
28 Use (up)
29 Wasn't faithful
31 Parenthetical remarks
33 1990s politico from Texas
34 1860s novel that is the basis for this puzzle's theme
37 Flightless birds
38 Electrify
41 Huck and Jim on the Mississippi, e.g.
44 Work that's been punningly called a "lex icon": Abbr.
45 63-Across, in France
46 Fixes
47 Waived the wake-up call
49 Mission ___, Calif.
50 Leave blank
53 Shark eater
54 You're not going anywhere if you're in this
55 Baby boomers, with "the"
58 Canal with 36 locks

59 Brightest star in Aquila
60 Reactor safety agcy.
61 Colors
62 College named for a Norwegian king
63 45-Across, in America

DOWN

1 Audrey Hepburn title role
2 "___ Odes" (classic work of poetry)
3 Staple of Mediterranean cooking
4 Münster "Geez!"
5 Like a freshly drawn draft
6 View
7 Malaria symptom
8 Lots
9 Lots of R.P.I. grads: Abbr.

10 Shakespeare play setting
11 Car service
12 Gertrude who swam the English Channel
13 "You've done enough"
18 H.S. proficiency test
24 Goes through a stage of babyhood
25 Spring time
26 Trite comment
29 Wrap (up)
30 Tiler's tool
32 Ribald humor
33 Foot: Lat.
35 ___ Américas
36 Subatomic particle with no electric charge
39 Creature in Rowling's Forbidden Forest
40 Price for forgiveness, perhaps
41 Answered, quickly

42 Place abuzz with activity?
43 Spenser's "The ___ Queene"
44 Pertaining to bone
48 Big belly
50 Some Swiss watches
51 Tuna-and-cheese sandwich
52 Digging
56 Narrow inlet
57 Whelp's yelp

by Ed Sessa

ACROSS

1 Put off
6 ___-American
10 Pen, e.g.
14 Not engaging
15 "Remove," to a typesetter
16 Oscar-winning Ben Affleck film
17 Not pass
18 [Canada]
20 Lighted tree, maybe
21 Zilch
22 Party with a piñata, say
23 "For sure, dude!"
26 Spoiled
27 ___ holiday
28 Cook's canful
29 "Wait just ___!"
31 [U.S.A.]
38 "Is this the spot?"
39 Big foot spec
40 Something to play
41 [U.S.S.R.]
46 Go a few rounds
47 Part of a round
48 Part of a science credit
51 One sharing a bunk bed, maybe
52 Athena's counterpart
55 Fortune 100 company based in Seattle
57 Salsa, e.g.
58 Wildcatter's investment
59 [Japan]
61 Sing with dulcet tones
63 Like many a beanie
64 Intl. association since 1960
65 Place of learning in France
66 Word after "&" in some store names

67 June 14, e.g.
68 Some protesters in China

DOWN

1 "You're dethpicable" toon
2 English pop singer Goulding
3 Hot chili designation
4 Very long period
5 '60s atty. gen. whose brother served as president
6 Start of a website manager's email address, maybe
7 All-natural
8 1992 Winter Olympics backdrop
9 C. S. Lewis's birthplace
10 Memorial Day weekend event
11 Take with force
12 Brightly colored rock
13 Diet food phrase
19 Source of soft feathers
21 Zilch
24 Where odalisques once worked
25 ___ White (Clue character)
26 Founded
30 Club
31 "Not another word!"
32 Crumpets go-with
33 Gets in the vicinity of
34 Place to play cards
35 Place to play cards
36 Pipe shape
37 Get
42 Office printing giant
43 Tlaloc, to the Aztecs
44 Overnight, maybe
45 + or – particle

48 Gaggle : geese :: exaltation : ___
49 Protein-building acid
50 Yacht club locale
52 Chop up
53 Part of a string quartet
54 "___ of God," 1985 film
56 Jerry Scott/Jim Borgman teen comic strip
57 1982's "Ebony and Ivory," e.g.
60 Place with robes
61 Toon's place
62 Developer of the U.S.'s first TV test pattern

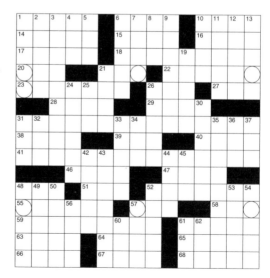

by Ian Livengood

ACROSS

1 Like some libelers
5 Spencer of "Good Morning America"
9 Emergency message, for short
12 Common flavorer in Italian sausage
14 In working condition
16 Line 22 on Form 1040
17 Long, involved story, in slang
18 Business, informally
20 Home of "The Gist" and "Political Gabfest"
21 Western tribe
22 Word with Man or can
23 Suddenly stops working, with "up"
24 Guinness superlative
27 Final order
28 Parabolic, say
29 John ___
30 Competition in marksmanship
37 About 8–15 mg. of iron, say
38 Email attachment attachment?
40 Modern term for "Roman fever"
45 Daresay
47 In groups
48 Holy ___
49 One who's been tapped on the shoulder?
50 Plagiarism and such
51 Queso-topped dish
54 100% . . . or words that can precede 17-, 18-, 30- and 51-Across
56 Sour
57 Mark Twain's boyhood home
58 Attacks
59 Alternative to -enne

60 Tiresome sort
61 Like Santa Claus

DOWN

1 "Damn Yankees" team
2 Relax
3 Hydroxyl compound
4 Show, informally
5 Miller character
6 Height
7 Coffee order: Abbr.
8 Comes about
9 Lit up
10 Certain metalworker
11 Bidding
12 Bone whose name is Latin for "pin"
13 Some jabs
15 "___ well"
19 "Well-bred insolence," per Aristotle
23 Look
25 Prefix with political
26 River bordering Tokyo

27 Track
29 It has four bases
31 Speaker of baseball
32 2013 Pawel Pawlikowski film set in post-W.W. II Poland
33 Fifth, e.g.: Abbr.
34 "Deck the Halls" contraction
35 One on a mission
36 What a hygrometer measures
39 Glacial formations
40 French ice cream flavor
41 Hawaiian exchange
42 Bedding
43 Nevil Shute's "___ Like Alice"
44 Forward, say
45 Chest part, for short
46 Kind of center
48 Fishing line
51 Company whose name is derived from a passage in Hosea

52 Locks up
53 Not be able to say "say," say
55 Item tied in a drum bow

by Mark Feldman

ACROSS

1 Some gobblers
5 Part of a fashion ensemble, maybe
9 Checkout procedures
14 Black-bordered news item
15 Plot-listing datum
16 Bindle toters
17 2001 best seller about competitive Scrabble
19 Scarlett's suitor
20 Prefix with Freudian
21 Bridal path
22 Tiny bits
23 Without ___ (riskily)
24 Interpreter of omens
26 Japanese "soft art" (max opening score of 92 points)
29 Sounds of censure (max opening score of 80 points)
33 Where to hear "Bravo!" and "Brava!"
34 Fathoms
35 Author Levin
36 Courtroom team: Abbr.
37 While away
39 "God is the perfect ___": Browning
40 Alternative to "x," in math
41 Quark's place
42 Feather in one's cap
43 Totally inept sorts (max opening score of 104 points)
45 Ran off, in a way (max opening score of 94 points)
47 Fare that may be rolled
48 In the thick of
49 Sewing kit item
52 Column style
54 Napkin's place

57 Wonderland cake message
58 What you'd need to play 26-, 29-, 43- or 45-Across
60 Some hotel lobbies
61 Newport Beach isle
62 A.C.L.U. part: Abbr.
63 Financial resources
64 M.Y.O.B. part
65 Guinness word

DOWN

1 Mini-metro
2 Light wind?
3 Barcelona's Joan ___ Foundation
4 Norm: Abbr.
5 Is inconsistent
6 1974 Mocedades hit whose English version is titled "Touch the Wind"
7 One-named singer who married Heidi Klum
8 Stops for a breather

9 Fun house noises
10 Partner in crime
11 Help in crime
12 "___ problem!"
13 Former Air France fleet members, for short
18 Fruity soda brand
23 What snobs put on
25 Abbr. before a founding date
26 Steinbeck family
27 On the observation deck, say
28 Volkswagen model since 1979
30 Wounded Knee tribe
31 Sweet filling, in product names
32 Full, and then some
34 It has its setting
37 Editor's override
38 "It could happen"
39 Lumber along
41 Cousins of rhododendrons

42 Balloon's undoing
44 Magnify an online map
45 Setting of Kubla Khan's palace
46 Key of a Bach "Bourrée"
49 Baseball part
50 Cracker topper
51 ___ vez (again: Sp.)
53 Mixed bag
54 Car that may have a bar
55 Some brews
56 Smart-alecky
59 Pompom's place

by Amy Johnson

ACROSS

1 What group founded in 1960 currently has 12 members?
5 What Fox series was set in Newport Beach?
10 Cab locale
14 What sport has divisions called chukkers?
15 Rock band?
16 Wizards
17 Classic 1940s–'50s quiz show
20 Of a bodily partition
21 Winter warmer
22 What are Greek P's?
23 What automaker makes the Yukon and Acadia?
26 Pace
27 What is the popular name for daminozide?
28 The Police and others
30 CBS procedural
32 What do four gills make?
33 Invited to one's penthouse, say
34 Muddle
35 À la a siren
37 School head, slangily
38 Thundered
39 What is hopscotch called in New York City?
40 Some tides
41 What company owns MapQuest?
42 What notorious 1999 computer virus was named after an exotic dancer?
45 States of madness
49 What rating does the Michelin Guide give to "a very good restaurant"?
50 Sacred petitions
51 Mentally pooped

53 Directional suffix
54 Incredulous response
55 ___ Palmas, Spain
56 Response to an oversharer
57 Pots
58 W.W. II inits.
59 Multitude
60 Mercedes roadsters
61 "Scientia potentia ___"
62 C train?

DOWN

1 Goes (for)
2 Juice provider
3 What do mahouts ride?
4 Twister
5 What best-selling 2004 young adult novel was written entirely in the form of instant messages?
6 What is the oldest academic quiz competition in the U.S. (since 1948)?
7 Contents of Suisse banks?
8 What is 1/100 of a Danish krone?
9 Carry's partner
10 Fastidiousness
11 Kama Sutra illustrations, e.g.
12 Converts to currency
13 What California congressman heads the House Oversight Committee?
18 Future profs, maybe
19 Dress smartly, with "out"
23 What were Russell and Anna Huxtable on "The Cosby Show"?
24 Tiny pests
25 Was able to
27 One who makes an impression?
28 Superskinny
29 What was Caleb in the Bible?

31 What word precedes "Eyes," "Girl," "Love" and "Mama" in Top 40 song titles?
36 Ones with breaking points?
39 Exhibiting the most civility
41 Oxygen users
42 Sacred pieces
43 What is French for "huge"?
44 Neighbor of Teaneck, N.J.
45 Country singer West
46 Disturbed
47 Not acquired, say
48 Solicits from
52 Morse bit

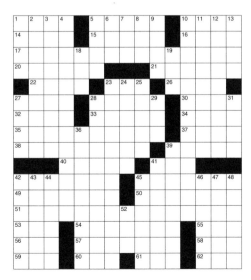

by Timothy Polin

ACROSS

1 Breather
5 Car radio button
9 Back of a 45 record
14 Telephone keypad abbr.
15 Wild hog
16 Reporting to
17 Where there's smoke
18 "I'm game"
19 It's rattled metaphorically
20 Goodyear employees when they're on strike?
23 Feed
24 "Goody, goody!"
25 Porch light circler
28 The Buckeyes' sch.
29 He's to the right of Teddy on Mount Rushmore
32 Site with a "Time left" display
35 Scenery chewer
37 It might reveal more than a simple X-ray
39 Result of Santa misplacing his papers?
42 Like some potatoes
43 Cotton seed remover
44 Puts in
45 Düsseldorf-to-Dresden direction
46 Prop in a western
48 Maryland athlete, for short
50 "Me, too"
52 First name in cosmetics
56 What the Red Sox had to start using in 1920?
61 Women's golf star Lorena
62 "Like that's gonna happen"
63 Some investment opportunities, in brief
64 One who's not from around here
65 Lime green 25-Across
66 Field for Gérard Depardieu and Audrey Tautou
67 Experimental division, for short
68 Drop when one is down?
69 The "K" in James K. Polk

DOWN

1 Some sleeping areas
2 Like the Statue of Liberty at night
3 Prefix with science
4 Story set on Mount Olympus
5 Up to the job
6 Homer Simpson's watering hole
7 Round one
8 Woman in "A Wrinkle in Time"
9 It may be diagrammed on a city map
10 Serpentine
11 "___ much obliged"
12 Traditional meat in a humble pie
13 Fouls up
21 Baseball's Durocher . . . or his astrological sign
22 Censorship-worthy
26 Nickname for filmdom's Lebowski
27 Holds
29 Liquid that burns
30 Posse, e.g.
31 Some M.I.T. grads: Abbr.
32 Admiral Zumwalt
33 Skewed view
34 Helper: Abbr.
36 Knicks' home: Abbr.
38 Buster Keaton genre
40 Theme park based on a toy
41 Tailor's concern
47 Margarita option
49 ___ room
50 Did a farrier's job on
51 People output
53 Easy basketball two-pointer
54 Prefix with metric
55 Earl of ___, favorite of Queen Elizabeth I
56 Waterfall sound
57 Sch. near Beverly Hills
58 Like dangerous ice
59 Fey of "30 Rock"
60 Miles and miles away

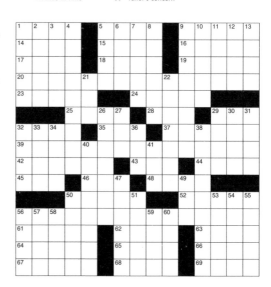

by Patrick Merrell

ACROSS

1 U.N. V.I.P.'s
5 Eats
8 Novelist Allende
14 Composer Schifrin
15 Yellowfin, on a menu
16 Robust
17 *___ Motel
19 Some shots
20 Reacted in horror, say
22 Hillock
23 2008 action thriller with Liam Neeson
24 *Dressing choice
27 Tornado siren, e.g.
30 Like a fifth wheel
31 Homes, colloquially
32 Campus digs
34 Pulitzer-winning biographer Leon
35 Inn patron
36 "Dear" one
40 How breakfast may be served . . . or how the answers to the eight starred clues should be entered?
41 Ending with peek
45 Released early
47 Kind of format for some data
49 *Longtime TV weatherman
51 Fit to be tied
52 Eight bells, maybe
53 Imprudent
56 ___ Quimby (Beverly Cleary heroine)
58 *Divide up
60 Heretofore
61 Mamie's man
62 Villainous visage
63 Aftermarket options
64 Capital of Texas?
65 Small vortex

DOWN

1 It's between B.C. and Sask.
2 Cooking wine
3 *Bit of hair
4 Parasailers, e.g.
5 "You crack me up"
6 Kiss interrupter, maybe
7 Rod Stewart's "Maggie May," for one
8 Periodical output: Abbr.
9 "Tristram Shandy" novelist
10 Outer ear
11 *Bit of excitement
12 Reagan cabinet member who was previously counselor to the president
13 Fleur-de-___
18 Bit of dough
21 Group beaten in a battle of the bands?
23 Dance genre
25 Court fig.
26 Broadband inits.
28 More out there
29 Habitual drunkard
33 Yank's foe
36 Manhunt letters
37 Seven Sisters college
38 *Leeway
39 46-Down's partner
41 Radiant light around the head
42 *Like Pisces, in the zodiac
43 Cereal grain
44 Pay dirt
46 A Beatle
48 One, for one
50 Red ink entry
54 It may be upside-down
55 Swiss Surrealist
56 Blues rocker Chris
57 Cribside cries
59 Like pinot grigio

by Pawel Fludzinski

78

ACROSS

1 Fix
5 Sauna garment
9 Needing a new muffler, say
14 Jessica of "Dark Angel"
15 Isle of exile
16 When prompted
17 MOUNTAINS TICK OFF TOY DOGS
20 Honshu honorific
21 Has control of
22 Caricatures and such
23 "Now or never" time
25 Netflix menu heading
28 SOUTH AFRICANS ARE UNEXCITED BY SWINE
32 Big name in fancy chocolates
33 Give ___ of approval
34 Play about Capote
35 Piece of Slate, e.g.
36 Sex columnist Savage
37 Crime in much insurance fraud
39 ___ brown
40 "Pics ___ didn't happen" ("Where's the proof?!")
41 ___ poker (dollar bill game)
42 COUPLES PEEL FRUIT
46 Cost of maintenance
47 ___ grease
48 Antiquity, in the past
49 Shrek, e.g.
51 Any of T. S. Eliot's "practical" creatures
54 PASTORAL POEMS INCAPACITATE TEEN FAVES
59 Author Zora ___ Hurston

60 One sleeping "in the jungle, the mighty jungle," in song
61 ___ Major
62 Lecherous goat-man
63 Didn't spoil
64 Sign of spoilage

DOWN

1 Chumps
2 "Don't shoot!," e.g.
3 Final order from the captain
4 Tibetan source of butter
5 Makes good on
6 Lena of "Havana"
7 Tailgaters' activities, for short
8 La mer contents
9 "You got it"
10 Pugilistic combo
11 "E-e-e-ew!"
12 Boy of song who hated his name
13 Sycophant's standard reply
18 Wisenheimer
19 Like fur seals
24 "___ means nothing" (1918 manifesto declaration)
25 Any of three literary sisters
26 Becomes worthy of the Guinness Book, say
27 Rarities for Gold Glove winners
28 Guinea-___ (West African nation)
29 Unjust verdict
30 Radio booth sign
31 Catches some rays
32 Grand jeté, e.g.
37 Kosygin of Russia
38 Iranian currency
40 Printed points of view, for short
43 Singer with the 1994 hit "Bump n' Grind"
44 Many a Craigslist user
45 PepsiCo, to Frito-Lay

49 Often-kicked comics canine
50 Zero-star fare
52 "In addition . . ."
53 Pre-1917 autocrat
54 Networkers' hopes
55 Bust-making org.
56 China's Sun ___-sen
57 Kind
58 Indigo Girls, e.g.

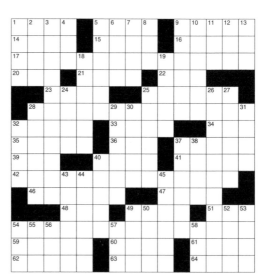

by Dick Shlakman and Jeff Chen

ACROSS

1 Sheepish
6 Compass drawings
10 Secretaries may collect them: Abbr.
14 Jones for
15 Aptly named Olympics star
16 Maker of the Insignia
17 Woman's name with an accent
18 Under tight control
20 Suffix with bass
21 Purse or pocket item, briefly
23 Go over and over
24 French cop
26 Go off
28 Half of hip-hop's Black Star
31 Game in 2006's "Casino Royale"
34 Treasure of the Sierra Madre
35 Must give
36 It's not unusual
38 "Two for me. None for you" candy
39 It left parts of itself in 11 states in 1980
43 Had pity (for)
44 One of the music industry's former Big Four
45 [Ha!]
46 Info for an airport car service, briefly
47 "It Takes Two" co-star
52 Licks
56 "Here Come the Warm Jets" musician
57 All right
58 Like limeade
59 Grind
61 Brit. military decoration
62 Like seashells at high tide
66 Bad-mouths
68 Three-piece piece
69 First name in long jumping

70 Two ___ (double-teaming situation)
71 Pro competitor
72 Pops
73 What locks may cover

DOWN

1 Early 2000s attorney general
2 Anatomical ring
3 Detective of 1960s–'70s TV
4 Female rapper with the 2002 hit "Gangsta Lovin'"
5 Thought-provoking
6 On
7 Howard who narrated "Arrested Development"
8 Not go together at all
9 Attack en masse
10 Ones woolgathering?
11 Landing for many an Apollo mission
12 "Who'da thunk it?!"
13 /
19 U.S. truck maker until the early '50s
22 X
25 Leave the casino, say
27 Cold-blooded sort
29 Dwarf planet beyond Pluto
30 Hottie
32 Keep
33 Start of a tile game
37 Need for support
38 Enlightens
39 Kind of lab
40 Illusion creator
41 Chart-topper
42 Throne room at Buckingham Palace
43 Like April, typically
48 Co-author of "The Communist Manifesto"
49 Place to get a malted
50 Early Semite
51 Deadly constrictors

53 One-named singer with the 2003 hit "Rock Wit U (Awww Baby)"
54 Fraction of a watt-hour
55 Hidden (away)
60 Olympic decathlon gold medalist ___ Eaton
62 Home of Marshall Univ.
63 Colorless
64 Eggs
65 Sunburned
67 Code carrier, sometimes

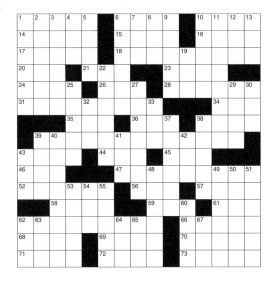

by Luke Vaughn

80

ACROSS

1 Where buses are parked
6 Where buffalo roam
11 ___ Harbour, Fla.
14 Big Indian
15 "___ case of emergency"
16 When août occurs
17 *Words on a birth announcement
19 Aurora's Greek counterpart
20 Ending with farm
21 Has coming
23 Magazine with a back-cover fold-in
26 *Quota for a rep to achieve
29 2009 Peace Nobelist
31 Island setting for "Pirates of the Caribbean"
32 Title island of a 2005 DreamWorks animated film
36 Only non-U.S. M.L.B. team, on scoreboards
37 *Oldest continuous democracy in Central America
40 Say further
43 Words from class clowns
47 Sisterly
50 Landscapist's prop
51 *Where to find money exchange shops
55 Before now
56 Pitchers?
57 Title for a French nobleman
59 "Kidnapped" monogram
60 Like the Oscars . . . or the answers to this puzzle's seven asterisked clues?
66 Driving need
67 First name in cosmetics
68 Question before takeoff
69 Suffix for braggarts
70 Tournament favorites
71 Follow

DOWN

1 N.B.A.'s Erving, to fans
2 Agua, across the Pyrenees
3 Slumber party attire, informally
4 Bran muffin topping
5 "Let's roll!"
6 Like most of Wyoming
7 Out of the way
8 Harry Reid's state: Abbr.
9 Bestow on, to Burns
10 Win over
11 Opposite of six-pack abs, ironically
12 In a single try
13 *Cigarette ad claim
18 Stephen of "The Crying Game"
22 Mobiles, stabiles, etc.
23 Alice, to Dennis the Menace
24 Litigators' org.
25 Henry, to Dennis the Menace
27 *Preflight psych job
28 Cheerio-shaped
30 ___ 'n' cheese
33 ___ expected (predictably)
34 Circus prop
35 ___ in cat
38 Kind of comfort
39 Top-rated
40 *Ancient fertility goddess
41 Marginal things?
42 It often shows a band's name
44 Rebs' org.
45 Bud holder, of sorts
46 ___-mo
48 Some Scandinavian coins
49 Salon supplies
52 Like a land baron
53 Derby bouquet
54 CPR pro
58 Original sin locale
61 "Cats" inspirer's monogram
62 Scarfed down
63 Hip-hop's ___ Racist
64 Dot follower, on campus
65 Food factory supply

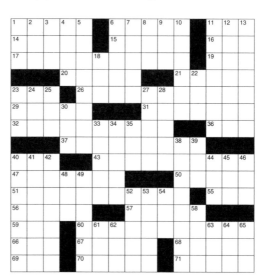

by Bruce Haight

ACROSS

1 Takeover
5 Hit 2006 horror film based on a video game series
9 Curses
14 Seltzer lead-in
15 Cousin of a cor anglais
16 Lock combination?
17 Brains
19 Having a bite
20 Art lovers
21 German chancellor between Schmidt and Schröder
22 Film series
23 Probes
26 Fangorn denizens
28 Spacecraft designer ___ Musk
29 3-Down issuer
32 Cleverness
34 Start of a director's cry
38 ___ point
39 Buster Keaton hat
41 Milk
42 Once in a blue moon
44 Cries of exasperation
45 Breaking a world record, e.g.
46 JFK-to-TLV option
48 Kind of paste
50 "Every good boy does fine," e.g.
54 Seminal 1962 book on the environment
58 Exude
59 Company providing financial assistance to college students
61 Chapter part
63 Some passive-aggressive behavior
64 Fatuous
65 Pizazz
66 Yours, in Tours
67 Car with a "rolling dome" speedometer

68 Times Sq. watcher
69 Condé ___

DOWN

1 Rio residences
2 Dweller in San Lorenzo Tenochtitlán
3 Decree
4 Business associate uninvolved in management
5 What a girl becomes after marriage, in an old expression
6 Sarcastic "Sure you can!"
7 Squanders
8 Tenant
9 Vaccine combo
10 One way to prepare chicken
11 Jules Massenet opéra comique
12 Popular Christmas carol
13 Pen, in Paris
18 Segue word

24 Great Hall locale
25 Mousseline de ___ (fabric)
27 Rugby official, whether male or female
29 What there may be a lot of interest in, for short?
30 Zodiac starter?
31 Punch
33 What a punch may result in, briefly
35 Rose, e.g.
36 Carry-on inspector, in brief
37 Collector's desire
39 Preppy wear
40 Poe title character
43 Lord's estate
45 Overseer
47 Tune in
49 Narrow projection of land into the sea
50 Almost any pre-1927 Hollywood production

51 Ceaselessly
52 Pound and Stone
53 Singer Simon
55 ". . . ___ man with seven wives"
56 Certain iPods
57 "Is that clear?"
60 Big step
62 Reef dweller

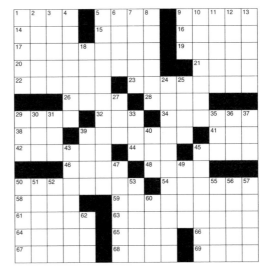

by John Guzzetta

82

ACROSS

1 Run up __
5 Marks for life
10 "__ be in England"
14 Big shot
15 Also-ran of 1992 and 1996
16 Frond bearer
17 Bootleggers' foes
18 Begin to correct, maybe
19 "Exodus" hero and others
20 Cabinet department until 1947
21 Like the figure formed by the three circled letters in the upper left
23 East of Germany?
24 Snobbishness
26 1996 Olympics city
28 Highlights show
29 Somerhalder of "The Vampire Diaries"
31 Skin-and-bones sort
32 Anti-D.U.I. ads, e.g.
33 A dog might catch one
35 Newcastle's river
36 Like the figure formed by the three circled letters in the upper right
39 He tapped Ryan in 2012
42 Something to lean on
46 "If the shoe fits, wear it," e.g.
47 "Alice" waitress
50 Shopaholic's binge
51 "Alice" diner owner
52 Traffic problem
54 1936 opponent of Franklin D.
55 Like the figure formed by the three circled letters at the bottom
60 Make a comeback

62 Overlay material
65 "In the Heat of the Night" Oscar winner
66 Rules for hunters to follow
67 Some distracted drivers
68 Sucker in

DOWN

1 Belgian seaport
2 Wrapped Tex-Mex fare
3 Stephen Colbert's "I Am __ (And So Can You!)"
4 Football's Roethlisberger
5 Blueprint details, in brief
6 Ming vases, e.g.
7 __ Sea (Asian body)
8 Comic with a "domestic goddess" persona
9 Artery implant
10 All __ sudden

11 Nesting area for wading birds
12 Isolde's beloved
13 Treading the boards
21 Nurse at a bar
22 N.Y.C.'s Third and Ninth Avenue lines, e.g.
25 Zapping, in a way
27 Starts malfunctioning
30 Early nuclear org.
33 Kind of milk
34 Special attention, briefly
37 Get the idea
38 Triage spots, for short
39 Flock member
40 Horatian work
41 The symbol for the Roman god Mars represents it
43 Refrain syllables
44 Disney collectible
45 Playboy nickname
47 Manicurists, at times
48 Grazing area
49 Loss of power

52 Ty Cobb, for most of his career
53 Praline nut
56 Conk out
57 The munchies, e.g.
58 Dream states, for short
59 ". . . __-foot pole!"
60 Queue after Q
61 Season after printemps
63 La Brea gunk
64 39-Down's mate

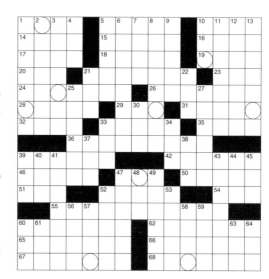

by Daniel Raymon

ACROSS

1 Stars
5 Blood group?
9 Oscar nominee for "Affliction"
14 Draft status for someone in the Public Health Service
15 Inspect the figures?
16 Huge, in verse
17 Singer in the sea, literally
19 Wrap up
20 "Smack"
21 B's tail?
23 Long-distance inits.
24 Something slipped under the counter?
25 Feel one's ___ (be frisky)
26 Fiction's Atticus Finch, e.g.: Abbr.
27 Plan B, literally
30 Place with a waiting room: Abbr.
33 Some intellectual property, for short
34 Literary Leonard
35 One side of a hot-button social issue
38 Ticked off
39 Skylights?
40 A.C.C. school
41 Multinational carrier
42 Gridiron maneuver, literally
46 Comprehensive, in edspeak
47 Baseball Hall-of-Famer Aparicio
48 Dime novels and such
52 Stocking stuffer
53 Ollie's partner in comedy
54 Negotiator's refusal
55 One of Donald's exes
57 Little kid's lift, literally

59 Frankincense or myrrh
60 Read but not comment, in Internet lingo
61 Unlikely mate for a princess
62 Big name in cosmetics
63 Summer Olympics event
64 Stimulate

DOWN

1 10 students, for short?
2 Like overly optimistic goals, typically
3 Intro to biology?
4 Teach
5 Singer Marc with the 1991 hit "Walking in Memphis"
6 JFK alternative
7 Indicator of stress
8 Must
9 Hasbro brand
10 In dire need of gas, say
11 Spots
12 Vino spot
13 Fisherman's bane and hockey player's boon
18 Plans to
22 Core
25 "All ___" (Steve Martin/Lily Tomlin comedy)
26 Bread producers
28 Guilty
29 Pier grp.
30 Gut
31 Soul mates
32 45 degrees
36 Petty around Hollywood
37 Grp. in a 1919–'21 war of independence
38 Tolkien's Prancing Pony and others
40 Exhausting
43 Bush successor

44 How individual firecrackers are priced?
45 "Friends" co-star
49 O'Hara portrayer
50 Tony Gwynn, notably
51 Hard fall
53 Ready to stand trial, in a way
54 Sponsor of Michael Jordan and Tiger Woods
56 Never: Ger.
58 M.A. hopeful's hurdle

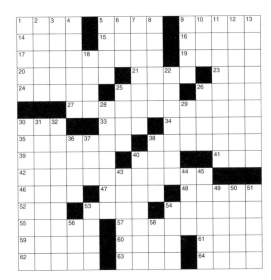

by Alan Arbesfeld

84

ACROSS

1 Truffle-seeking beast
5 Like some orders or tales
9 Bits in marmalade
14 Works of Goya, e.g.
15 Utah skiing mecca
16 Words after "You can't fire me!"
17 Speed Wagons of old autodom
18 *Movie stand-in
20 Toddler's banishment to a corner, say
22 Talkative bird
23 It may be bid in the end
24 Singer/songwriter Corinne Bailey ___
25 ZZ Top, for one
29 *Crowd noise, for example
33 Devoid of wool, now
34 Keep in touch, in a way
35 Palindromic girl's name
38 Bach work
41 iPhone data: Abbr.
42 Join, as a table
44 End of a Greek series
46 *One's physical or emotional burdens
52 Love-letter letters
53 A "little word" in charades
54 Enjoy to the max
55 Like a soufflé's texture
57 What the moon does during a lunar eclipse
59 Complete freedom . . . and a hint to each half of the answer to each starred clue
63 Sign of virtue
64 Tilter's weapon
65 Anthony's longtime partner on satellite radio
66 "___ option . . ."
67 Where sailors go
68 Like odor-indicating lines, in comics
69 The latest

DOWN

1 Tippler's account
2 Tater Tots maker
3 Superprecise, as some clocks
4 Tries for again, as an office
5 Fragrance name that's forbidden-sounding
6 Jillions
7 Old Ford model
8 Nonprofessional
9 Promised Land, to Rastafarians
10 Where it's always zero degrees
11 Benchwarmer
12 Up to, briefly
13 Fr. woman with a 63-Across
19 Got away from one's roots?
21 Should
24 What your blood may do when you're frightened
26 Completely screw up
27 Infatuated with
28 Praiseful works
30 Pal of Pooh
31 Humanoid monster of myth
32 Walk with an attitude
35 Nile reptiles
36 Asset of an oceanfront home
37 First razor with a pivoting head
39 Diplomatic fig.
40 Word before set or service
43 With suspicion, as a look
45 Shiite leader who claims direct descent from Muhammad
47 Buster?
48 "As I was saying . . ."
49 Anxiety-free
50 The Brady Bill is one
51 Popular printers
56 Certain superstore
57 604, in old Rome
58 Solution to the classic riddle "What force or strength cannot get through, / I, with gentle touch, can do"
59 Crunchy sandwich
60 Mekong Valley native
61 T or F, perhaps: Abbr.
62 Water-quality org.

by Howard Barkin

ACROSS

1 Bunch
5 Game similar to euchre
11 "Arsenal of democracy" prez
14 Auto datum
15 Credit card lure
16 ___ Highway, classic New York-to-San Francisco route
17 Area in front of a chancel
18 Linoleum alternative
19 Place of rest
20 "Looky here!"
22 -
23 Nabokov novel after "Lolita"
24 Mario ___ (Nintendo racing series)
27 A series of "insurmountable obstacles on the road to imminent disaster," per Tom Stoppard
29 Flight setting
32 -
34 Helmet part
35 Greater part of Turkey
36 -
37 Sound a hot dog makes?
38 End of a fairy's wand
40 Outwit, in a way
42 Goose : gaggle :: ___ : knot
45 Wedding feature, in two different senses
47 Interrupts, as a broadcast
49 -
50 South Australian exports
52 Chosen people
53 -
54 Overlook, as someone's flaws
56 ___ notes
58 Writer Philip
59 Not worry about something annoying
61 -

65 Choler
66 California county between San Francisco and Sacramento
69 Similar
70 "No ___!"
71 Digs deeply
72 Small price to pay
73 Kind of fever
74 Prophet on the Sistine Chapel ceiling
75 Evil "Get Smart" organization

DOWN

1 In ___ with
2 Genesis matriarch
3 Place for a wasp's nest
4 Hit 2012 Disney film
5 Went around
6 Men's formalwear feature
7 Picked locks?
8 Good or bad name
9 Means of enforcement, metaphorically
10 It's just a guess: Abbr.
11 Pebbles, e.g.
12 "GoodFellas" co-star
13 Jeremy of "The Avengers"
21 Corn syrup brand
23 1966 Rolling Stones hit . . . or an instruction to be followed four times in this puzzle
25 -
26 -
28 "Casino Royale" Bond girl ___ Green
29 KLM competitor
30 Big bang maker
31 Remote power source, maybe
33 Booze
37 One of the Wailers of Bob Marley and the Wailers
39 -
41 Don Quixote's love

43 Took in
44 Tango twosome?
46 Org. for which Edward Snowden once worked
48 "Hard" or "soft" subjects: Abbr.
50 Beastly
51 Bradley University site
52 Stanley Kowalski's woman
55 Dark-skinned fruit
57 -
60 Rikki-tikki-___
62 Furniture megastore
63 11-Down pet
64 Middle-earth creatures
66 Reagan's Star Wars program: Abbr.
67 -
68 -

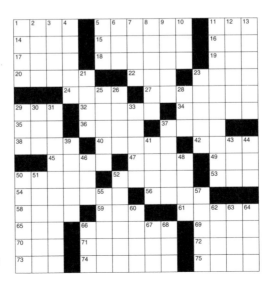

by David Phillips

ACROSS

1 Sandwich usually served with mayo
4 Like messy beds
10 Scott Pelley's network
13 Tyler of "The Lord of the Rings"
14 April to September, for baseball
15 Stadium closed in 2008
16 Like some stocks, for short
17 List of user IDs?
19 "I'm surprised to see you!"
21 Run some water over
22 Undergarment fitting device?
25 Tag . . . or a word that can precede tag
26 Plains Indians
30 Jailer with a key ring?
35 The Rosetta Stone is one
36 Massachusetts or Connecticut in D.C.
37 Was livid
39 Cowboy moniker
40 Card combinations
43 Hardly an attraction for a surfer?
46 Impersonate
48 ". . . ducks in ___"
49 Directors in charge of downsizing?
55 Elementary start
57 Textile artist, perhaps
58 Attractive but annoying date?
61 TurboTax alternative, for short
62 Features of many late-1950s cars
63 ___ greens
64 Vessel that was 300 cubits long
65 Poison ___

66 Jerks
67 Fish eggs

DOWN

1 What century plants do only once
2 Limber
3 Just 2 to 13, once
4 Sch. with a noted marching band
5 Opposite of paleo-
6 Most Cook Islanders
7 Welcome at the door
8 "___ anything later?"
9 "Romanian Rhapsodies" composer
10 Food Network V.I.P.
11 Gripe
12 College Board creation
15 Patronize, as a store
18 Noted children's "doctor"
20 Golfer Aoki

23 One crouching at home
24 Snorkeling spot
27 Aid for a bank heist
28 Peak figure: Abbr.
29 ___-Coburg (former German duchy)
30 Summer getaway
31 Former Chevy subcompact
32 Book before Deut.
33 British record giant
34 Cam button
38 Bummer
41 Some coffee orders
42 Arab kingdom native
44 Planet, e.g.
45 Pinocchio material
47 Hospital implants
50 Dress smartly, in old parlance
51 Hindu warrior king
52 German refusals
53 Not an original

54 Rapper with the 3x platinum single "Hold On, We're Going Home"
55 Karmann ___, classic German sports car
56 Arrange in order
58 Exec in charge of $$$
59 ___ card
60 Some PCs and printers

by Jean O'Conor

ACROSS

1 Financial writer Marshall
5 Girl of Guatemala
10 Captain played by Patrick Stewart
14 Shade provider
15 Chinese province known for its spicy cuisine
16 Plumb crazy
17 Be long and boring
18 Prayer starter
19 Ruined, in a way
20 55-Across, e.g.
23 Shark
25 Dangling piece of jewelry
28 55-Across, e.g.?
32 Come to
33 "Amazing!"
34 Antipolio pioneer
35 Second of all?
36 Sardonic Larry
38 Journal
39 Low state
42 Drops
45 Lender's assessment
46 Mars, e.g.
47 Edit
50 Easily prepared lunch item, informally
54 Fire truck item
55 Visual representation of this puzzle's theme
59 Jackie's #2
60 Insults
62 Left or right
63 Short news item
65 Sign word after "Ye"
66 Ottoman V.I.P.
67 ___ rings
68 One with a staff position?
69 ___ Noire (Russie borderer)
70 Lather

DOWN

1 Trailblazed
2 Stroke, in a way
3 Empties
4 Irish oath
5 Who said "The less you open your heart to others, the more your heart suffers"
6 Alternative to standard TV
7 "How could ___?"
8 Attention to detail
9 Bargnani of the N.B.A.
10 Home of Banff National Park
11 People swear by it
12 Strikeout star
13 Where the nose is
21 Whimper
22 Nebr. neighbor
23 You, on the Yucatán
24 Pilot's place
26 ___ rings
27 Feature of some cuts
29 Howard of Ayn Rand's "The Fountainhead"
30 Part of U.S.S.R.: Abbr.
31 Word with honey or flower
36 You might need a lot of it for your files
37 It's far out
40 Master
41 Areas that may be protected by military jets
43 Regions within regions
44 Nine-digit no. issuer
47 It might make one's shadow disappear
48 The Roman dramatist Seneca, once
49 Proceeds indirectly
51 Pacific nation once known as Pleasant Island
52 Like prunes
53 Agrees
56 Hit 1996 live-action/animated film
57 We're living in it
58 Name for 55-Across
61 Fetch
64 Bev. units

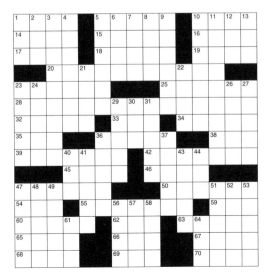

by Jeff Chen and Jill Denny

ACROSS

1 Tribal symbol of luck
5 Printout problem
9 Some brothers
13 Actress ___ Rachel Wood
14 Singer David Lee ___
15 Dust collector
16 Where business is picking up?
17 Memorable 2005 Gulf hurricane
18 Prudential rival
19 French chicken dish garnished with kernels?
22 Whitish
25 Philosopher who asked "What is enlightenment?"
26 Quartet on an online help page?
30 This: Sp.
34 Rapper with the 2008 hit "Paper Planes"
35 It can give you a lift
36 Lie in the hot sun
37 Frequent, in odes
38 Dancer Duncan
41 Company's end?
42 Totally puzzle
44 Key periods
45 M.M.A. decision
46 Bad character?
47 What Ben stitched for his business partner?
50 Quad part
52 Jets' victory over the Colts in Super Bowl III, famously
53 Royal ending to a mathematical proof?
59 Functional
60 Lower-class, in Leeds
61 Warhead carrier, for short
65 Central
66 The Time Traveler's hosts
67 Longtime teammate of 12-Down

68 Something good for a scout, say
69 Trick-or-treater's wear
70 Ones working on a case-by-case basis?: Abbr.

DOWN

1 Black
2 Cavalier's sch.
3 Florida port, briefly
4 Trick-or-treater's cause
5 "It's f-f-freezing!"
6 Choice cut
7 "Smoke Gets in Your Eyes" lyricist Harbach
8 1998 Alanis Morissette hit with a slangy misspelling
9 Swifter
10 Big source of coll. scholarships
11 53 for I, e.g.
12 Longtime teammate of 67-Across
15 "High Hopes" lyricist Sammy

20 How the police might investigate someone
21 Driveway topper
22 Not more than
23 Deceitful
24 Intensify
27 Play callers, for short
28 Drone regulator, in brief
29 "Atten-TION!," e.g.
31 "You're right about that"
32 Cat collar sound
33 Literary giant from Concord, Mass.
36 Like the sport of jai alai
39 "Catch-22" character who "hasn't got brains enough to be unhappy"
40 Flat fish
43 Patterned (after)
47 Yearbook sect.
48 Rapper with the autobiography "The Way I Am"

49 John who won two Pulitzers for fiction
51 British pound, informally
53 British pound, informally
54 ___ Reader
55 Article in Arnsberg
56 Dreyfus Affair chronicler
57 Book of Mormon prophet
58 Classic Nestlé drink
62 Trig. function
63 Summer event, briefly . . . or a phonetic hint to 19-, 26-, 47- and 53-Across
64 Año part

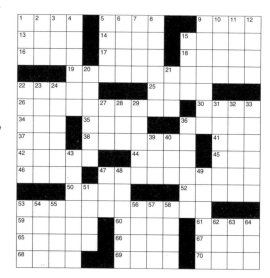

by Brendan Emmett Quigley

ACROSS

1 Extends credit
6 Exam for a future G.P.
10 Sot
14 Possible score before winning a game
15 Figure on a Utah license plate
16 China setting
17 Like a dingbat
18 Stonewaller's response
20 Part 1 of a wordplay-related quip
21 Quip, part 2
22 Temple of ___
23 Saturn's wife
24 City bonds, informally
27 Golfer Sorenstam
29 What thumb drives provide
31 Cheaper-looking
34 Take a little off the top?
35 Quip, part 3
39 ___ shot
40 Spark
41 Italian Riviera resort
44 Trap
48 Still liquidy
49 Lead-in to a 2000s "-gate"
51 Singer with the 1971 hit "Mercy Mercy Me"
52 Quip, part 4
55 End of the quip
56 Bag lady?
58 Formal response at the door
59 Chip, maybe
60 Site of one of the world's most famous onion domes
61 Bad strain?
62 Fleet on the street
63 Spotted
64 They may be taken to the next level

DOWN

1 Pretentious
2 Westinghouse adversary
3 Concept
4 Tiny creature that can trigger allergies
5 Trough locale
6 "Stop being such a wuss!"
7 Pen name
8 ___ no.
9 Radiohead frontman Yorke
10 Dorothy of old "Road" films
11 What an anonymous person may lack
12 Sloth, for one
13 It may be tipped
19 Kind of pad
21 ___ Löw, coach of Germany's 2014 World Cup-winning team
25 Composer Stravinsky
26 Tie up some loose ends?
28 Kit ___ bar
29 Slip (through)
30 Three-horse carriages
32 Lotto variant
33 Department of the Treasury dept.
35 Jackson with 13 #1 country albums
36 Doesn't pay immediately
37 Prefix with lateral
38 Approving remark after "By Jove . . ."
39 Sch. of 2013 Heisman Trophy winner Jameis Winston
42 Signs up for more
43 They may be delayed by weather, for short
45 Wordsmith who wrote "Last but not least, avoid clichés like the plague"
46 Looks at covetously
47 Negligent
49 Training group
50 "Um . . ."
53 Figs. on some résumés
54 Oversize sunglasses, these days
56 Company with a bucket list?
57 Styled after
58 O.R. devices

by Joe DiPietro

90

ACROSS

1 Eurasian plain
7 Sugary punch, slangily
15 Like McJobs
16 Worker's advocate, in brief
17 Class for the hotheaded
19 Deliver by wagon, say
20 Storage buildings with elevators
21 H.R.H. part
22 ___-a-brac
24 Cirrus cloud formation
27 ". . . ___ can't get up!"
29 Covered with goose bumps
33 Cardiologist's insert
35 One with a habit
36 Partner of then
37 Result of a buzz cut
41 ___ rule
44 Veterinary school subj.
45 "I'm outta here!"
49 Miller Park crew
53 Tended to, as a strain
54 They know beans
55 Loser to paper
57 Something to trip on
58 ___ year (annually)
62 NBC anchor before Williams
64 Foreigner's obstacle . . . or a hint to hidden words in 17-, 29-, 37- and 49-Across
68 Transpired
69 Nutbag
70 Diving board locales
71 Ropes in

DOWN

1 Diminutive, in Dundee
2 Like variety stores of old
3 Fighting words, of sorts
4 Fishing place
5 Medicare component
6 Twain's New York burial place
7 Brat holder
8 Señora's "some"
9 Caron title role of 1958
10 Billy a.k.a. the Piano Man
11 Like golf course roughs, typically
12 Work stoppage declaration?
13 2000s, e.g.: Abbr.
14 Competent, facetiously
18 Indigo source
21 Is down with
23 Desktop problem
25 ___ Poke (classic candy)
26 Seat for a service
28 Good folks to know
30 Volcanic spew
31 White-glove affair
32 Body part used in some recognition systems
34 Seafarer's adverb
38 Exclamation point's key-mate
39 Lacking polish
40 Big name in outdoor gear
41 Get-together: Abbr.
42 "Well, well!"
43 Music star with an accent in her name
46 Oblong pastries
47 "You take credit cards?" response
48 Interpose
50 Excellent, as a job
51 L.B.J. in-law
52 Doctor's penmanship, stereotypically
56 Home to Samsung
59 Smoke or salt
60 Bring in
61 Kept in the cellar, maybe
63 Jenner of reality TV
64 Israeli air hub locale
65 Big club?
66 Times V.I.P.'s
67 Children's author Asquith

by Dan Schoenholz

ACROSS

1 Former Ford full-sizes
5 Divide by zero in a computer program, maybe
8 Huck Finn and Tom Sawyer, e.g.
12 One who gets a charge out of charging?
14 Grassy expanse
15 -
16 Calculated
17 Commercial start for Pen
18 -
19 Lovable 650-pound TV character
20 ___-de-Marne (French department)
21 -
22 New Mexico county or its seat
23 Service station sign
24 Display one's guts
25 Big bird
26 First mass-production auto company outside the U.S.
30 Mess up
31 "Just leave!"
33 Outlier
35 Epitome of thinness
36 Start of a massive renovation, for short
37 Biblical betrayer
40 37-Across, e.g.
44 ___ pop (music genre)
45 Head of Olympus?
47 Open kimono preventer
48 "I am a man more sinn'd against than sinning" speaker
50 It has an analytical writing component, for short
51 Dug up some dirt?
52 One of two engineering features depicted in this puzzle

54 Czech reformer Jan
55 -
56 Reflexive response to an accusation
57 Wordplay, e.g.
58 -
60 Writes briefly
61 One way to see a talk, for short?
62 -
63 Avant-garde
64 "___-haw!"
65 Material used in many high-end chess sets

DOWN

1 Flashback cause, maybe
2 Rapper whose 2006 album "Doctor's Advocate" was #1
3 Apportion
4 Short drives
5 One reason for a 52-Across
6 Withdraw (to)

7 Another reason for a 52-Across
8 Went carefully (over)
9 One side in college football's Iron Bowl
10 Like some interpretations
11 Trees, hills and streams, e.g.
13 N.Y.C.-based dance group
15 Daughter of Loki
22 Business card abbr.
26 Green formerly of "The Voice"
27 Building component with two flanges
28 Summer time in Buenos Aires
29 Another name for Odysseus
32 Hosp. procedure
34 Reply of mock indignation

37 Co-star of "The Cannonball Run," 1981
38 Changed
39 Kind of dock
41 "We're not joking about that yet"
42 Michelle Obama campaign target
43 Relieve
46 Compete without a struggle
49 "I Am Woman" singer
51 "I ___ idea"
53 Urgent care workers, for short
55 Org. concerned with pupils
59 Big ___ (Dallas fair icon)

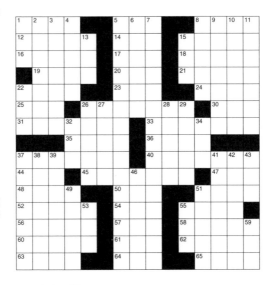

by Jason Flinn

92

ACROSS

1 Start to grunt?
6 Air freshener scent
11 Tabloid paper, slangily
14 Shudder at
15 Plain People
16 Subj. for U.S. citizens-to-be
17 *Fare for those 17 and up
19 Lunes or martes
20 Google Earth offering
21 Watered down
22 *Astronomical red giant
24 Runoff conduit
26 Steal the show from
28 *"Invest With Confidence" firm
31 Swelled heads
32 Top of a platter
33 Black keys, in some key signatures
35 Schumer of Comedy Central
36 Publicist's handout
39 G.M.'s Mary Barra, beginning in 2014
42 Land on the eastern Mediterranean
43 Imam's Almighty
45 "As seen ___"
48 *Best-selling novelist who wrote the children's poetry volume "Father Goose"
51 Anticipate
53 Windblown soil
54 *"It's Gonna Be Me" group
55 Symbol of authority
56 Autograph seeker's encl.
59 Cries of surprise
60 *The Boss's backup musicians
64 ___ Offensive of 1968
65 "Julius," e.g., in Gaius Julius Caesar

66 Like the number 8, to the Chinese
67 Masthead listings, for short
68 Road signs may warn of them
69 Spaniard's "these"

DOWN

1 "What's the ___ in that?"
2 Start of a magic incantation
3 Liszt piece
4 Umlaut half
5 Tired
6 Hedy of "Ecstasy"
7 "Don't worry about me"
8 Tyler of "Stealing Beauty"
9 "Just ___ expected"
10 Game in which pieces can be forked
11 Sale item attachment
12 Cheese that's often grated

13 Gives the evil eye
18 Almost to the outfield wall
23 Fr. holy women
25 Wearer of a natural wool coat
26 Rose Bowl stadium sch.
27 Wasabi ___ (bar snack)
28 Org. with a no-shoes policy?
29 Wheel part
30 "Sadly . . ."
34 Whistler in the kitchen
37 First name in mysteries
38 Subject of a search on Mars
39 One to admire
40 Mer contents
41 Resistor unit
42 Name that's Old Norse for "young man"

44 Abbr. in a birth announcement
45 Worth mentioning
46 Snacked
47 No-tell motel meetings
49 Many Astounding Stories cover subjects
50 Aroma
52 Hot spot
55 Like the initial letters of the answers to the six starred clues, on "Wheel of Fortune"
57 "My Way" lyricist
58 Brand known as Dreyer's in the West
61 "Hel-l-l-lp!"
62 Things Coke and Pepsi have: Abbr.
63 Work tables?

by Zhouqin Burnikel

93

ACROSS
1 Pace
5 Serfs, e.g.
10 Absorbed
14 Is __ unto oneself
15 American __
16 26-Across of a North Carolina "-ville"
17 Clump up
18 First place
20 Roman road
21 Besmirched
22 Carrier to Tokyo
23 Cozy thing?
25 One that's HI-strung?
26 See 16-Across
28 Biota part
30 To-do
32 Ayatollah Khomeini, e.g.
34 Super Mario Galaxy platform
35 Mickey Mouse pics, e.g.
39 Mail conveniences . . . or a hint to eight squares in this puzzle
42 Cryptozoological beast
43 Many, many moons
44 Hose attachment
45 Friend of Homer on "The Simpsons"
47 Intermediate, in law
48 Mark Twain's belief
51 John of Liverpool
53 Freeloader
56 Legal borders?
57 Wagnerian heroine
60 H.S. exam
61 Means of murder in some Agatha Christie novels
63 Core
64 Cocktail order
65 Knightley of "Pirates of the Caribbean"
66 Like Olympic years
67 Seasons in Lyon

68 Utopian settings
69 Edit menu command

DOWN
1 Left unsaid
2 Send
3 Prepare to give blood, perhaps
4 Throwing one's weight around, in international relations
5 Benjamin
6 [I'm not listening . . . I can't he-e-ear you!]
7 "__ bag of shells" (Ralph Kramden malapropism)
8 Sleep-inducing
9 Return mailer, for short
10 Mobster's "canary"
11 __-American
12 Impostor
13 Common break time
19 Bean product?
24 Film pooch

27 Feature of many a movie house
29 Direct
31 Feudal lord
32 Plant, maybe
33 Aid in weed control
34 __ big
36 Large-scale
37 Spike in movie sales?
38 Byelorussian __: Abbr.
40 Succeeded
41 Stereo control
46 Last name in despotism
47 Hip
48 Testify
49 1948 Literature Nobelist
50 Offspring
52 Almost any hit by Prince or Queen
54 Like some retirement communities
55 Prefix with botany

58 Umbrella part
59 Pitching stats
62 Choice connections

by Jules P. Markey

94

ACROSS
1. Showing hopelessness
7. "West Side Story" weapon
11. Do Not Call Registry org.
14. Truckers' contest
15. Colombian city of 2+ million
16. Dig this!
17. Libretto for "Eel Trovatore"?
19. FEMA offering
20. Green-light
21. Want ad abbr.
22. Lightning setting
24. Microwave for hot dogs?
27. Sequel to "Twilight"
31. 90° from sur
32. Sound of an allergic reaction
33. ___ factor
34. Porter's cousin
37. Actor Sheen after starting a new career in piano maintenance?
42. "Salem's ___"
43. DVR brand
44. Subject of King Abdullah
45. Union station?
48. Lacking the traditional comforts
50. One who knows the earnings report by heart?
53. Get the lead out?
54. Hauler's choice
55. Once, quaintly
59. Lucy of "The Man With the Iron Fists"
60. Actor in a Mr. Potato Head costume?
64. Gig part
65. Scrape, in a way
66. Make bubbly
67. Wood used to make the original Stratocasters

68. Neurosurgeons' readouts, for short
69. George's friend in "Of Mice and Men"

DOWN
1. Oil giant that's part of the Tesoro Corporation
2. Reserve
3. 1998 Wimbledon champ Novotna
4. Pushing the boundaries of propriety
5. Daycare center?
6. Fighter in a ring
7. Descendant
8. Solo on the big screen
9. Land in la mer
10. Prospects
11. Bit of packaging detritus
12. Horsefeathers
13. Chest wood
18. Like ostrich meat
23. Abbr. in some addresses
24. Hornswoggle
25. ___ brothers, noted political donors
26. First name of the wolf in Disney's "The Big Bad Wolf"
27. Salt, chemically
28. Parrot
29. "That is SO stupid!"
30. Country on the Strait of Gibraltar: Abbr.
33. "Keep ___ secret"
35. Helen of Troy's mother
36. Hibernia
38. Early 2000s war zone
39. Color similar to almond
40. Winter Palace resident
41. Political alliance of 1958: Abbr.
46. "___ Girls," 1957 musical comedy

47. Sub-Saharan menace
48. Badge shape
49. One who might have a collection of foreign stamps
50. 1965 civil rights march site
51. Curious, action-oriented sort, supposedly
52. Pizzeria needs
55. Pull in
56. Romney's 2012 running mate
57. ___ Institute, org. that makes use of the Allen Telescope Array
58. Family ___
61. Relative of a cuatro, informally
62. All over the news
63. Victor at Chancellorsville

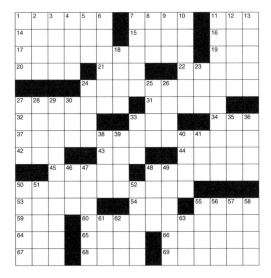

by Gareth Bain and David Poole

95

ACROSS

1 Much of Brides magazine
8 Wall St. operator
11 [as per the original]
14 In the general vicinity
15 Toscanini, for one
17 Kitschy quality
18 Cornered
19 Bust ___ (laugh hard)
20 Retailer owned by Gap
22 "We Three Kings of Orient Are," e.g.
23 Part of a spiral galaxy farthest from the center
27 Ones who cry uncle?
31 Feed a line to again
32 1960s TV's Cousin ___
34 Stable color
35 Query for clarification
36 Adolf Hitler, e.g., according to a 1983 hoax
38 Depression Era architectural movement
39 Exit
40 H2O, to a tot
41 What makes a top stop?
42 Manage
43 Pretenses
45 Diner or sleeper
47 Party request
50 Rot
53 Where most of Russia is
54 Something not seen on a nudist, maybe
57 Compensates for
59 Approval for un hombre
60 1920s–'30s Ford output
61 Parabola, for one

62 Some washers
63 Event at Victoria's Secret or Nordstrom

DOWN

1 Boutros-Ghali's successor as U.N. chief
2 Golden, in Guadalajara
3 21-/40-Down to a doctor
4 Good for planting
5 Yanks
6 This, in Tijuana
7 Writer/ illustrator Silverstein
8 Nearly perfect
9 Attacked
10 21-/40-Down on 1950s–'60s TV
11 Orchestra section: Abbr.
12 Something a fund manager may manage, for short
13 Lift

16 Disposable cup material
21 With 40-Down, how rain falls . . . or a literal description of the answers to the four themed clues
24 21-/40-Down in Hollywood
25 Trashes
26 Rations (out)
28 21-/40-Down to a penologist
29 Carriage puller, in rural dialect
30 Not fast
32 Clarification lead-in
33 "Easy there, ___"
35 Los Angeles's U.S.S. ___ Museum
37 Give an alias
38 Bud
40 See 21-Down
43 Certain soundboard knobs
44 Wipes out
46 Dugout, for one

48 Key
49 Out
51 Bausch & ___ (eye-care brand)
52 ___ effort
54 Screening org.
55 It's mostly nitrogen
56 Presidential advisory grp.
58 Rx overseer

by Ned White

ACROSS

1 2013 Tonto portrayer
5 Artwork and furnishings
10 Flaky mineral
14 Word at the bottom of a page, perhaps
15 Eye: Prefix
16 Slippery ___ eel
17 Metaphorical mess
19 Bloods or Crips
20 Working stiff
21 Stage, say
23 Monarch's advisers
26 1960s TV show featuring the cross-eyed lion Clarence
29 Wizards of aahs, for short?
30 Postings at LAX and ORD
31 Twice tetra-
34 Sharply dressed
37 ___ Lemon ("30 Rock" role)
38 "St. Louis Blues" composer
40 Period sometimes named after a president
41 Author Calvino
43 Himalayan legend
44 Push
45 "Get Smart" adversary
47 Micronesia's home
49 Only president to win a Pulitzer
53 Manhattan region
54 "You're wrong about me!"
58 Mex. miss
59 Race advantages . . . or a hint to 17-, 23-, 38- and 49-Across
62 ___ Parker, first president of Facebook
63 Fired up
64 "Oh, why not?!"
65 "Giant" novelist Ferber
66 Jolts, in a way
67 Bean staple

DOWN

1 Official paperwork, for short
2 FEMA request, briefly
3 Phnom ___
4 Memory triggers
5 Big name in chemicals
6 "The Name of the Rose" author
7 Rice spice
8 Ancient Mexican
9 Mobster's gun
10 Burgundy relative
11 Musician with a Presidential Medal of Freedom
12 "Ple-e-e-ease?"
13 Guardian ___
18 Words with time or song
22 Undercooked, as an egg
24 Old stock car inits.
25 French spa locale
26 Place where people pick lox?
27 Bickering
28 Former Soviet republic
32 ___ Bo
33 Chekhov or Bruckner
35 "Star Trek: T.N.G." counselor
36 One-third of "et cetera"?
38 Scares a cat, in a way
39 Chop up
42 Showy flower
44 Biweekly occurrences, for many
46 Part of Waldo's wear in "Where's Waldo?"
48 Shorten, say
49 Track great Owens
50 Worked on a trireme
51 Plant swelling
52 Minimum-range tides
55 Traditional ingredient in cookies and cream ice cream
56 Certain court order
57 Workplace rules setter, for short
60 Joey ___ & the Starliters
61 1960s antiwar grp.

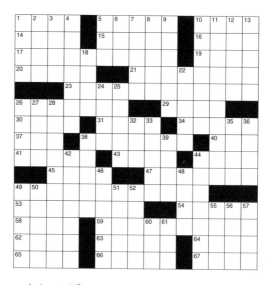

by Peter A. Collins

ACROSS

1 Sober
6 Improper way to take the SAT
11 Not a very big invention
14 Cash holders
15 Many a museum marble
16 Stir
17 Sherlock Holmes accessory
19 Hot ___
20 Intense hunger
21 Part of a Latin 101 conjugation
22 Not to term
24 "The Raven" start
26 Mold, as clay
28 Biker gear
31 Siesta shader
34 Thumb ___
35 Loki's brother, in movies
36 2nd-yr. student
37 Volleyball team count
38 Appointment holder
41 Contend
42 The economist Adam Smith, for one
44 Preprinted gift tag word
45 Place for playing games
47 Orthodox trademark
49 Sinatra cover
50 Source of the headline "Study Finds Blame Now Fastest Human Reflex," with "The"
51 Take ___ (sample some)
52 Strip locale, informally
54 "Aw, heck!"
56 Kellogg's brand since 1970
60 Parlement assent
61 Go crazy . . . or a hint on how to enter five answers in this puzzle

64 Subj. of the book "Many Unhappy Returns"
65 Small intestine section
66 Softly
67 What's the point?
68 Recipe amts.
69 Slashed conjunction

DOWN

1 Lower-left keyboard key
2 Stead
3 Game with horns
4 In sum
5 Org. whose annual budget is classified
6 "Who's there?" reply
7 Dunn formerly of "S.N.L."
8 Briefing site
9 Atlanta-to-Charleston dir.
10 Partner's refusal
11 Very distant
12 Bedroom poster subject
13 Part of a shampoo promise
18 Dash dial
23 Black-and-white alerts, briefly
25 Scholarship criterion, maybe
27 Lover of Leander, in myth
28 French cup
29 ___ Aybar, 2014 All-Star shortstop on the Angels
30 Bartender
31 "This is exciting!"
32 Offer one's two cents
33 Harvester's bundle
35 Oppressive regimes
39 Big do
40 Byron of "MythBusters"
43 ___ salad
46 Corrals
48 Outcast, often
49 Part of A.A.A.: Abbr.

51 Small parts
52 Like a redeemed coupon
53 Mark's successor
55 "___ and away!"
57 Big name in trash
58 Pop singer Vannelli
59 Something found in the trash?
62 Legal deg.
63 Evil org. in "The Simpsons Movie"

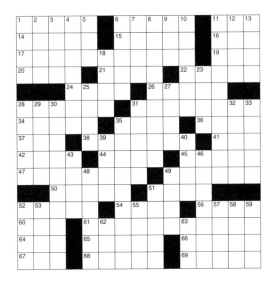

by Samuel A. Donaldson

98

ACROSS

1 Missing links
7 Place for a mud bath
10 Abductees' destinations, in some hard-to-believe stories
14 Cleanser brand that "hasn't scratched yet"
15 Shorten, perhaps
16 Styptic pencil target
17 Architect ___ Mies van der Rohe
18 Half an exorbitant fee?
19 Prefix with matter
20 Riders in 10-Across
21 "What's goin' on?"
24 Fuel rating
26 Motorized racers
27 "I need my ___"
30 Coquettish sorts
32 "Let's shake!"
34 Celestial strings
38 Inheritance tax target
39 "Yours truly" alternative
41 Actor Jackie who's his own stuntman
42 "Don't worry, I'm O.K."
46 Scoundrel
48 Cary of "The Princess Bride"
49 Online birthday greeting
52 Sinatra's big band leader
54 "Hand it over!"
56 ___ alai
59 Be caught in ___
60 Mauna ___
61 Some collectors' "vinyl"
64 Cameron of "Bad Teacher"
65 Electric bill abbr.
66 Turn the page, say
67 Common-sense

68 Recent U.S.N.A. graduate: Abbr.
69 Where you might see the message formed by the last words in 21-, 32-, 42- and 54-Across

DOWN

1 Up to the job
2 Wear a puss
3 Some touchdown scorers
4 Gaping mouth
5 Universal Music Group label
6 Like all World Series games, now
7 Tecumseh's tribe
8 How salaries or rainfall may be reported
9 Bandoleer filler
10 In an open, no-apologies manner
11 In better condition, to collectors
12 The black pawns, e.g.
13 Washington pro team, informally
22 "I do solemnly swear . . . ," e.g.
23 "Aloha Oe" instrument, for short
24 Beachgoer's cooler-offer
25 Part of C.D.: Abbr.
27 Design detail, briefly
28 Market aggressively
29 Lead-in to "boy!" or "girl!"
31 Blacken on a barbecue
33 Watch over
35 Say for certain
36 Tennis great Lacoste
37 Secret Service's charge: Abbr.
40 Jolly Roger crewman
43 Historic section of a city
44 Big kerfuffles

45 Gillette brand
47 Halsey or Nimitz: Abbr.
49 "OMG!," old-style
50 Eyelashes, anatomically
51 For the birds?
53 Boot up
55 Sommer of "A Shot in the Dark"
56 Oscar winner Dench
57 Love, in Lisbon
58 "___ it ironic?"
62 WKRP's Nessman
63 "Rubbish!"

by Jim Peredo

ACROSS

1 Computer purchase
6 "Much ___ About Nothing"
9 Rooster's roost
14 Canadian pop singer Lavigne
15 Hawaii's Mauna ___
16 Pretty person
17 Dismantle
19 Goody two-shoes
20 Hum follower
21 Stomach muscles
23 Brazilian baker?
24 Further to the right on a number line
27 Yellow-centered bloomer
30 Archaic "Curses!"
31 Fish oil source
32 Sticky stuff
33 Reading material, for short
34 It can be saved or cured
36 Leader of the pack?
40 Simon & Garfunkel's "I ___ Rock"
41 False show
42 Gives a thumbs-up
44 Repair
45 Under attack
47 Starsky's partner
49 President between James and Andrew, briefly
50 First state: Abbr.
52 Excellent drivers often break it
53 Supernatural being
54 Rely on
56 Piece of office equipment
59 "Adios!"
60 Tier
62 "___ Joey" (Sinatra film)
63 Deduce logically
66 Sideshow performer
71 "I have no idea!"
72 Slew
73 Georgia campus

74 Priest of ancient Gaul
75 Exclamation of discovery
76 Perez of film

DOWN

1 Pin cushion?
2 Some germ cells
3 Sturdy tree in the beech family
4 Filter in the kitchen
5 Cow in Borden ads
6 ___ broche (cooked on a skewer)
7 "Rico Suave" rapper
8 Swear words?
9 "Angel dust"
10 U.K. locale
11 Spring (from)
12 Autumnal quaff
13 Command to a canine
18 Friskies eater
22 Moderate decline in prices
24 "Johnny B. ___"

25 Label anew
26 "Planet of the Apes" planet [spoiler alert!]
28 /
29 Cambodia's Lon ___
30 Exerciser's enemy
34 They may be drawn before bedtime
35 Tune for nine
37 Sufficiently old
38 Float like a helicopter
39 Brought down, as a tree
43 Abrasion
46 Partner of Dreyer
48 Improvement
51 Item in an env.
54 Pavarotti or Caruso
55 Evoking the past
57 Rapunzel's prison
58 "Me ___ Patricio" ("I am called Patrick")
59 Cowboy's home, familiarly
61 Old Spice alternative
64 London-based record company

65 Word before Sox or Wings
67 Cell stuff
68 ___-Mex
69 "___ tu" (Verdi aria)
70 Manhattan part

by Patrick Blindauer

100

ACROSS

1 Hatcher who was a Bond girl
5 Medicate again
11 Letters at Indy
14 Complaint
15 Words from the agreeable
16 Like early morning hours
17 Drink made with Jameson, maybe
19 "The Lord of the Rings" creature
20 Fix
21 Eric, in Finland
22 Geoffrey of fashion
24 Dumb as a box of rocks
26 Genie's reply
29 Original "Veronica Mars" airer
31 Spartan serfs
32 "Behold," to Brutus
35 Tough time
38 Mountain __
40 Landlocked land
41 Cheated, slangily
42 "S O S!," e.g.
43 "Yummy!"
44 Supply with goods
45 Rubber-stamped
46 Circus clown car, often
48 Witty sort
50 Literary hybrid
53 Raid
57 Biathlete's weapon
58 Clueless
60 Absorbed, as a loss
61 Author LeShan
62 Job done by the insects seen above the circled words in 17-, 26- and 50-Across
66 Shape of Mork's spacecraft on "Mork & Mindy"
67 Plaza Hotel girl
68 "Freedom __ free"
69 Bridal bio word
70 Backspace over
71 Bare it all

DOWN

1 Car in the Beach Boys' "Fun, Fun, Fun"
2 Like "Dark Shadows" episodes
3 Hold the scepter
4 Hypotheticals
5 Bed of __
6 Atlanta university
7 Friday's creator
8 Neanderthal
9 About 5:00, on a compass
10 Look over, informally
11 Cajole
12 Home of Fort Donelson National Battlefield
13 One of Hollywood's Farrelly brothers
18 Dickens's scheming clerk
23 "__ Beso"
25 Seeks damages
27 Word before cake or music
28 Place for a lark
30 Totally useless
32 Horror film street
33 Where Stephen Hawking and Charles Darwin went to school
34 Reach adulthood
36 Loggers' contest
37 Internet access option
39 Snookered
42 Okefenokee possum
44 Like hot tea
47 Subj. for a future bilingual
49 Mennen shaving product
50 Congratulate oneself for achievement
51 "Dallas" matriarch
52 Like a well-prepared turkey
54 Poker ploy
55 Set things straight, in a way
56 Gender-bending role for Barbra Streisand
59 Old dagger
63 "__ ELO" (1976 album)
64 [That cracks me up]
65 Line on a restaurant bill

by Zhouqin Burnikel and Don Gagliardo

ACROSS

1 Spicy quality
5 Like more than a third of U.S. immigrants nowadays
10 Female motorcyclists, in biker slang
15 Airport shuttle route, commonly
16 Man trying to clarify the spelling of his name in 21-, 25-, 38-, 52- and 57-Across
17 Tequila source
18 Takes responsibility for
19 Sound of an incoming text, e.g.
20 Martin Sheen's real first name
21 Unhelpful spelling clarification #1
23 Outs
24 Bébé's need
25 Spelling clarification #2
27 Circles around the sun
30 Team that last won an N.F.L. championship in 1957
31 Place often named after a corporation
32 Firing locale
33 Nicknames
37 Sch. whose team is the Violets
38 Spelling clarification #3
42 Nearly nada
43 Fair
45 Setting for "Gladiator"
46 "The Last Supper," e.g.
48 Not fair
50 Copy
52 Spelling clarification #4
55 "Ooh-la-la!"
56 Places where you can hear a pin drop?

57 Spelling clarification #5
61 Courtroom fixture
62 Rhythmic feet
64 Sp-[gasp]-speaks like th-[sniffle]-this
65 Busybody
66 What the listener might think 16-Across's name is?
67 "Would ___ to you?"
68 Like many indie films
69 Beats it
70 A whole bunch

DOWN

1 Blue Dog Democrats, e.g.
2 One of 14 in the Big Ten
3 A whole bunch
4 Elasticity symbol, in economics
5 Tree in a giraffe's diet
6 General reception?

7 "Hmm . . . is that so!"
8 ___ Lingus
9 W.S.J. alternative
10 "The Old Man and the Sea" fish
11 Con
12 Tree-dwelling snake
13 To have, in Toulouse
14 Meaning
22 Some sitters
23 Together
25 Dress style
26 Feels bad
27 Support staff
28 African antelope
29 Go for additional service
32 Celebrity couple portmanteau
34 Air
35 Part of a black cloud
36 It's always underfoot
39 First sign
40 PlayStation maker
41 Friends of Firenze

44 Situates
47 Something set in a place setting
49 Soon
50 Soon
51 Wife, informally
52 College softball?
53 Tailor, say
54 Pitch
57 Song that was a hit for a spell in the 1970s?
58 Modern acronym suggesting "seize the day"
59 Life lines?
60 Exercises
62 Geniuses' prides
63 Chip shot's path

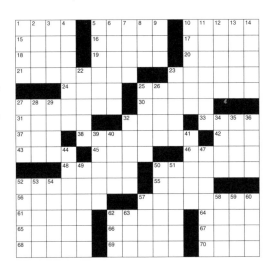

by Joel Fagliano

102

ACROSS

1 Bums around
6 Bellini opera
11 Night light, perhaps
14 Shoptalk
15 Weest of wee hours
16 Mint
17 Film about a Communist invasion? (1996)
19 Enthusiast
20 Casanova
21 Ties down
23 Moroccan headwear
25 Line on a baseball
26 Film about the woman most likely to catch men's attention? (2001)
33 Computer mode
34 It's usually between 3 and 5
35 Logic game with matchsticks
36 Battery containing a liquid electrolyte
39 The statue "David" on open-air display in Florence, e.g.
42 Well-suited
43 Take a gander at
45 Captain and others
46 Film about an elegantly made crossword? (2009)
51 Collaborator with Disney on the film "Destino"
52 Add-on charge
53 First family of Germany, 1969–'74
56 Licit
62 Brit's washroom
63 Film about a romantic dentist's daily routine? (2010)
65 Israeli gun
66 "Delphine" author Madame de ___
67 Fray
68 Lo-___

69 Absorbent cloth
70 4 x 400-meter relay, e.g.

DOWN

1 Genie's home
2 Kind of vaccine
3 Site of a famed mausoleum
4 Guileful
5 Poke holes in
6 "Hold on a sec"
7 ___ lark
8 Geom. shape
9 Confirm
10 Brewery named after a Dutch river
11 Like a bass voice or a hairy chest
12 "___ not!"
13 Dominates, informally
18 Vegetarian's protein source
22 Son of Noah
24 Élan
26 Beth preceder

27 Actress with the iconic line "What a dump!"
28 Old trade inits.
29 Mime
30 Away's partner
31 Shaving boo-boos
32 Holiday associated with 44-Downs, in brief
33 Whack
37 Get off the ground?
38 Caustic material
40 Old hand
41 Easygoing
44 See 32-Down
47 Acronym for linked computers
48 Like Jackie Jackson, in the Jackson 5
49 How the swallows returned to San Juan Capistrano
50 Actor Lugosi
53 Memory of a very busy day, maybe

54 Level
55 Lead
57 Instrument for Orpheus
58 King Harald's father
59 Told, as a yarn
60 Level
61 Shoulder muscle, for short
64 Member of the MTV generation, informally

by Andy Kravis

ACROSS

1 Oscar-winning Hanks role
5 Reinstate, in a way
9 Oklahoma tribe
14 About
15 Exude
16 Corrective
17 Golden girl?
19 Polite word in Palermo
20 Czech playwright who coined the word "robot"
21 It may be raised in a company's new building
22 Jockey, e.g.
25 Protein generators
27 Series of watering troughs?
28 Usurper
29 Big guns
31 Delta hub, briefly
32 Many a modern game
35 Rampaging
37 Yerevan is its capital
40 37-Across was the smallest one: Abbr.
41 Nickname
43 Wine judge, e.g.
44 Comes to light
47 TV character who says "Captain, you almost make me believe in luck"
48 Enterprise, for one
51 Perfects
52 Soft rock
53 God on whose name Iago swears
55 Setting for van Gogh's "The Yellow House"
56 New Americans of 1898
60 Walter ___ Theater (part of Lincoln Center)
61 Like some punished 1-Down
62 Lifeguard's concern
63 Aware, with "in"

64 They're big on Wall Street
65 Gold-medal skater Vasiliev

DOWN

1 Ones on base?
2 Argentine article
3 Howard Cunningham, informally
4 "Later, bro!"
5 Dish contents
6 Air traffic control sites
7 Book that describes the destruction of Gog and Magog
8 Hot spot?
9 Counter
10 Imp
11 Time to retire, maybe
12 Figure on Mexico's flag
13 Tart fruit

18 Rapper who co-starred in 2002's "Half Past Dead"
21 According to legend, at age 2 he identified a pig's squeal as G sharp
22 "Parenthood" actress Sarah
23 Millions of millennia
24 Thick smoke
26 Nickname for Angel Stadium, with "the"
30 "Fifty Shades of Grey" topic
32 Russian composer Arensky
33 King or queen
34 City department purview
36 Overnight, maybe
38 Mixed media?
39 First N.H.L. player to score 100 points in a season

42 Literally, "northern capital"
44 Acquiesce
45 Not thrown away, say
46 Villain in "Indiana Jones and the Kingdom of the Crystal Skull"
48 Bare
49 Gay ___
50 Assuage
54 Cheese ___ (Nabisco product)
56 Mothra or MUTO, to Godzilla
57 Zip
58 Sapphic work
59 Line div.

by Alex Vratsanos

104

ACROSS

1 "Take ___" (1994 Madonna hit that was #1 for seven weeks)
5 Formal, maybe
9 Formal wear accoutrement
13 St. Petersburg's river
14 "Peanuts" kid with a security blanket
16 Build muscles, with "up"
17 Genre of Verdi's "Jérusalem"
19 Lens holders
20 "Come in!"
21 "Fist of Fury" star, 1972
23 Chapter 52, formally
24 Guacamole base, in British lingo
27 Making the rounds?
29 Yang's go-with
30 Cause of a blowup?
31 Cannes showing
32 Sound from a window ledge
34 Do some housekeeping
36 Used a crowbar on, say
40 ___ facto
42 Crime lab sample
43 Amt. of cooking oil, maybe
47 Spanish she-bear
48 Face the pitcher
51 Boorish
53 Robert Redford's "great" 1975 role
56 Vote for
57 Where you might pick fruit while it's still green
58 Palliates
60 Something false in the Bible?
61 Lowdown . . . or a hint to 17-, 24-, 36-and 53-Across
64 Tizzy
65 "Please, I can do it"
66 Violinist Leopold
67 "Hey, José!"
68 Tire swing part
69 Appalachians, e.g.: Abbr.

DOWN

1 Good-looking?
2 "Apollo and Daphne" sculptor
3 Warm response from a crowd
4 Decline
5 Gaza grp.
6 Engraved letters?
7 End of an ancient period
8 Lexicographer James who was the O.E.D.'s first editor
9 ___ throat
10 Facilities
11 Accidental
12 Much of Arabia
15 ___ Arabia
18 In need of some color
22 Publisher Nast
25 End of a famous boast
26 Platte Valley native
28 Workout count
33 Screwy
35 Golden rule preposition
37 Bomb squad member
38 "Movin' ___"
39 Glazier's unit
40 Words before ". . . and that's final!"
41 Soap ingredient
44 Takes over the assets of, as a partner
45 Make more inclined
46 "Star Trek" weapons
47 Studious-looking
49 Shower time
50 Many a Taylor Swift fan
52 Tribe of the Canadian Plains
54 What a big mouth might have
55 Basil-flavored sauce
59 Singer Lambert
62 Little handful
63 Syllable repeated after "fiddle"

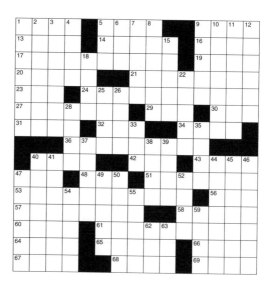

by Elizabeth C. Gorski

ACROSS

1 Nasty stuff
5 Symbol of authority
9 TV's "___ Bridges"
13 Lush
14 Member of an old empire
15 "___ bene" ("Very well": It.)
16 Finalizes, as a contract
17 Hilo do
18 2003 summit participant with Sharon and Bush
19 20th-century figure with a famous 56-Across represented literally six times in this puzzle
21 NBC parent beginning in 2011
22 "Te ___"
23 One of the grains in Nutri-Grain
24 Agitate
25 Backer
27 Sore loser
31 Nickname for Fogell in "Superbad"
33 He's asked to "please shine down on me," in song
34 It can be cast in a tragedy
37 Stash seeker
39 "___ it ironic?" (1996 song lyric)
40 Near the hip
42 Woodstock producer
44 "Parallel Lives" writer
46 Promiscuous guys
50 Word after back or break
51 ___ book
52 ___ mai (Asian dumplings)
53 Art store buy
56 See 19-Across
58 Broadcasting

59 Admitting a slight draft, maybe
60 Not squishy
61 Like many shut-ins
62 They follow arcs
63 Soup thickener
64 Crack up
65 Blind as ___
66 Rock's ___ Music

DOWN

1 Top in the pool?
2 Low points
3 Disentangle
4 Eject, as from a game
5 Most important movies
6 Ice man?
7 Pore over
8 19th of 24
9 Recognition received by 19-Across
10 Co-star of 2005's "Fantastic Four"
11 Boarding spots: Abbr.

12 Have over, say
15 Little Red Book ideology
20 Drive (along)
21 Gloucester haul
24 It has hands and brands
26 Subject explored by 19-Across
27 Kind of beer
28 Old spy org.
29 String
30 Cable channel that revived "Dallas" in 2012
32 Explorer ___ da Gama
34 One of hearts?
35 Comprehensively
36 Actress whose last name is a New York school's inits.
38 Tirade, e.g.
41 Singer
43 "Livin' la Vida ___"
45 QB protectors
47 Italian cheese

48 Chest
49 Miscellaneous
51 Jordanian port
53 Admits (to)
54 Obsessive, say
55 Org. with lofty goals?
56 Unfulfilling work
57 "___ she blows!"
59 Like

by David Woolf

ACROSS

1 Try to sink, maybe
4 "Rhyme Pays" rapper
8 Fantasy league figures
13 TBS competitor
14 Knock silly
15 "Ah, I didn't know what you were referring to"
17 Put on a blacklist
18 The Auld Sod
19 Honest with
20 "Hot to trot" or "cold feet"
22 Many a PX shopper
24 The Dow, for one
25 "Amerika" novelist
26 Many, many moons
27 Jeans brand
28 Shoreline raptor
30 "The Rachael Ray Show" creation
32 ___ Lanka
35 Father-and-son rulers of Syria
37 Homer Simpson's mother
38 One with a checkered existence?
39 Quickly write
40 "Foolish" singer, 2002
42 Time to revel
43 First-goal link
44 Jockey's control
45 Privy to a practical joke, say
47 Pastrami go-with
48 Cornerstone abbr.
49 Porn
50 Onetime tribe of the Upper Midwest
52 Official with a whisk broom, for short
54 Positrons' places
57 All, in Alba
59 "___ your request . . ."
60 Commerce pact signed by Clinton
61 Incite, as trouble

63 Dr Pepper Snapple Group brand
65 Be sociable
66 Italian sandwich
67 Slave away
68 Gator's tail?
69 Marriott competitor
70 Humane org.
71 "N.Y. State of Mind" rapper

DOWN

1 Inventor of a six-color puzzle
2 Carne ___ (Mexican dish)
3 Expansionist doctrine
4 Election loser's cry
5 Vacation rental, maybe
6 Slate or Salon
7 Text on tablets
8 Elbow-bender
9 Big 1975 boxing showdown

10 Carry ___ (sing on key)
11 Darwin work . . . with a hint to three consecutive letters in 3-, 4-, 7-, 9- and 11-Down
12 Fill beyond full
16 Poison sci.
21 Gumbo need
23 Result of a leadoff single
29 Handy Scrabble tiles
31 Nay sayers
33 Beatle George's sitar teacher
34 "Fat chance!"
35 Cracked a bit
36 Maker of Aibo robotic pets
41 Ask, as for a loan
46 Eke ___ living
51 Skylit rooms
53 Before surgery, informally
55 Crete's highest peak
56 Big band section

57 Rx amt.
58 One of its symbols is the sego lily
62 Indy service area
64 Sound from an 8-Down

by Mary Lou Guizzo and Jeff Chen

107

ACROSS

1 Corn or cotton
5 Western wear
9 Where the Pilgrims first landed in the New World
13 Put on a scale
14 Many a fête d'anniversaire attendee
15 Homer Simpson's workplace
16 Subject of National Federation of Independent Business v. Sebelius
18 Parkinson's disease drug
19 Engage in an extreme winter sport
20 La starter
22 Mil. mess personnel
23 Sixer rival
25 Feature of Polyphemus from "The Odyssey"
27 Dessert often made with cream cheese frosting
31 Comic Cenac formerly of "The Daily Show"
33 Red as ___
34 "Sure, go ahead"
35 White's counterpart
39 English county closest to Continental Europe
40 Places where wheat is stored?
41 Org. with an antipiracy stance
42 Swirl
43 Meaningful sets, for short?
44 New U.N. member of 2011
45 Resolution unit
47 Lab item
48 Alternative to a fade-out in a movie ending
51 Israel's Barak
53 Hold up
54 Seven-time Rose Bowl winner, for short

56 Buffalo hunters, once
61 Skirt
63 Be unsuited?
65 Recovers from injury
66 Diving position
67 Be a fall guy?
68 Ben & Jerry's alternative
69 2014 N.B.A. champ
70 What a prophet may look for

DOWN

1 -
2 Rhyme scheme for "Stopping by Woods on a Snowy Evening"
3 Have the lead
4 Blood: Prefix
5 -
6 Letters that don't go to the post office
7 Canada or Jordan preceder

8 Bygone brand in the shaving aisle
9 -
10 Came to
11 Animated
12 Record over, say
15 -
17 Quaint wear
21 First name in children's literature
24 Sing like a bird
26 Word origin
27 -
28 Not up
29 Tear apart
30 Correct, as a manuscript
32 Half of a vote
34 -
36 Great work
37 At nine and a half months, say
38 Architect Louis
40 -
44 -
46 Some preppy shirts

47 -
48 -
49 Didn't stay put
50 Deep black
52 "An old silent pond / A frog jumps into the pond / Splash! Silence again," e.g.
55 Offerer of package deals, in brief
57 Firebug
58 Leader of a race?
59 It's a snap
60 Store sign
62 T.S.A. requirements
64 Currency of Laos

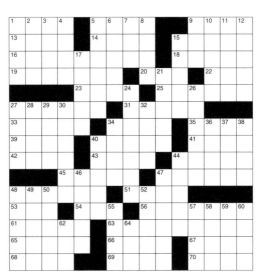

by Joel Fagliano

ACROSS

1 Attempt
5 Places longshoremen work
10 Pickle flavoring
14 Mozart's "___ Fan Tutte"
15 Internet giant that purchased Flickr in 2005
16 "The Time Machine" vegetarians
17 *Drifter of literature
19 Flow stopper
20 Sorrowful 1954 Patti Page hit
21 Pragmatic person
23 Swiss/Austrian border river
24 Degree for many a 58-Down
26 One-third of a triptych
27 Cube creator
28 *Potent potable in "Arsenic and Old Lace"
30 Parrot
31 It can take your breath away
32 Big ___ (hallux)
33 *Nicole Kidman, hairwise
38 Brynner of "The King and I"
39 ___ Savage, player of the boy on "Boy Meets World"
40 Dr. J's league, once, for short
43 *1985 Prince hit
47 Screenwriter Sorkin
49 Pop singer Mann
50 Story assigners, in brief
51 "You had me at ___" ("Jerry Maguire" line)
52 Like preserved flowers and writers under deadline
54 Surrendered to gravity
55 Man or Mull

56 One of the original Rock and Roll Hall of Fame inductees, whose name is a hint to the answers to the four starred clues
59 Shoulder muscle, to a gym rat
60 Cornball
61 Forever and a day
62 Comes out with
63 Spanish "others"
64 Where Citigroup is C, for short

DOWN

1 Astronaut Wally, the first person to go into space three times
2 Airbrush, e.g.
3 Attributes
4 Two-piece suit
5 Brunette no more, say
6 Bumbler
7 Tai ___
8 German chancellor Adenauer
9 Unit of loudness
10 Rendered harmless, in a way
11 "Fighting" Big Ten team
12 Relax
13 Lilliputian
18 Vichyssoise vegetable
22 Plane's parking place
24 Request for milk, maybe
25 Spilled the beans
29 View from Windsor Castle
31 Christian in Hollywood
34 Prepares for proofing
35 Hayseeds
36 Court replays
37 Tea choice for TV's Frasier Crane
41 Short jackets worn open in front
42 Pain reliever
43 Canoeist's challenge
44 Like some rescues
45 Ripe
46 Flying off the shelves
47 Starbuck's superior
48 Greece/Turkey separator, with "the"
53 Bounce back
54 "The ___ the limit!"
57 Kiev's land: Abbr.
58 Many a Fortune profilee, for short

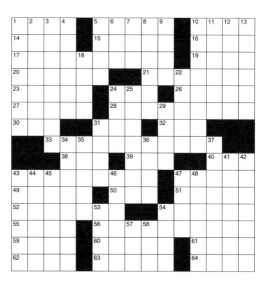

by David Poole

ACROSS

1 City with a view of the White Cliffs of Dover
7 "David," e.g.
11 "L'Amore dei ___ Re" (Montemezzi opera)
14 Certain homecoming attendee
15 Some Michelin Guide readers
17 Bonkers
18 Cream-filled chocolate treats
19 Mark of dishonor
21 Place for a saint's image, maybe
22 ___ Reville, Hitchcock's wife and collaborator
23 "Fear and Loathing in Las Vegas" drug
25 Villainous Luthor
26 Defeat
29 Iraq war issue, for short
31 Fall guy's partner?
33 Bustle
34 Walker alternative
36 Chilled coffee drink
39 "If Winter comes, can Spring be far behind?" poet
42 Inspiration for Johann Strauss II
43 Deer John?
44 Great ___
45 "Land of the sun" native
46 Science advocate with a bow tie
47 Tournament passes
48 Efron of "Neighbors"
50 What you get for bringing someone home
52 Edomite patriarch
55 One taking an unscheduled flight?
57 All-time scoring leader for the U.S. men's soccer team
62 Official residence at the Vatican

64 The Ramblers of the N.C.A.A.
65 Dish often served au jus
66 R-rated movie attendees
67 Computer language named for Lord Byron's daughter
68 Studies
69 What three-letter words do in five answers in this puzzle

DOWN

1 Home security devices, for short
2 ___ Trevelyan, Agent 006 in "GoldenEye"
3 "Two-horned queen of the stars," per Horace
4 Pacific Surfliner operator
5 Collectively
6 "Days of Our Lives" town
7 Pond dweller
8 Maintained
9 Some haute couture designs
10 "The Island of the Day Before" novelist
11 Ultimate rally-killer
12 He wears #1 in "42"
13 Earl of ___ a.k.a. Robert Devereux
16 Put ___ fight
20 Golden brown
24 Goal of some industry lobbyists, for short
26 Hollywood force, in brief
27 "Whose ___ was this?"
28 Abundant supply
30 Convoluted
32 ___ d'Orcia (Tuscan region)
34 Relative of e-
35 Fiver
36 Govt. mortgage insurer
37 Penelope's pursuer in Looney Tunes toons

38 Sightseers?
40 Share
41 Cavalry mount
46 Vitamin B3
47 Bolster
48 "Don't Eat the Yellow Snow" rocker
49 Hope for a nominee
51 Trumpet
53 Renewable option
54 Point of contact in the automotive industry?
56 Getaway
58 Bird bills
59 Burrowing rodent
60 Opposite of baja
61 Father of the American Cartoon
63 Had followers

by John Farmer

ACROSS

1 Actor Gerard of "Buck Rogers"
4 Bit
7 Target of trimming
10 12-Down from meditators
13 U.K. award
14 Catherine de' Medici is said to have eaten it at every meal
16 Losing line in tic-tac-toe
17 Words to a baby
20 One with a mister in Münster
21 Ballot marker
22 Another time, in "Li'l Abner"
23 Fjord explorers?
25 Robert of "The Sopranos"
27 Summon, with "for"
28 Emulated Pacino in a "Scent of a Woman" scene
30 Adages
32 & 33 Meeting with someone in person
34 Straighten out
37 Reading for a king's herald
41 Body in a bed
42 Strong punch
46 Vote on Scottish independence
47 Amiss
49 Shakespearean title character
50 Copper
51 Urban blight
53 Ballot topic for decriminalization
54 Subj. with Riemann sums
55 Factors in wine competitions
57 Some carnival rides
59 007 film of 1981
63 Vegan-friendly protein source
64 "Impression, Sunrise" painter
65 Czolgosz who shot McKinley
66 Like some radios
67 Form of 10-Down
68 Uffizi display

DOWN

1 Die
2 Largest airline of Spain
3 "I Hope You Dance" singer Womack
4 Org. with the Precheck program
5 "Dragnet" alert, briefly
6 Compound containing 10-Down
7 Like Snow White, per the magic mirror
8 Some LG appliances
9 United States Constitution's first article
10 Element #8
11 Cattle yard 12-Down
12 See 11-Down
15 Coward who said "I love criticism just so long as it's unqualified praise"
18 A master of this really knows his chops
19 Not so knotty
24 Shoots up
26 French for "grape"
29 Lots of sparkle
31 Facility often referred to by its first letter
34 Anytown, ___
35 Anchor's place
36 "Carmina Burana" composer
38 "I wonder what the word for 'dots' looks like in Braille," e.g.
39 Model of chivalry
40 Rent
43 Winter chill
44 Biotechnology output, for short
45 Poppycock
48 "The Mikado" maiden
50 ___ oil
52 Image in Tiananmen Square
54 G.M. and G.E.
55 Aqua Velva alternative
56 Bare-chested sport
57 Basketball legend Maravich
58 End of a Burns poem heard annually
60 Cartoonist Chast
61 Ambient music composer Brian
62 Urge

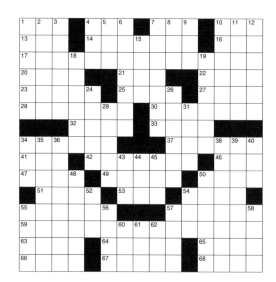

by Patrick Blindauer

ACROSS

1 "Attack!"
7 They're often dipped in wasabis
15 Best at a buffet, say
16 Tabasco turnover
17 Camry competitor
18 ___ Brewster, "Arsenic and Old Lace" role
19 Classic Jag
20 Common street name
22 The French way?
23 Spanish pronoun
24 Competitor of Clark and Emerson in coll. athletics
26 Range wear?
29 "Give me a break already!"
32 Chat
33 Sacrifice, e.g.
34 Griffin who created "Jeopardy!"
36 Under cover?
40 Michael of "Weekend Update" on "S.N.L."
41 Go for a quick cruise, say
43 One of 17 on a Monopoly board: Abbr.
44 Copycat's comment
46 ___-serif
47 Comment often after "Hmm . . ."
48 Cricket club
50 Holds
52 Bosom buddies
56 Where the ball drops on New Year's Eve . . . as depicted literally in four places in this puzzle
57 ___-eyed
58 Want-ad abbr.
59 Speed
61 California's ___ River
64 Bounding

67 One of the Brothers Karamazov
69 Brewed beverage
70 Laudanum, e.g.
71 Ran out on
72 Dirty

DOWN

1 Sweet-talk
2 Any Mr. Olympia
3 Went for
4 Big name in camping gear
5 Life starter
6 Library indexing abbr.
7 Part of a sch. year
8 2006 million-selling Andrea Bocelli album
9 Out, in a way
10 Letters that are hard to read?
11 Pasta name ending
12 "American Buffalo" playwright
13 Cousin of "exempli gratia"
14 Singers Bareilles and Evans
21 Strolls
25 Paris's ___ Saint-Louis
27 Milan-based fashion house
28 Arabic "son of"
29 Tolkien's Gorbag and Bolg
30 Old Ritz rival
31 Org. backing Obamacare
35 Go poof
37 Lead, e.g.
38 First name in daredevilry
39 Odd couple?
41 Pipe measure
42 "Was ___ passiert?" (German "What happened?")
45 Strip of paper around a Japanese book
47 Uganda's ___ Amin

49 White Cloud Temple worshiper
51 "Resume speed," musically
52 Lollygagged
53 Clue for a car mechanic
54 Some subs
55 Jittery
60 Merger agreements?
62 Designer who wrote "Things I Remember"
63 Wasn't veracious
65 Tick off
66 Prayer object
68 Trailer for "Rocky" or "Rambo"?

by Patrick Blindauer

112

ACROSS

1 Actress Ward
5 Church bell location
10 Shade at the swimming pool
14 Skating competition entry, maybe
15 Barkin of "The Big Easy"
16 Void
17 *Chilled appetizer or dessert
19 Actress Lollobrigida
20 Port of Algeria
21 Like one side of Mount Everest
23 State that borders Bangladesh
25 Comic strip makeup
26 Brand in a bowl
27 Sponsorship: Var.
29 Illustrious
32 Baseball great Hodges
33 Foot specialist?
34 Its capital is Pristina
35 Geisha's sash
36 *Billboard listing
38 He's a real doll
39 Holy Communion, e.g.
41 Very, in Vichy
42 Temper
43 Grps.
44 Part of a planet
45 Pay (up)
46 Ruin, as a dog might shoes
48 Stoners' purchases
50 Reasons for some street closures
52 One being strung along?
53 Dentist's instruction
54 Longtime Prego slogan . . . with a hint to the answers to the five starred clues
59 Safe-deposit box item, maybe
60 Surface anew, in a way
61 Yellow sub?
62 Payroll IDs
63 Bottom of the barrel
64 Something to match

DOWN

1 Tanning lotion letters
2 Canal zone?
3 Actress Lucy
4 Bach composition
5 Ingredient in much Asian cooking
6 __ B
7 Feeling flush, say
8 Rodeo ropes
9 Culminate with
10 Frank McCourt's "__ Ashes"
11 *Kick the habit, say
12 Forearm bone
13 Ex-Fed head Greenspan
18 Part of a chorus line?
22 Obscures
23 Excuses, excuses
24 *Feature of many a TV interview
25 *Time to retire?
26 Ancient market
28 Follow
30 Turns inside out
31 Gifted person?
33 Gradually introduced, with "in"
34 Leg strengtheners
37 Canadian-born hockey great
40 Lets go of
44 Big name at Little Bighorn
45 "You said it!"
47 Remarkable, as a coincidence
49 Bran name?
50 Acacia features
51 Copiers
52 Bookstore sect.
55 Seattle-to-L.A. direction
56 Yalie
57 Part of AARP: Abbr.
58 Canon camera

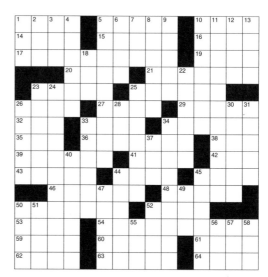

by Elizabeth C. Gorski

ACROSS

1 Moving
6 Wizard's wear
10 Actor Guy of "Memento"
11 Indivisibly
13 They may be blocked in the winter
14 Last line of many a riddle
16 Entertainers with something to get off their chests?
19 Funeral masses
20 ___ Dome (old Colts home)
21 Milk source
22 Green sci.
23 Wise one?
27 Transfer ___
28 Jokester
29 Contribute
30 Focus of The Source magazine
32 John McCain, for one
35 Baby seal
36 Summer abroad
37 French woman's name meaning "bringer of victory"
42 The Bahamas, e.g.
46 Word before an advice columnist's name
47 Tar Heels' sch.
48 A tot may have a big one
49 Engage in oratory
51 Slimming technique, briefly
52 What a well may produce
54 Burns with a camera
55 O.C.'s home
56 Treat represented visually by this puzzle's answer
61 One using acid, say
62 Wore
63 Good Samaritan, e.g.
64 Arena, maybe
65 Development on the north side?
66 Mountain nymph

DOWN

1 Anise relative
2 Hails
3 Major figure in space?
4 NATO member with the smallest population: Abbr.
5 Hot spot
6 Spreadsheet input
7 Lab safety org.
8 Benefit
9 Pass
10 Popular Polish dish
12 Mideast chieftains: Var.
13 Aston Martin DB5, for 007
15 Qom resident, e.g.
16 Tribe of the Upper Midwest
17 Writer John who was an authority on cards
18 Abbr. on a music score
23 Kind of gland
24 Covert maritime org.
25 Fight against
26 Nonhuman singer of a 1958 #1 song
29 Fast-food chain named after a spice
31 News inits.
33 Last thing learned in kindergarten?
34 Long-billed wader
38 Teller?
39 Like liquor, in an Ogden Nash verse
40 Like volunteer work
41 Place for un instituteur
42 "Wait ___!"
43 Nouveau ___
44 They may be made with pitching wedges
45 Vehicles that often have unlicensed drivers
50 Group associated with many tourist destinations
51 Took stock?
53 Philosopher William of ___
55 ". . . ish"
57 Lima's place
58 Eye part
59 Upbeat
60 Eye part

by David Woolf

114

ACROSS

1 React to a haymaker
5 "Song of the South" appellation
9 Pair on a yawl
14 Take the edge off
16 Many a Greenlander
17 1964 hit for Manfred Mann
19 Is the first act
20 Perpendicular to vert.
21 It sells, it's said
22 Home in the sticks?
23 Viagra rival
26 1968 song from the Beatles' "White Album"
32 ID thief's target
35 Flick with a duel, maybe
36 Small wonder?
37 1965 hit for the Dixie Cups
39 1954 hit for the Chords
41 What snobs put on
42 Place for high living?
45 Golf club V.I.P.
46 1994 hit for the Crash Test Dummies
50 Introduce to the mix
51 Like a legal deposition
55 "They're ___ Delicious!" (Alpha-Bits slogan)
58 Ex-president Tyler sided with it: Abbr.
59 Super
60 1973 song by the Rolling Stones subtitled "Heartbreaker"
65 "Beats me"
66 Hollywood's Hollywood and Vine do it
67 Dish sometimes served au poivre
68 Swimmer Kristin ___, the first woman to win six gold medals at a single Olympics
69 Amor's counterpart

DOWN

1 Cause of some poisoning
2 Pursue "I do's" when the parents say "don't"
3 Cary who played Robin Hood
4 Makeshift shelter
5 eBay action
6 Bollywood star Aishwarya ___
7 Flight board abbr.
8 Feature of one nicknamed "Ginger"
9 Leaf's central vein
10 Singer DiFranco
11 Beer, slangily
12 Sand castle's undoing
13 River ferried by Charon
15 Pre-DVD format
18 Modern acronym meaning "carpe diem"
23 "Cool" guy
24 Chemical suffix
25 Hearty slice
27 ___ choy (Chinese cabbage)
28 Vientiane native
29 Surmounting
30 Symbol of opportunity
31 Armory supply, informally
32 Pre-1939 atlas name
33 Milk option
34 Standard
38 Ideologies
39 Alastair of "A Christmas Carol"
40 Tailor's edge
42 Medium for much political talk
43 U.K. record label
44 Watergate inits.
47 Highest peak in N.Z.
48 Soup served at a sushi bar
49 Down in the dumps
52 Equestrian, e.g.
53 BP merger partner of 1998
54 Pillages
55 Introduces to the mix
56 Ring event
57 Baskin-Robbins order
59 ___ favor (Spanish "please")
61 "CSI" test subject
62 It borders four Great Lakes: Abbr.
63 Mel with 511 homers
64 To God, in hymns

by Gareth Bain

ACROSS

1 Winter plantings?
9 First name in "Star Wars"
15 One who's just out for a good time
16 Junk shop transaction
17 So to speak
18 More Serling-esque
19 Leader of a noted 37-Across
20 Left for good
22 "Nebraska" star, 2013
24 Turn blue?
25 Feast of unleavened bread
28 Southernmost U.S. capital
32 Gardner namesakes
33 Nonmusical Abba
35 Diamond complements
36 -
37 See 19- and 54-Across and 11- and 41-Down
39 -
40 Not perfectly put
42 Subject of a onetime Nepali hunting license [true fact!]
43 Belated observation of 4/14/12
44 Home of Charlotte Amalie
46 Like the people of Siberia
48 Unanimously, after "to"
49 Stadium projection, maybe
50 Co-signer, say
54 Location of the 37-Across
58 Priestify
59 2014 World Cup host
61 Strange bird
62 Spare item?
63 Airplane with the propeller at the back
64 "As if you could kill time without injuring ___": Thoreau, "Walden"

DOWN

1 Leveler
2 Many a state lottery game
3 Mythical Greek who slew Castor
4 Impersonated
5 "Just a mo!"
6 Hoopster Jeremy
7 European city of 500,000+ whose name translates as "to eat"
8 Result (from)
9 Snake's place, in part
10 Party game
11 Beneficiary of the 37-Across, in modern times
12 "Just a moment!"
13 Captain's direction
14 Filmdom's Napoleon Dynamite, for one
21 "You can count on me"
23 Flightless bird
25 Setting for much of "Inglourious Basterds"
26 Schedule listing
27 October War leader
28 Bad feelings?
29 Last name of three Indianapolis 500 winners
30 Bad looks
31 Copy editor's concern
34 Bear on a field
37 Product of organic decay
38 Pending, as a legal decree
41 Loser on account of the 37-Across
43 Deal
45 Sort
47 Eye
49 Blue eyes, e.g.
50 Hair gel, e.g.
51 Language from which "cummerbund" comes
52 Tots
53 Bone: Prefix
55 First name in space
56 What cabalists do
57 One of eight for Stephen Sondheim
60 Vein filler

by Matt Ginsberg

116

ACROSS

1 Now or never: Abbr.
4 Sounds from test cheaters, maybe
9 Bris officiant
14 Moo goo ___ pan
15 Erect
16 Have ___ to pick
17 Nanette's nana
19 Parachute parts
20 William who wrote "What is originality? Undetected plagiarism"
21 "Bonne ___!"
23 Those, to José
24 Geographical name that's another geographical name backward
25 One of two N.T. books
26 Leave in the lurch
28 German town
30 World headquarters of LG Electronics
32 Civil War inits.
33 Wee bit
35 Numerical prefix
36 ___ Lingus
37 & 40 Repeat offender? . . . or something found, literally, in four rows in this puzzle
42 ___ Paulo
43 Like one for the ages
45 Racket
46 Airport approximation, for short
47 Shade of brown
49 Mexican cigar brand
53 Less likely to be G-rated
55 Car starter?
57 Vitamin amts.
58 Uptight, informally
59 "His/her" alternative
61 Bone near the funny bone

62 Georges who wrote "Life: A User's Manual"
64 Making a father of
66 Serengeti scavenger
67 Name hollered in the "Flintstones" theme song
68 See 69-Across
69 Participated in a 68-Across
70 True
71 Ones who are so last year?: Abbr.

DOWN

1 Texas A&M team
2 "Rats!"
3 Product touted by Hugh Hefner
4 Mail order abbr.
5 Poison ___
6 They tend to be fast typists
7 Flush
8 Graf ___ (ill-fated German cruiser)
9 Buddy
10 Small section of an orchestra
11 Transportation in Disneyland's Main Street, U.S.A.
12 Backed
13 Cigarette ad claim
18 Must
22 Drew out
27 Draw out
29 Start to a baseball song
31 "The Star-Spangled Banner" preposition
34 Send away for good
37 React, just barely
38 Baseball Hall-of-Famer mistakenly listed in "The Chanukah Song" as a Jew
39 Actor Cage, informally
41 Minimal baseball lead
42 High-ranking angels
44 "Ta-ta!"
48 With bitterness
50 Does improv

51 Way
52 Plains Indians
54 Chaiken who co-created "The L Word"
56 Slangy commercial suffix
60 Laugh uproariously
63 No great catch
65 Confident finish?

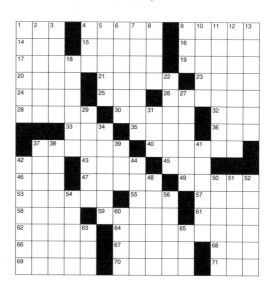

by Daniel Landman

ACROSS

1. Get down to business
5. Plum or peach
10. Straddling
14. Others, in Latin
15. Exercise in brevity
16. Literally, with 19-Across, a Western state capital
17. Literally, with 20-Across, ski resort purchases
18. Swallowed a loss
19. See 16-Across
20. See 17-Across
22. Prickly plants
24. Ideology
26. Rotten
27. Captain Morgan competitor
30. Reacted to, as fireworks
34. Scintilla
35. Literally, with 39-Across, head doctor
37. Part of a collegian's email address
38. It's north of Den.
39. See 35-Across
41. Hollywood's Howard
42. Something that might be left at the scene of a crime
43. Common daisy
44. Desiccated
45. Baltimore's I-695, e.g.
47. Buck
50. Firm ending
51. Botanical opening
52. Toscanini and Maazel
55. Literally, with 62-Across, longtime action star
59. Literally, with 63-Across, distinguished chef
60. Ancient region of Anatolia
62. See 55-Across

63. See 59-Across
64. "America's Got Talent" airer
65. "The Praise of Chimney-Sweepers" essayist
66. Go hand to hand?
67. Honkers
68. ___ job

DOWN

1. Upper-crust sort, stereotypically
2. Olive, to Ovid
3. Narrow estuaries
4. Between-innings feature on a Jumbotron
5. Took off after
6. Lead-in to cake or meal
7. More than mislead
8. Dust Bowl migrant
9. Vegetable whose name comes from Swedish
10. Bow
11. Shadow
12. Table scraps
13. Stage name for 2012 singing sensation Park Jae-sang
21. Muff
23. Semiarid region of Africa
25. Big name in parks
27. Motel alternative, informally
28. In agreement (with)
29. Pinkish
30. Halt
31. John who played Joshua in "The Ten Commandments"
32. Flip over
33. One pulling strings?
36. 180
39. Graduation attire
40. Strict
44. Gobbled (down)
46. At deuce, say
48. Native Arizonan
49. Physicians' org.
51. "___ U Been Gone" (Kelly Clarkson hit)
52. Mobster's gal
53. Bay ___
54. It's a wrap
56. Capacity
57. Spring bloomer
58. Where I-90 and I-29 cross: Abbr.
59. Ottawa-based media inits.
61. "___ a miracle!"

by Tracy Gray

118

ACROSS

1 Like a new recruit
4 Raise, as Old Glory
9 Fritter away
14 Patterned after
15 Come to mind
16 "In the red," e.g.
17 NAFTA signatory: Abbr.
18 With 64-Across, words of certainty . . . or a hint to 23-, 40- and 56-Across
20 At attention
22 One headed for Ellis Island, say
23 "Silkwood" screenwriter
26 Gaelic tongue
27 ___ Croft (Angelina Jolie role)
28 Clerical nickname
30 Cuisine in which "phat mama" is a noodle dish
33 Little pain in the you-know-where
35 Archipelago makeup
40 Like Advil vis-à-vis Vicodin
44 Mormon's obligation
45 Make darts, say
46 Bit of dinero
47 "Fire away!"
50 Instrument in the painting "The Spirit of '76"
52 Contest with seconds
56 Convention outcome
61 Where the Joads were driven from
63 Presto or largo
64 See 18-Across
67 Adopt-a-thon adoptee
68 Krupp Works city
69 Took a spin
70 Bard's preposition
71 Dirty looks?

72 "Cowboy and the Senorita," e.g.
73 One in knickers

DOWN

1 Noodle dish
2 Last Oldsmobile
3 Car wash machine
4 Cold sufferer's drink
5 Gaelic "Gee!"
6 It might go away for the summer
7 Not so iffy
8 Something a seismograph picks up
9 Buffalo ___
10 Be wild for
11 Instrument with sympathetic strings
12 Dots on a map
13 Act badly, in a way
19 It has a reciprocal function
21 Self-proclaimed leader of ISIS, e.g.
24 ___-dieu
25 Prosciutto and others
29 Big wheel
30 Discharge letters?
31 ___ polloi
32 Aardvark's morsel
34 IBM-compatibles, e.g.
36 Tropicana Field site, informally
37 Factor in club selection
38 Canon offering
39 Nestlé ___ Caps
41 Stephen of "Citizen X"
42 Lower one's A.P.R., perhaps
43 "Heads ___, tails . . ."
48 Elitist
49 ___ dragon (huge lizard)
51 Like a "before" versus "after" photo subject, say
52 Carpentry peg
53 Czar's edict

54 "Family Ties" mother
55 ___ tag
57 Tierney of "ER"
58 Urge forward
59 Record store section
60 Jotted down
62 A Katzenjammer kid
65 Rug rat
66 "You're all ___ got"

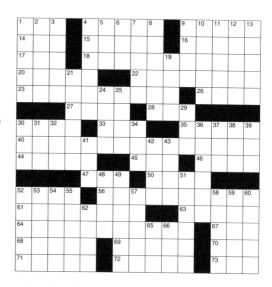

by Jacob Stulberg

119

ACROSS

1 Century, for one
5 Skip over water, as stones
8 "Brr-r-r!"
14 One of the 12 in the Pac-12
15 "Huzzah!"
16 Descriptor for olde England
17 Show inattention, say
18 Pince-___
19 Bold
20 What Set committed when he slew Osiris
22 "M.Y.O.B."
23 Sea urchin, at a sushi bar
24 Woodstock artist who performed while six months pregnant
25 They're hooked up to breathing tubes
29 Initial offer?
33 British paper vendor
34 Ultimate
35 Littoral eagle
36 Displayed conspicuously
38 Weapon in Clue
39 Bygone Chevy subcompact
40 Like Baha'i houses of worship
42 Slit made with a saw
43 How zombies act
44 Author Grey
45 "Life doesn't imitate ___, it imitates bad television": Woody Allen
46 Member of the buttercup family
50 "The spur of industry," per David Hume
54 Skink, e.g.
55 New York's Tappan ___ Bridge
56 Sea of ___, outlet of the Don River

57 Difficult kind of push-up
58 100,000 picojoules
59 Colloquial denial
60 Some statuary
61 Diva's accessory
62 Certain panegyrics

DOWN

1 Fictional rabbit hunter
2 Historical buffalo hunter
3 "Judgment at Nuremberg" defendant
4 With 29-Down, first story to feature 44-Down (1919)
5 With 37-Down, real name of 44-Down
6 One way to turn a ship
7 Kind of dispenser
8 Steeps

9 Ricardo landlord, in 1950s TV
10 Suffix with theo-
11 Little pasta
12 Place
13 It might be hammered out
21 "___ Dinka Doo" (Durante tune)
22 Lift others' spirits?
24 Petroleum ether
25 One not to be trusted
26 Pluck
27 Manual reader, maybe
28 Having a sense of pride?
29 See 4-Down
30 Etching supplies
31 Get going
32 Clinging, say
37 See 5-Down
41 Antivenins, e.g.
43 Little green ones come from Mars
44 Subject of this puzzle
46 Often

47 Young muchacho
48 Israel's Weizman
49 Goat sounds
50 Designed to minimize drag
51 Lacoste competitor
52 Hack it
53 Brinks
55 "The Waltons" grandpa

by Timothy Polin

120

ACROSS

1 Buried treasure site, maybe
5 Eagles' band?: Abbr.
8 What confirmed bachelors avoid
14 Wet missile
16 Jay ___, onetime Obama press secretary
17 Potato?
18 Benefits
19 "Bewitched" spinoff
21 Take in, as patients
22 Major tanker port
24 Ebb tide?
26 Fled or bled
27 Not quite enough
28 Philanthropist Broad
29 Sci-fi author Stanislaw
30 Most of the symbols on a traditional slot machine
32 Willow shoot
34 Inoculation order?
38 Rotten tomato's sound
39 Put into law
42 Org. originating the three-point shot
45 Suffix with super
46 Neither his nor hers
48 ___ mag (Maxim or FHM)
49 "Clean out your desk!"?
52 Goes down
53 Commencement participants, for short
54 Eases
56 Like Superman and Spider-Man
58 1983 sci-fi drama . . . or a possible title for this puzzle
61 Actress Bynes of "She's the Man"
62 Letterman's favorite activity?

63 Took home
64 A, B and C, in D.C.
65 See 50-Down

DOWN

1 Suffix with sex
2 Masseuse's workplace
3 "Pay attention!"
4 Allen who captured Fort Ticonderoga
5 Exile
6 Like the toves in "Jabberwocky"
7 E'en if
8 Signature Obama health measure, for short
9 Some microphones
10 Major League Baseball news
11 Savage
12 Go through again
13 What an anarchist rails against, with "the"
15 Pal

20 "Give it ___!"
22 Toy sound
23 Historical org.
25 Director Kazan
27 Words of welcome
31 Code letters?
32 One side of Niagara Falls: Abbr.
33 Watergate initials
35 Tough trek
36 Doo-wop group with the 1963 hit "Remember Then," with "the"
37 Infomercial figure
40 Cool ___
41 Scores of Vikings, for short
42 Warm blanket
43 Old galley
44 Biblical debarkation point
46 Baby
47 Aquarium fish
50 With 65-Across, "Not a clue"

51 Midwest tribe
52 Snide comments
55 Humpty Dumpty, e.g.
57 Scoundrel
59 Music genre
60 Chicago-to-Houston dir.

by Michael S. Maurer

ACROSS

1 Modern traffic director?
10 Punk theme
15 London's __ Barnett School
16 News anchor O'Donnell
17 One who's not out all night?
18 Steer
19 T-Pain and Ice-T output
20 Time's 1963 Man of the Year, informally
22 Pick up
23 John or James
26 Fashion designer Marshall
28 Et __
29 Back
31 Ship captained by Vicente Yáñez Pinzón
32 West of Nashville
34 "Martin Chuzzlewit" villain
35 Silver screen name?
39 "__ Pleasure" (Charlie Chaplin movie)
40 Fixed, as lining
41 Abdominal and lower-back muscles, collectively
42 Embarrassed
43 Unleashes on
47 Writes a Dear John letter, say
49 Novelist Isabel
50 Where one might take a bullet: Abbr.
51 Some seaweeds
54 Actor Franco of "Now You See Me"
55 Skateboard trick named after its originator
57 Not reserved
60 Female lead in "Brigadoon"
61 They'll never hold water

62 Big celebrations
63 Paid a visit

DOWN

1 President beginning in 1995
2 Delaware Valley Indians
3 Hip place
4 Strabismus
5 1901 Kipling book
6 Big __
7 Words before "to be born" and "to die" in Ecclesiastes
8 Not this type?: Abbr.
9 Change course at sea
10 Physicist __-Marie Ampère
11 Common conjunction
12 Looking sheepish, say
13 Southern city that's the setting for "Midnight in the Garden of Good and Evil"
14 Beauty's partner
21 Celeb who got the 2,500th star on the Hollywood Walk of Fame in 2013
24 Easy runs
25 Trellis strip
27 Messiah
29 Hung out to dry
30 Groks
33 Kind of pump
34 Beauty
35 Goes head to head
36 "Trust me"
37 "My Big Fat Greek Wedding" writer/star
38 "Go, team, go!," e.g.
42 GPS line: Abbr.
44 Wove (through)
45 Sooner or later
46 Wee
48 U.S. chain stores since 1985
49 Cartoon dog
52 Setback
53 It's by no means a long shot
56 Football stat: Abbr.
58 Scammer's target
59 Mark on a card

1	2	3	4	5	6	7	8	9		10	11	12	13	14
15										16				
17										18				
19					20			21			22			
23			24	25			26		27					
28						29	30			31				
		32			33			34						
35	36	37					38							
39				40										
41			42			43			44	45	46			
47		48			49									
50		51		52	53			54						
55		56		57			58	59						
60				61										
62				63										

by Brendan Emmett Quigley

122

ACROSS

1. Is guilty of disorderly conduct?
11. Not much
15. Accompaniment for a 17-Across
16. Film featuring Peter Sellers as a matador, with "The"
17. Kid getting into treble
18. Gym request
19. Indication that you get it
20. ___ & Watson (big name in deli meat)
22. Indication that you don't get it
23. Played a club, maybe
24. What to call some femmes: Abbr.
26. Hand-held game device
28. Wedding gown accessory
30. 1997 role for Will Smith
31. David, e.g.
34. Fish also known as a blue jack
35. One with long, luscious legs
38. Wagers
39. Trail
40. Geek Squad service
43. Internal development?
44. Many party hacks
46. Word in the titles of six songs by the Beatles
47. TV monitor, for short
50. Quantity that makes another quantity by adding an "m" at the front
51. Intimated
53. Sociologist Mannheim
54. Teriyaki go-with

56. 1971 song that was the "CSI: NY" theme
59. Cry that makes children run away
60. Performed hits at a concert?
61. Some home-schoolers get them, briefly
62. 1920s scandal

DOWN

1. Brand paired with On the Run convenience stores
2. Strike ___
3. Excited, with "up"
4. Source of the word "trousers"
5. Common word on a Portuguese map
6. Tour tote
7. Organized crime enforcers of the 1930s–'40s
8. Morales of film
9. Power cord?
10. Burns's land, to Burns
11. ___ of steel
12. First place
13. "Since you mentioned it . . ."
14. Cut it
21. Slalom path part
24. What some formulas are based on
25. 24-Down producer, informally
27. Large magnets?
28. One hanging by a thread?
29. Want from
31. Boston, Chicago or Kansas
32. Follower of the Sultan of Swat in career homers
33. Email attachment?
35. Warren Buffett's college fraternity, informally
36. Where to find Edam and Gouda: Abbr.
37. Bond film?
41. Tour part

42. Moderator of Tribal Councils on TV
45. Like some humor
47. "Nurse Jackie" star
48. Bygone publication subtitled "America's Only Rock 'n' Roll Magazine"
49. 1967 title role for Warren Beatty
52. Rhyme pattern at the end of a villanelle
53. Clement
55. Coneheads, e.g., for short
57. Lead-in to meter
58. Singer

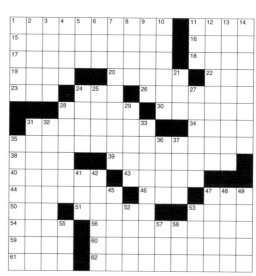

by Sam Ezersky

ACROSS

1 Toast often given with Manischewitz
7 Nobel-winning economist who wrote "Fuzzy Math"
14 Precipitate
15 Longtime Tab competitor
16 In the best- or worst-case scenario
17 Like things in "Ripley's Believe It or Not!"
18 Psychobabble, say
20 In the 29-Down, e.g.: Abbr.
21 "___ do, so he shall do": Numbers 15:14
22 Put to work
25 Hell
29 Like players who sweep things
34 Digs in the snow?
35 Olympian in a shell
36 Pitches
38 "Luncheon on the Grass" painter
39 Like much unheeded advice
40 Pick up something common?
43 Line of tugboats?
44 Dye containing indigotin
48 Jackasses, e.g.
51 "It's all good"
53 Actor with the line "Say hello to my little friend!"
56 Take stock of
57 Feature of a Shaw show
58 Ominous final words
59 Accessories purchased just for openers?
60 Big player in the Suez Crisis

DOWN

1 Source of very soft wool
2 Whale constellation
3 Oh-so-dramatic
4 Acrobat producer
5 "___ happens . . ."
6 Perfect expression
7 Pet food in the form of pellets
8 "Luncheon of the Boating Party" painter
9 ___-Aztecan
10 [This is so frustrating!]
11 Storyteller who needs no words
12 ___ impasse
13 Dickens protagonist surnamed Trent
15 Horror film antagonist surnamed Thorn
19 King Arthur's father
23 1971–'97 nation name
24 Drove (on)
26 Pat material, maybe
27 Low-class, in Leeds
28 Royals manager Ned
29 Devil dog's outfit: Abbr.
30 Org. affected by Title IX
31 It may be a sacrifice
32 Approve for office installation
33 E'en if
36 Fault, in law
37 "Father Knows Best" family name
39 Like some things you can't handle
41 Shop shelter
42 The Furies, e.g.
44 Timber dressers
45 Nativity numbers
46 Not free
47 Shunned one
48 Be a high-tech criminal
49 Allure or Essence alternative
50 Fix, as a pointer
52 Major star of 2-Down
54 Domain of 38-Across and 8-Down
55 Grp. with many operations

by James Mulhern

124

ACROSS

1 Prop for Kermit the Frog
6 It's big in the suburbs
15 Kind of acid
16 Something you shouldn't knock?
17 What dots may represent
18 "Stay cool!"
19 ___ mix
20 Ready to play, with "up"
21 N.F.L. stat: Abbr.
22 ___ pants
24 Source of the phrases "cakes and ale" and "milk of human kindness": Abbr.
25 Belize native
26 What "II" or "III" may indicate
28 Profession of Clementine's father in "Oh My Darling, Clementine"
29 R.A.F. award
32 Shrimp
33 Small job for a gardener?
34 Noble one
36 Spelunker's aid
37 High
38 Something cited in a citation
39 Suffix with transcript-
40 Über ___
41 Origin of the word "behemoth"
43 Architect ___ van der Rohe
44 Knockout
45 Where Chekhov lived and Tolstoy summered
49 Big Apple ave.
50 Half of a matched set
51 Inadequate
52 Girl in "The Music Man" with a floral name
55 Nil
56 Desktop item
57 Elite unit
58 Capital on the Raccoon River
59 Something from the oven

DOWN

1 Mangle
2 ___ Tower (Pacific landmark)
3 More green
4 Spelling problems?
5 Brass maker: Abbr.
6 Year that Chaucer died
7 It follows a pattern
8 Stick
9 2001–'05 Pontiac made in Mexico
10 Org. in 1950s–'60s TV's "Naked City"
11 Govt. lender
12 Where Syracuse is a port
13 Elderly
14 Relative of ocher
23 Where many accidents occur
24 Lies out
25 Philadelphia tourist attraction
27 Target of a squat, for short
28 1960s dance, with "the"
29 State of sleep
30 Student loan source, familiarly
31 Third-year hurdles, for some
33 2008 Libertarian presidential candidate
35 Lycée breaks
36 Temporal ___
38 It may come with a cookie
41 Kentucky county in a 1976 Oscar-winning documentary
42 Forest ranger?
44 Melvin who was called "The King of Torts"
46 Ruy ___ (chess opening)
47 Relative of ocher
48 Something from the oven
50 Shot deliverer
53 Radiation unit
54 French possessive
55 Use a laser on

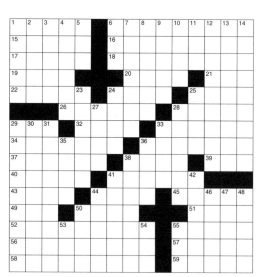

by Barry C. Silk

125

ACROSS

1 Director in "A Chorus Line"
5 Pistol packer in a 1943 #1 hit
9 Make eyes pop and jaws drop
14 Paradoxical assertion, perhaps
15 Writer of the 644-line poem "Ibis"
16 Stage
17 Seasonal servings
18 1969 Rolling Stones album
20 Like some long flights
22 Part of une fraternité
23 He called the U.S. pres. a "glorified public relations man"
24 Abbr. on some clothing tags
27 Part of a filled-out survey: Abbr.
29 Admiral who bombarded Tahiti in 1914
30 It often results in changes across the board
38 1959 hit with the lyric "One day I feel so happy, next day I feel so sad"
39 At any price
40 Not meant for specialists
41 Some Blu-ray players
42 First of 66 books: Abbr.
43 Fix
44 Couch problem
47 March Madness, with "the"
51 Charges at the door
55 Swan song
58 "Who ___?"
59 Emmy-winning Ed
60 The "O" in F. A. O. Schwarz
61 Looking up
62 Nelson Mandela's mother tongue

63 Sound heard during a heat wave
64 Event with touches

DOWN

1 Corrosion-preventing coating
2 Not very affable
3 With 56-Down, refuse to be cleaned out from a poker game?
4 Literature Nobelist before Gide
5 Stream on the side of a mountain, perhaps
6 Car name that's Latin for "desire"
7 McConnell of the Senate
8 "Peace out"
9 Black-and-white transmissions, briefly?
10 Like most brain neurons
11 Had a beef?
12 Actress Kazan or Kravitz
13 One may get a pass
19 Picture on a chest, for short?
21 They often spot people
25 Withdraw
26 Minor parish officers
28 Jason of "How I Met Your Mother"
29 Five to nine, maybe, but not nine to five
30 Big bass, in fishing lingo
31 Ones remaining
32 Activity that proceeds hand to hand?
33 Heart-to-hearts
34 ___ Jon (fashion label)
35 "Give me ___"
36 Product for young string players?
37 Ones remaining
44 Good name for a worrywart?
45 Achilles' undoing

46 Wayne's pal in "Wayne's World"
48 Extremely excited
49 Ancient master of didacticism
50 Pick up
52 Drag racers' governing grp.
53 ___ Grey, alter ego of Marvel's X-Man
54 Extraocular annoyance
55 Like some oversight
56 See 3-Down
57 ___-cone

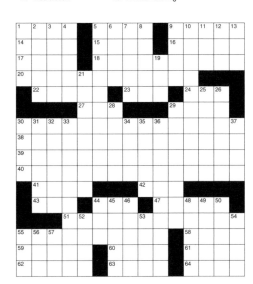

by Martin Ashwood-Smith

ACROSS

1 Gallop
9 "Our Town" family
14 Three- to six-year financial commitment, usually
15 Eponym for a day of the week
16 Livid
17 Where Mozart's "Don Giovanni" premiered
18 Infamous settler on Galveston Island, 1817
19 Fail at stoicism, say
20 Dating inits.
21 Result of pushing too hard?
22 Revlon brand
24 Road sign silhouette
25 Natural barrier
27 Domain name element
28 Tree-dweller that sleeps 20 or so hours a day
29 Recipe for KFC chicken, e.g.
32 Italian artist with the largest painting in the Louvre
35 "Guys and Dolls" number that ends with the rolling of dice
36 Gray ones spark debate
37 Umpire's call
38 "Bonanza" brother
42 Like poodle hair
43 "The Marshall Mathers LP" co-producer
45 Home of Utah Valley University
47 Parlor with simulcasts, briefly
48 Seabiscuit, notably
49 Urge
51 Cousin of a zombie
53 It's often canned
54 Composers Bruckner and Webern

55 Couldn't keep cool
56 Anthem singers at the closing ceremony of the Salt Lake City Olympics
57 Lengthy undertakings

DOWN

1 Denali National Park sits on one
2 One who puts others to sleep?
3 Suppress
4 Show time, in some ads
5 ___ du jour
6 Trunk line
7 Once-common desert fighting force
8 There are three in an inning
9 Not easily taken
10 Air ticket info
11 Sources of chronic annoyance
12 Many watch his movies for kicks
13 Run down
15 Quick
19 Stand for a photo
23 Posed
24 Number of signos del zodiaco
26 Ballistics test units: Abbr.
28 Country whose currency is the shilling
30 Tommy of 1960s pop
31 Stuff sold in rolls
32 Group living at zero latitude?
33 Tartness
34 Allow
35 Classic Doors song in which Jim Morrison refers to himself anagrammatically as "Mr. Mojo Risin'"

39 Exercise in a pool, say
40 Kindle
41 River crossed by a ferry in a 1965 top 10 hit
43 Recitation station
44 It's dangerous to run on
46 Touches
48 French seat
50 "As if that weren't enough . . ."
52 Slew
53 Opposite of hence

by Brad Wilber

ACROSS

1 Tears
9 Philatelist's abbr.
13 Blow up
15 Zero, for one
16 When Winesap apples ripen
18 Genesis source
19 Weapons in Olympic shooting events
20 Actress in a best-selling 1979 swimsuit poster
22 Braves' division, briefly
23 Make less attractive?
24 Mythical hunter
25 Notable buried at the Cathedral of Lima
26 Inside opening?
27 Downs rapidly
28 N.F.L. positions: Abbr.
29 Blew away
30 Ottawa electees, for short
33 Flusters
34 Existed
35 Bungler
36 Soda, at times
37 Tattooed temporarily
38 Red-eye remedy
39 Mitsubishi model whose name means "huntsman" in Spanish
40 Describing an ancient tragedian
41 One of the books in the Book of Mormon
42 Rosalind Russell title role
44 Ball __
45 Lied
46 Filmmaker __ C. Kenton
47 Worker who often takes leaves

DOWN

1 It doesn't hold water
2 Proving beneficial
3 Camp David and others
4 Purple-flowered perennial
5 Patriotic chant
6 Means of attracting publicity
7 Takes courses?
8 World Series of Poker champion __ Ungar
9 Affected sorts
10 Extremely
11 Fulminates
12 Kind of jacket
14 Crooked bank manager, maybe

17 Arizona city across the border from a city of Sonora with the same name
21 Belled the cat
23 Confused
25 Solve
27 Ben of "Run for Your Life"
29 Moon of Saturn
30 Latin America's northernmost city
31 Matthew, Mark, Luke and John
32 Least flustered
33 Life insurance plan
34 Member of a biblical trio
35 Kitchen bulb?
36 Democrat in the Bush cabinet
37 It's a long shot

38 "Casablanca" actor Conrad
39 Emulate Eeyore
40 Capital of France's Manche department
43 Head, in slang

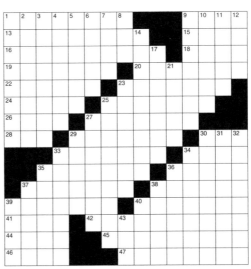

by David Steinberg

ACROSS

1 Talk, talk, talk
9 Give stories
14 Basis of comparison
15 National tree of India
16 "Good going!"
17 Words before many a commercial
18 Singer who wrote
19 Battle of Albert setting, 1914
21 United hub, briefly
22 Traditional Christmas gift for a child
24 Accent reduction may be a subj. in it
25 Italian title
26 Unwelcome closet discovery
29 Their sizes are measured in cups
30 1967 album that included "I Can See for Miles"
34 Fiddled
35 "A Study in the Word" host
36 Make a comeback?
37 Old cinema
38 Round stopper, for short
39 Merrie Melodies sheepdog
41 Schoolmarmish sound
46 ___ Brum (car accessory)
47 Having depth
50 Recipient of much 2010s humanitarian aid
51 Giant in test prep
53 Succeeded
55 "Er . . . uh . . ."
56 Boss

57 Largest minority in Croatia
58 "Sounds about right"

DOWN

1 Took downtown
2 Jägermeister ingredient
3 Talking pet
4 Complain
5 Pie-in-the-face scenes, say
6 Sacred thing, to Ayn Rand
7 Sharing word
8 Indie rocker Case
9 Flap of fashion
10 Pub
11 Command to pay attention
12 It may include laundering
13 Down, in a diner

15 They're often seeking change
20 Text, e.g.
23 Loud complaints
27 Life starts in it
28 Certain beach phony
29 Obscure
30 "The King's Speech" director
31 Horace man?
32 Field fungus
33 Subprime mortgagee, to detractors
34 Handle
35 Kawasaki products
39 Doctor's orders
40 Dahlia in Wodehouse novels, e.g.
42 Surrealist known for self-portraits
43 Like many ribbons
44 All- ___
45 Bud

48 One who has a hunch
49 Mooring spot
52 Media ___
54 Classic Bogart role, in slang

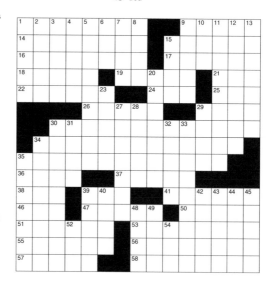

by Peter Wentz

129

ACROSS

1 Any of the three authors of "Pull My Daisy"
9 They produce minimal distortion
14 He may have many lines memorized
16 Monomer of proteins, informally
17 Elicit a "T.M.I."
18 Like about 30% of 51-Across, belief-wise
19 Head of communications?
20 1,000-pound weight units
21 Suffered a face-plant
22 Rugby-to-Reading dir.
23 Novel title character called "My sin, my soul"
25 Cry of contempt
26 Trip
27 Appeal to
28 Light on TV or Broadway
31 Star of Bombay, e.g.
33 Cousin of cumin and coriander
34 Arrested
35 Riveting piece, perhaps
39 Nickeled-and-dimed?
40 Award with a Best Upset category
41 Its flag includes an image of a nutmeg clove
43 Appeal formally
44 À gogo
45 Prefix with pressure or point
48 "Our Gang" girl
51 Its flag includes an image of a cocoa pod
52 Old Brown Dog and others
53 Old pitcher of milk?

54 Next to
56 Budget alternative
57 Try
58 DuPont development of 1935
59 Subject that includes women's suffrage and the Equal Rights Amendment

DOWN

1 Stains
2 Homebuilders' projections
3 Best New Artist Grammy winner of 2008
4 One needing pressure to perform well
5 Ovid's foot
6 Midwest city named for a Menominee chief
7 Potential virus sources
8 Bone preservation locations

9 Reaction to a card
10 Tag statement
11 Often-overlooked details
12 "Imagine" Grammy winner of 2010
13 County seat on the St. Joseph River
15 Beverage brand portmanteau
23 Engine measure
24 Twitter, Facebook or Instagram
26 Like areas around waterfalls
27 Major cocoa exporter
28 Oscar nominee for playing Cal Trask
29 Very, very
30 Opposite of aggregation
32 What "ruined the angels," per Ralph Waldo Emerson

36 Prod
37 One of Time magazine's cover "Peacemakers"
38 Wily temptress
39 Jason, for one
42 "For real"
45 Co-worker of Kennedy starting in 2006
46 Cigar box material
47 Words before a date
49 Wheels of fortune?
50 Unit in a geology book
52 ___ supt.
55 Juice

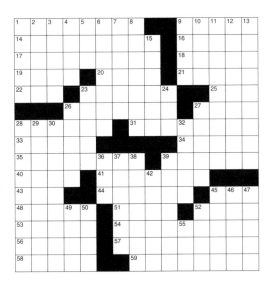

by James Mulhern

130

ACROSS

1 Cause of an artery blockage
11 Some working parts
15 Foam item at a water park
16 Coming up, to milady
17 Follower of Roosevelt
18 Jordan's Mount ___, from which Jericho can be seen
19 Innards
20 Black hat
22 Sect in ancient Judea
23 Lacking backing
24 E.R. units
25 Protective, in a way
26 Missouri city, informally
29 Knuckle-bruiser
30 "Discreet Music" musician
31 Ludwig ___ van der Rohe
32 "In"
33 Seizure
34 Field of fields?: Abbr.
35 Acoustic units
36 Hunter of a 20-Across
37 Standbys
39 "___ Nibelungenlied"
40 Like hospital patients and much lumber
41 Ephemeral
45 "Saving Fish From Drowning" author
46 Carry on
47 Mom on "Malcolm in the Middle"
48 Free
50 James of jazz

51 Hallmarks of Hallmark
52 Old TV news partner of David
53 Visual expertise

DOWN

1 Tear
2 Pluto and Bluto, e.g.
3 Debacles
4 Some Prado hangings
5 Intensify
6 Conservative side
7 Some candy wrappers
8 Interjects
9 ___ Sainte-Croix
10 Established in a new place, as a shrub
11 Hymn leader
12 They may be thrown out to audiences
13 Flip out

14 One left shaken?
21 Lead role in the film known in France as "L'Or de la Vie"
23 Brokers' goal
25 Some lap dogs
26 Class clown, e.g.
27 A woolly bear becomes one
28 Springsteen, notably
29 Like diamonds and gold
32 Trysting site
33 Dished
35 Overseas deb: Abbr.
36 Hobby
38 Distresses
39 1978 Broadway revue that opens with "Hot August Night"
41 Rialto and others
42 Cuckoo

43 Cuckoo
44 Big V, maybe
46 Veronese's "The Wedding at ___"
49 Bleu body

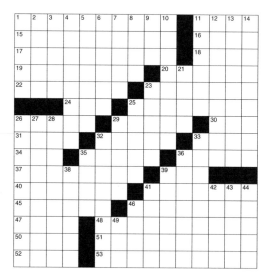

by John Lampkin

131

ACROSS

1 Decision theory factor
5 Athletic short?
10 Coolers, in brief
13 Indie rock band whose "The Suburbs" was the Grammys' 2010 Album of the Year
15 Jiffy
16 British author of the so-called "London Trilogy"
17 Feature of a Norman Rockwell self-portrait
18 Agitation overseas
19 Hot, spicy brew
21 ___ Records
22 Washboard parts
25 "Sic 'em!"
26 Popular Japanese manga seen on the Cartoon Network
29 "Bonanza" setting
30 Language originally known as Mocha
34 Turkish money
35 Miscellany
36 Tochises
38 Diego Rivera's" ___ Sandías"
39 Ceilings
41 Exotic annual off-road race
43 Dead reckonings?
45 Admits
46 In wait
48 Best-selling food writer ___ Drummond
49 "Bad!"
52 Become dazedly inattentive
54 Ryan of Hollywood
56 One with a password, maybe
57 Writer, director and co-star of the Madea films
61 Master's counterpart
62 Belief in human supremacy
63 Buffoon
64 Goes on and off diets, say
65 ___ Modern

DOWN

1 Pickup line?
2 Furious
3 Rugby formation
4 Subject of Spike Lee's "When the Levees Broke"
5 Reed section?
6 1962 film "___ Man Answers"
7 Energy
8 Actor Stoltz
9 Gaga contemporary
10 Notable Senate testifier of 1991
11 Florida's so-called "Waterfront Wonderland"
12 Password requirer, maybe
14 10-watt, say
15 Old-fashioned shelter along a highway
20 Phone inits.
22 Proceeded like a rocket
23 Time capsule event
24 Tough problem
27 Grayish
28 Downer
30 South African leader beginning in 2009
31 Reanimation after apparent death
32 Insipidity
33 Short
37 Kind of hotel, for short
40 David Ogden ___, actor on "M*A*S*H"
42 Colony unit
44 ___-cone
47 Bold
50 Opera ___
51 Land formation known for its caves
53 Printed slip
54 Unlock, in poetry
55 Old ___, Conn.
58 Willy ___, pioneering writer on rocketry
59 Green start?
60 "___ for rainbow"

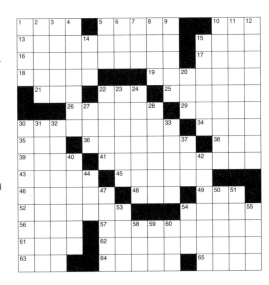

by Kameron Austin Collins

132

ACROSS

1 Web nuisance
8 With 26-Down, dramatic end to a game
15 Modern-day sanctuary
16 Mostly
17 "The Hurt Locker" setting
18 Jumps all over
19 Place for un bateau
20 Donkey : mule :: ___ : huarizo
22 Admission ticket
23 Cut down to size, maybe
25 Sweet Jazz sound?
27 Meant ___
28 Serape wearer
30 Have ___ at
32 Nick, say
33 Complex data
35 The middle Andrews sister
37 Heartening words
40 Corrupted
41 Show up at dinner?
42 WorkCentre maker
43 Elect
44 Construction material for several theme parks
46 Ruptures
50 Where 24-Down began his managerial career
52 Proverbial battlers
54 Eastern wear
55 Flavorer once labeled a "milk amplifier"
57 Burn to the ground
59 Bunkmates, often

60 Orion's hunting companion
62 #1
64 Jumped all over
65 Professor ___
66 Like some Hmong
67 Solution for storing contacts?

DOWN

1 All ___
2 Flaunt
3 Relief provider since 1916
4 1974 John Wayne title role
5 Not just tear
6 What many racers race on
7 Lightning strike measure
8 River between two Midwestern states
9 Malt finisher?
10 Enrich
11 Reuben ingredient
12 Denouements
13 Plant said to repel bugs
14 Decayed
21 Yearn for
24 See 50-Across
26 See 8-Across
29 Kind of artery
31 Pipe accompanier
34 Las, e.g.
36 People plot things around it
37 Recreation hall staple
38 High
39 Confirm
40 Yellow type?
42 Valentine letters
45 Boards
47 One might get past a bouncer
48 Blue, in Burgundy
49 Moral duty?
51 Get 180 on the LSAT, say
53 Boob
56 Wyndham alternative
58 Elevator at the bottom?
61 Suffix with 28-Across
63 Mate

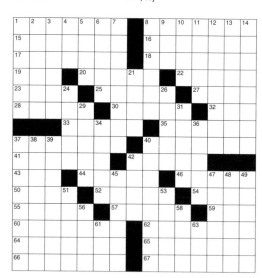

by John Lieb

ACROSS

1 Family guy
8 Create some ties
15 It often has chips
17 1974 #1 hit written by Bob Marley
18 Almost equaling
19 Brat's place
20 With 24-Across, "The Pianist" star
23 Unlikely donor
24 See 20-Across
25 Common shower garment
29 First name in westerns
30 Conditioning apparatus
34 Family guy, affectionately
35 Once-common commercial fuel
36 Skippered
37 Extremely long string
39 ___ Robles, Calif.
40 Like some symmetry
41 Congolese, e.g.
42 Word menu option?
45 Criminal activity
46 Khloé Kardashian's married name
47 Like St. Catherine
51 Rapper with the 2009 hit "Kiss Me Thru the Phone"
56 Classroom films, e.g.
57 Like opinion pieces
58 World of DC Comics

DOWN

1 Sprint competitor, once
2 Physical reactions?
3 "I'm such a fool!"
4 Deforestation, e.g.
5 Assorted
6 TV foodie Brown
7 Informal rejections
8 Rail construction
9 Say again
10 Nail site
11 Less direct, say
12 Steinbeck have-nots
13 It can kick back
14 Fermented milk drink
16 Souvenir shop purchase
20 Feminist with the 1984 book "Gender Gap"
21 Product under a sink
22 Dial-O-Matic maker
23 ___ van der Rohe
25 Animal whose tongue is more than a foot long
26 Brand that's a shortened description of its flavor
27 Topper of der Tannenbaum
28 Munchies, in ads
30 "Storage Wars" cry
31 Scrabble player's asset
32 Durango direction
33 Unlisted?
35 Dog breed distinction
38 Scapegoat for many a failure
39 Driver's warm-up
41 In a vulgar way
42 Día de San Valentín bouquet
43 Lefty out in left field
44 Cheese burg?
45 Fix, as some roofs
47 Stat for a pitcher
48 Term paper abbr.
49 Canon shooter
50 Stooge syllable
52 Insignificant amount
53 Blitzed
54 Japan's ___ Castle
55 ___ Explorer

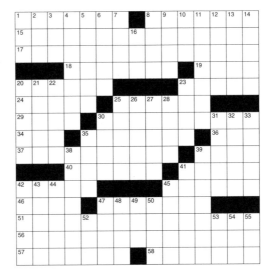

by David Steinberg

134

ACROSS

1 "Diamonds and Rust" singer, 1975
9 Add in large amounts
15 "Is that a gun in your pocket, or are you just happy to see me?," e.g.
16 Surround with light
17 Disappoints
18 More legible, say
19 Marvin Gaye's "___ Tomorrow"
20 Gambling
22 One often seen at the door
23 River of Hesse
25 Undermine
26 Wound around the body?
27 Reasons for some joyrides
29 Cause of an insurance increase, for short
30 National card game of Mexico
31 Call for a meeting?
34 Part of many a symphony
37 Visit
38 Many a Cape Cod locale
40 Multitudes
41 Multitude
42 Some settlers, before settling
46 H. G. Wells's "Empire of the ___"
47 Teatro Costanzi premiere of 1900
49 Kind of engr.
50 Pull (out)
51 New Testament money
53 ___ Andric, Literature Nobelist before John Steinbeck
54 Ornament at the top of a spire
56 Sign at the end of a freeway, maybe
58 Like God, in the olden days
59 Former Egyptian president Mohamed Morsi, for one
60 Team whose playing venue appears on the National Register of Historic Places
61 Dumps

DOWN

1 Dumped
2 Six Nations tribe
3 Provider of bang for the buck?
4 Greek consonants
5 Twins, e.g.
6 Make ___ of
7 Best Actor nominee for "American History X"
8 Fall asleep fast
9 Cylindrical pasta
10 Rare blood type, for short
11 Ching preceder
12 Asian capital
13 Wild olive
14 Boreal
21 Kojak's love of lollipops or Reagan's love of jellybeans, e.g.
24 Starts on a righteous path
26 Disobey directives, say
28 Gathers on a surface, chemically
30 Charms
32 Novel ending?
33 Time keeper?
34 "America's oldest lager beer"
35 First person outside NASA to receive a moon-rock award, 2006
36 Accelerated
39 1937 film based on a Gershwin musical
43 ___ of life
44 Work over
45 Nursery brand
47 Bringer of old news
48 Sitter's choice
51 Longtime soap actress Linda
52 "Take ___ a sign"
55 Group awaiting one's return, for short
57 Some rock

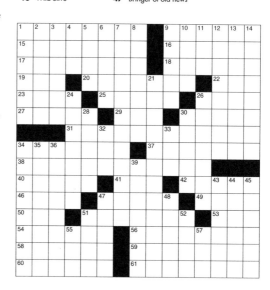

by Alex Vratsanos

ACROSS

1 Prepare to speak, say
16 Nurse
17 Not now
18 Puts somebody out
19 FICA fig.
20 ___ corde (piano direction)
21 Ganders, e.g.
22 "Bummer"
25 President's first name on "The West Wing"
26 Slicker go-with
29 With 35-Down, slightly stale
30 Choice for bow-making
33 Inexperienced
34 Their contents have yet to be dealt with
36 Tenor Vickers
37 Defense Department dept.
38 She played Detective Sasha Monroe on "Third Watch"
39 Greetings
40 Dummy in "Stage Door Canteen"
41 Cellphone feature, informally
42 Fr. religious title
43 Hotel waiter?
46 Florida preserve?
52 Keen insight, with "the"
53 Peak performance in 1953?
54 Focus of HGTV's "House Hunters"

DOWN

1 Philistine
2 "August: Osage County" playwright Tracy
3 Westphalian city
4 Looking down on?
5 DVD-___
6 Snack since 1912

7 Fish with iridescent blue stripes
8 Automaker Bugatti
9 German boys
10 The old you?
11 Snack since 1900
12 Named names, maybe
13 Crazy quilts
14 "Look ___ now!"
15 Alternative to cafés
22 Raid target
23 Top 10 hit for Eminem or 3 Doors Down
24 Eponymous German physicist
25 Aerosmith's titular gun carrier
26 Gandhi opposed it
27 ___, amas, amat
28 Crime writer Rankin
29 China shop purchase
30 Intro to biology?

31 Business bigwig Blavatnik
32 Composition of Accent seasoning
35 See 29-Across
39 Big name in oratorios
40 Scottish island that's home to Fingal's Cave
41 First stabber of Caesar
42 1930 tariff act co-sponsor
43 Joe, for one
44 "___ of Rock 'n' Roll" (1976 Ringo Starr hit)
45 Propensities
46 "Hug ___" (Shel Silverstein poem)
47 Exhibit upward mobility?
48 Some paddle wielders, briefly

49 Propose in a meeting
50 Bass line?
51 Romance novelist ___ Leigh

by Martin Ashwood-Smith

ACROSS

1 Keister
8 Soft drink company based in California
14 Comfortable way to rest
15 Cigar with clipped ends
16 Winter Olympics group
17 Edible in a cone
18 Onetime White House resident with a cleft palate
20 Onetime capital of the Mughal Empire
21 Only man ever to win an L.P.G.A. Tour tournament (1962)
22 Handy talent?
24 Govt. medical agency
25 Fountain spirits
27 Travelocity competitor
29 Saw home?
32 ___ d'agneau (lamb dish)
33 Harbors
34 El Greco, after age 36
36 Ate at
37 "Kramer vs. Kramer" novelist Corman and others
38 Crack, say
39 Energy company in the Fortune 100
40 Home pages?
41 Sierra Nevada evergreen
43 Like some verbs: Abbr.
44 Moon of Saturn
46 Strategic port raided by Sir Francis Drake in 1587
50 Anika ___ Rose, 2014 Tony nominee for "A Raisin in the Sun"
52 Java file, e.g.
54 Showed

56 Treats to prevent goiter, say
57 Delivers in court
58 Furthest stretched
59 Legs' diamonds?
60 Panel composition, often

DOWN

1 They rotate on Broadway
2 ___ Engineer (M.I.T. online reference service)
3 Gloria Gaynor's "I Will Survive," originally
4 Xenophobe's bane
5 Frozen foods giant
6 ___ Parker, founding president of Facebook
7 Author of the 87th Precinct series
8 Buff
9 One given to brooding
10 Bailiwick
11 Berlioz's "Les Nuits d'Été," e.g.
12 Printing on many concert souvenir T-shirts
13 Spots likely to smear
15 79, say
19 Onetime Toronado, e.g., informally
23 Game in which top trumps are called matadors
26 Certain tax shelters, for short
28 Stone coal
29 Setting for "One Day in the Life of Ivan Denisovich"
30 Helicopter-parent, say
31 University of Phoenix specialty
33 Dennis in "Monty Python and the Holy Grail," e.g.

35 Like roots, periodically?
36 Voter with a Green button, once
38 Array of options
41 Chancel arch icons
42 Slick, in a way
45 River bordering the Olympic host cities Grenoble and Albertville
47 Sleepy sort
48 Namely
49 Some garnishes
51 Annual race, colloquially
53 Soft-soap
55 Animation fan's collectible

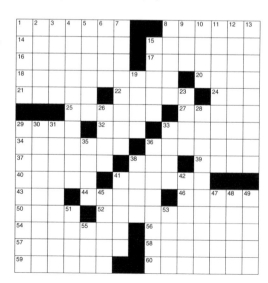

by Brad Wilber and Byron Walden

ACROSS

1 Hoping to get home?
7 Borrows without intending to repay
11 Therapy developers: Abbr.
14 In a slip
15 Government groups
17 Like many garments at the cleaner's
18 Hit the road
19 "I wouldn't lie"
21 Some linemen: Abbr.
22 Get in on the deal
23 Cross
25 Dreidel letter
26 It has a 30-min. writing skills section
30 Mtn. statistic
31 Surprising words from Shakespeare?
32 Ruined "rose-red city" of Jordan
33 Much of Mae West's wit
37 Line up
38 Mangrove menace, informally
39 It's often compounded: Abbr.
40 Lots
41 "___ to be!"
43 Approved
44 Language in which "talofa" means "hello"
46 What I can be
47 Sizzling
53 Celebrates wordlessly
54 Ferrari or Lamborghini
55 It may not be able to pick up something tiny
56 Bit of "Archie" attire
57 Elle's English-language counterpart
58 Bald-eagle link
59 One getting the picture

DOWN

1 Drop
2 ___ Barnacle, James Joyce's wife and muse
3 Drop in library use?
4 Will of "30 Rock"
5 Looks
6 Cause of some turbulence
7 Storied storyteller
8 "Casablanca" crook
9 Pea-brained researcher?
10 Real mess
11 Gucci contemporary
12 "Crucifixion of St. Peter" painter
13 Army E-6: Abbr.
16 Hoofed it?
20 Singer John with the 1984 #1 hit "Missing You"
23 Ready to dress down, say
24 Ecuadorean province named for its gold production
25 Bygone telecom
27 What half of a battery is next to
28 Concert itinerary listing
29 Easily taken in?
31 City on the Ouse
32 ___ Park (Pirates' stadium)
34 Its bottles feature red triangles
35 Big name in heating and air-conditioning
36 Hyperion's daughter
42 Cry when rubbing it in
43 Comparable (with)
45 Carne ___
46 Like some ancient Mexicans
47 Weapons inspector Blix
48 Hawaiian menu fish
49 No place for a free ride: Abbr.
50 Restaurant attachments?
51 It's at one end of I-79
52 Suez Crisis weapon

by Peter A. Collins

138

ACROSS

1 Tangy fruit pastry filling
11 Physical, say
15 There might be one after a bridge
16 The Rice Krispies mascots, e.g.
17 Georgia neighbor
18 Amazon icon
19 Raskolnikov's love in "Crime and Punishment"
20 City whose name is pronounced like the natives' word for "Where is . . . ?"
21 Something an aichmophobe fears, briefly
22 Old mount
24 Grandmotherly plaints
26 Abbr. at the end of some crossword clues
27 2003 Billy Bob Thornton crime film
32 Language of Middle-earth
34 Craigslist section
35 It's usually closed before leaving
36 Playground retort
37 Ax
39 Presidential debate mo.
41 Father of Paris
42 What may accompany a salute
44 With 51-Across, end of the London blitz?
46 Ruler with a palace near St. Mark's
47 San Diego's ___ Pines, site of the 2008 U.S. Open
48 Prerequisites for some overseas travel
50 On the q.t.
51 See 44-Across
53 New, informally
54 Valley girl's "no"

56 Cry over spilled milk?
58 Kung Pao chicken ingredient
63 Solstice time
64 Literally, "different lizard"
66 Some extracts
67 Advice of caution to a beginner
68 Midwest squad
69 Bizarre and alienating

DOWN

1 "What ___!" ("How fun!")
2 Two-time Oscar-winning screenwriter
3 Love at the French Open, essentially
4 Humble response
5 Changing place
6 Start of an "Ave Maria" line
7 Beer named for a port on the Yellow Sea
8 Guy from Tucson in a Beatles song
9 1960 historical film written and directed by John Wayne, with "The"
10 Well-off
11 Put on the surface, in a way
12 Superpower
13 Ventilation provider
14 Campers' relatives
23 Argentine ___
25 Spillover
27 Key of Schumann's Symphony No. 1
28 "Really?"
29 Not willing to give
30 "Popeye" cartoonist Elzie
31 Part of the Disney family, so to speak
33 "Falstaff" composer

38 Attention-getter, in some rooms
40 Company asset
43 Freebie on some airplane flights
45 Prefix with efficiency
49 Obsolescent media holder
52 It's around the mouth
55 Own (up)
57 Dedicatee of a famous Tallinn church
59 Runs smoothly
60 Setting for "Three Kings," 1999
61 Beaut
62 Vacation destination
65 "Come ___?" (greeting)

by Josh Knapp

ACROSS

1 Quickly gets good at
8 Summer hat
14 Restrained
16 "This isn't a good time"
17 First-century governor of Britain, whose name was Latin for "farmer"
18 Signer of the Kansas-Nebraska Act
19 Trade fair presentation
20 It means "council" in Russian
22 Apprehend
23 Roofing material
25 Cut short
26 Membre de la famille
27 Compact Chevys of old
30 G-rated oath
31 Poll calculation
34 "While we're on the topic . . ."
35 Marked by hostilities?
36 One of the Kennedys
37 Manhattan Project scientist
38 Emblem on Captain America's shield
39 All you can take with one hand
40 "Frida" actress Hayek
45 Williams nicknamed "The Kid"
46 Field strip
49 Automaker that introduced heated front seats
50 1950 short-story collection by Asimov
52 Cork bar
54 Dry up
55 Cause for complaint

56 Phalanx weapons
57 "Through the Dark Continent" author, 1878

DOWN

1 Witches' brew ingredients
2 Being in heaven
3 Cosmic payback
4 "I have measured out my life with coffee spoons" writer
5 Brief wait
6 Stop along the Santa Fe trail
7 Four-time host of the Nordic World Ski Championships
8 Upstanding one?
9 Pass over
10 Bart and Lisa's grandpa
11 Betrayed embarrassment
12 Not-so-fast food?

13 Amber-colored brew
15 Send-off for the dear departed?
21 To such an extent
24 Register
26 Empty
28 Creature outwitted by Hop-o'-My-Thumb
29 Tries to win
30 Columbian Exposition engineer
31 Addictive analgesic
32 Beauty magazine photo caption
33 Bit of paperwork
34 Call from home
35 Rouses to action
39 Finishing strokes
41 Pasty
42 Name tag location
43 "Never trust a woman who wears ___" (line from "The Picture of Dorian Gray")
44 "The Name of the Rose" setting

46 Two by two?
47 Veins' contents
48 Olympic skater Katarina
51 Burlesque accessory
53 Body treatment facility

by Patrick Berry

ACROSS

1 Neckwear slider
10 Domed dessert
15 "The highest result of education is ___": Helen Keller
16 Purpose
17 Continuing in its course
18 Hardly smash hits
19 Part of the Roman Empire in modern-day NE France
20 One forced into service
22 Bit of illumination
23 Tooth coating?
24 1994 Peace Prize sharer
25 Eschews money, say
26 Reduces the fare?
27 Big brand from Clermont, Ky.
28 Drill specialist, for short?
29 Minor documents?
30 "Poppycock!"
33 Producer of cheap shots?
34 "The Farm" painter, 1921
35 Dances with sharp turns
36 Biblical verb
37 What ruthless people show
38 Apollo, e.g.
39 Greek city where St. Paul preached
40 Los Angeles suburb once dubbed "Berryland"
41 ___ rock
42 "See!"
44 First name in the 1948 presidential race
45 About 90% of cotton fiber
46 "Magister Ludi" writer
47 Old-fashioned duds

DOWN

1 Greatly wanting
2 Good thing to keep in an emergency
3 A little of everything
4 Connects
5 Crunchy snack
6 Took for booking
7 "Young Frankenstein" girl
8 Drill specialist, for short?
9 Male issue?
10 Slums, e.g.
11 Not quite spherical
12 Winged prayer
13 Theodore of "The African Queen"
14 Computer programming command
21 Rather violent, perhaps
23 Old Pokémon platform
25 Woman in a leather jacket, maybe
27 Broadway inspector
29 Dot preceder
30 Consumed in copious amounts
31 Ignition technician?
32 Much-anticipated outings
33 Company with a game piece in its logo
34 1993 Peace Prize sharer
35 Orchard menaces
36 Get comfortable, in a way
37 Acapulco-to-Monterrey dirección
38 Château chamber
39 ___ crop
40 It's a blast
43 800s, e.g.: Abbr.

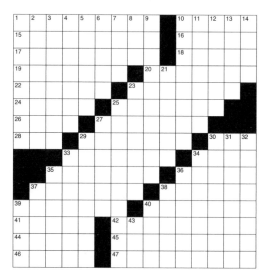

by David Steinberg

ACROSS

1 Displeases one's buds?
10 Dart maker . . . or dart
15 R.V. park hookup option
16 When New York's Central Park closes
17 Snack in a gym bag
18 Clog
19 Phrase cooed en español
20 Opposite of miniature
22 Uses a 49-Down
23 People thank God when it comes
25 What Kramer often called Seinfeld
26 Joseph of ice cream
27 Art ___, Steelers owner for 55 years
28 Cops, in slang
29 Moon views?
30 "Wiener Frauen" composer
31 They might like your comments
36 N.F.L. team that went 0-16 in 2008
37 Have an itch
38 Duncan of Obama's cabinet
39 Impound lot charge
41 Jump start?
44 Gomer Pyle, e.g.: Abbr.
45 Trees used to make shoe trees
46 Enfant bearer
47 Ad mascot in sunglasses
49 Spanish soccer club, for short
50 Spirit
51 Outerwear for moguls?
54 Battery for many a toy
55 Like a 1938 Andrew Jackson stamp
56 Writer featured in "The Electric Kool-Aid Acid Test"
57 409 and 410, but not 411

DOWN

1 Scary little sucker
2 12-book classic
3 Like many exercisers
4 The "2x" and "5" in 2x + 5, e.g.
5 Accordingly
6 Designing
7 Restaurant accessory
8 Knight who fell to the dark side
9 Knock sharply
10 Spot, to a tot
11 Large charge
12 Cousin of a carafe
13 It may cover a tear
14 Power line?
21 Unfavorable reply
23 Shot, informally
24 Tiller attachment?
27 Coats put on at barbecues
28 Part for a whack job?
29 Well, in Rome
30 Old change in the Vatican
31 Hotcake
32 Jet pack?
33 Cries uncle
34 What chickens have
35 Clothing, colloquially
39 Pro ___
40 Seat of Ector County, Tex.
41 Moved like a whiptail
42 Apprehended by a small group
43 Brewers' supplies
45 Pop singer ___ Rae Jepsen
46 Cry in a swimming pool game
48 He had a 1948 #1 hit with "Nature Boy"
49 Judge's perch
52 "___ no idea"
53 Kind of gravel

by Victor Fleming and Sam Ezersky

142

ACROSS

1 Army equivalent of a leading seaman: Abbr.
4 Lowered
11 Man on the street?
14 New England state sch.
15 Football helmet feature
16 Preposition with three homophones
17 Span since 1955
20 Middle of an Aeschylus trilogy, with "The"
21 Classic label in classical music
22 Try to pull off, say
23 Camera movement
24 Unwelcome neighbor
29 Get on board
30 Gouda and Muenster
33 Greeting at the head of a procession
34 Selfish response to a request
42 River that passes by the Hermitage
43 Wall hanging
44 Saint who is one of the Fourteen Holy Helpers
45 Squarely, informally
47 First name in late-night TV, once
48 Monumental
54 Pro athlete in a red-and-white uniform
55 Subway inits.
56 Bright spots
57 One being shepherded, say
58 It's double-hyphenated: Abbr.
59 Like many a sports car
60 Brutus' "but"

DOWN

1 Schnitzels, e.g.
2 Plain variety
3 Stick in a purse?
4 1950s–'70s defense acronym
5 Request often accompanied by "please"
6 Pasta eaten with a spoon
7 "That's enough," to a server
8 Banker/philanthropist Solomon
9 River into which the Vltava flows
10 Clear of vermin
11 Some corner shops
12 Move from A to B, say
13 Hero of 20-Across
18 Stanger a.k.a. Bravo's "Millionaire Matchmaker"
19 "You can't beat me!"
24 Sight-singing technique
25 54-Across, e.g., for short
26 Gender option on modern forms
27 Onetime center for the distribution of oranges
28 2008 World Series winners, to fans
31 Didn't get snapped up, say
32 Laura Nyro album "___ and the Thirteenth Confession"
34 They run up legs
35 Skips
36 Reproductive, in a way
37 Sportscaster Jim
38 Olympic gymnast Strug
39 Manhattan eatery referenced in Billy Joel's "Big Shot"
40 "Wow!"
41 Turned off and on
46 Shade
47 Ohio's ___ Point, home of the Top Thrill Dragster and Millennium Force roller coasters
49 Kind of day or job
50 Headlight?
51 Part of A.M.P.A.S.: Abbr.
52 Arum family member
53 TLC, e.g.

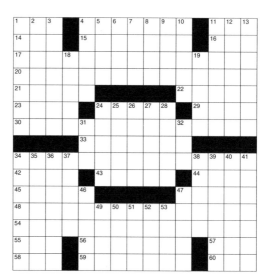

by Tim Croce and Alex Vratsanos

143

ACROSS

1 "Know what I'm sayin'?," in hip-hop slang
8 "Yep, alas"
15 Feature of many a reception
16 1998 N.F.L. M.V.P. Davis
17 Tablet alternatives
18 Laughed menacingly
19 Any of the Baleares
20 Political leader?
22 Bob of play-by-play
23 Squeeze
26 Kind of dye
27 Things that wind up on trucks
30 Sounded wowed
32 Days ___
33 Villainous organization in the 007 film "GoldenEye"
35 Sleep around
37 Like many Plains Indians
39 Football and basketball
43 Like innuendo
44 Electronics component
45 Ole Miss, athletically
47 What you might arrive two hrs. early for
48 Central American capital
49 Blue-flowered Mediterranean herb
52 Buff finish?
53 Nuzzling spot, maybe
57 Leader referred to as "His Imperial Majesty"
59 1994 memoir with a chapter on "New Robot Novels"
61 Oscar-nominated Greek-American actor

62 Crank
63 Certain solution holder
64 Figure in many a New Yorker cartoon

DOWN

1 Meditative sort
2 Big tree climbers
3 Something to catch from scolding parents
4 Box
5 Org. the Utah Stars belonged to
6 Public Enemy and others
7 Who wrote "Unless someone like you cares a whole awful lot, nothing is going to get better. It's not"
8 U.S. fraud watchdog
9 Breadth
10 ___ Arena (past Kings home)
11 Needles

12 Campus spot for Bluto, Otter and Boon
13 Scuzz
14 Motherland
21 Tender with Washington
24 Google browser
25 Ted Danson hit series
27 "Groovy!"
28 "All right already!"
29 Walk of Style locale
30 Flavorings in some root beers
31 Member of a loving trio?
34 Person on a mission?
36 Ordered
38 George Clinton was its first gov. (for 21 years)
40 K–12 grp.
41 "Whoops!"
42 Answers
44 Lower

46 "Quit your squabbling"
48 Switched to, as on a thermostat
50 Fictional boss of Stubb and Flask
51 River to the Colorado
54 Member of a loving trio?
55 Work for an artist, maybe
56 "Would I ___!"
58 Start of a kids' clothing line name
60 Letters on a track

by Ian Livengood

144

ACROSS

1 It has many giants and dwarfs
7 Profit-sharing figure: Abbr.
10 Part of the former Republic of Pisa
14 Run down a mountainside
15 Pour it on
17 One who winds up on a field
18 A kid might be punished for showing it
19 Scores
20 Marked up, say
21 Something pocketed in Italy?
24 Like Princess Leia vis-à-vis Luke Skywalker
27 Roller coaster feature with a food name
29 Celle-là, across the Pyrenees
30 Movie with the line "I'm a vulgar man. But I assure you, my music is not"
31 Be a very fast learner?
32 Title woman in a "Paint Your Wagon" song
35 Hybrid, maybe
36 Do a 35-Across chore
37 Romp
38 Brave, e.g.
40 "Who ___?"
41 1965 Yardbirds hit
45 Like many rodeo animals
47 Dweller near the Potemkin Stairs
48 Best seller
50 In
51 Track on "Beatles '65"
53 "Out!"
55 Scarab, e.g.
56 Tip for slips
57 Barreled

58 Like some broody teens
59 Folks working on courses?

DOWN

1 D preceder
2 Telescope part
3 Tuesday preceder
4 Be a juggler?
5 Ending of saccharides
6 Letters in old atlases
7 Seaweed derivative
8 Call for a timeout
9 Some body work
10 John in an arena
11 Chaises, in Cheshire
12 Flower child?
13 Had dogs, e.g.
16 Fail at falling asleep
20 Underdog playoffs participant
22 Character in many Baum works

23 Where Gray's "lowing herd wind slowly"
25 Biblical venison preparer
26 Artery connection
28 Noted acid studier
31 Noted 1-Across studier
32 Company with the King David Club
33 "Lost Horizon" figure
34 St. Patrick's Day order
36 "Saw" sights
38 Pity party plaint
39 Alternative to the pill, briefly
41 Snaps
42 Slip through, say
43 Like Cinderella's stepsisters vis-à-vis Cinderella
44 "___ Game"
46 Not iffy

49 Hungarian name meaning "sincere"
51 "___ me"
52 Battle-planning aid
53 Spring place
54 "Cap'n ___" (1904 novel)

by Barry C. Silk

145

ACROSS

1 It's part of a club
5 Place for vino
9 Like some floors and series
14 Ancient land east of the Tigris
15 Fur source
17 Repeated cry in a 1973 fight
19 High class
20 Mo. of Indian Independence Day
21 Annihilate, arcade-style
22 Many a New York Post headline
23 Geezers
25 Aptly named N.F.L. M.V.P. of the 1960s
28 Tudor who lost her head
29 The Glass Capital of the World
31 Thing, in Spain or Italy
35 Minority report?
36 Polish rolls
38 ___-eyed
39 Regardless of the repercussions
41 Fox in the Baseball Hall of Fame
43 Bring up to speed
44 They might become bats
47 Death, to Mozart
48 People often strain to make it
49 D.C.-based intercontinental grp.
50 Calls upon
54 Many Victoria Cross recipients
57 Heads with hearts
58 One hit on the head
59 Indian yogurt dish
60 "No ___ nada" ("It's all good": Sp.)
61 Journeyer through Grouchland, in a 1999 film

DOWN

1 Doc's orders
2 Palliation application
3 Demonstration of disinterest
4 Like God
5 Fall faller
6 Hens and heifers
7 "___ true"
8 Like God
9 Like yaks
10 Richard Pryor title role, with "the"
11 The "you" in "On the Street Where You Live"
12 Fold
13 Some cover-ups
16 Tanker's tankful
18 Currency of 46-Down
23 "Impressive!"
24 Elated
25 Touchstones: Abbr.
26 Bust a hump
27 Further
28 Liquor store, Down Under
30 Restrained
32 Beauvais's department
33 Institute in the 1997 sci-fi film "Contact"
34 N.R.A. member?: Abbr.
37 Agreement
40 Start of an alphabet book
42 Work first publicly performed at the Theater an der Wien in 1805
44 In open court
45 Junípero ___, founder of San Francisco
46 Where 18-Downs are currency
47 Home of minor-league baseball's Drillers
50 Ducky web sites?
51 Dollar bill feature
52 Quick cut
53 Europe's Tiger City
55 Cousin of a chickadee
56 The English Beat's genre

by Peter A. Collins

146

ACROSS

1 Faces facts
9 Cruise vehicle
14 Airline relaunched in 2009
15 A Ryder
16 Resort town near Piz Bernina
17 Like some migraines
18 "Home Alone" actor
19 Hot stuff
20 Schubert's "The ___ King"
21 Place for a shoe
23 Star material, maybe
24 Highlander, e.g.
28 Taking five
31 Public face
34 Scylla in Homer's "Odyssey," e.g.
35 Former hit TV show with the theme song "Get Crazy"
36 Eliza in "Uncle Tom's Cabin," e.g.
37 "Raising Hell" rappers
41 ___ de la Réunion
42 Phila.'s Franklin ___
45 Queenside castle indicator, in chess
46 Zigzag ribbon
49 Change for a C-note, maybe
53 Tops
54 Smashes to smithereens
55 Narrow soccer victory
56 Mark of affection
57 Undesirable element in the home
58 Deserve to be listened to, say

DOWN

1 Fixture in a chemistry lab
2 Las Ventas combatant
3 Opportune
4 Cry to a tickler
5 ___ bird
6 Whiffenpoofs, e.g.
7 Common aspiration?
8 Region of Italy that includes Rome
9 Material also known as cat-gold or glimmer
10 ___ probandi (legal term)
11 Set off easily
12 Caught
13 Bringing forth fruit, as corn
15 Provider of "!!!"
22 Voice actress in Disney's "The Princess and the Frog"
25 Horse ___
26 Feature of breakfast . . . or dinner?
27 Like the lifestyle of many a monk
29 African political movement
30 Fire sign?
32 Check for size, say
33 Some semiconductor experts: Abbr.
34 Set apart
35 Dutch queen until 1980
36 Reflect
38 Beaut
39 Some Renaissance music
40 Baby
43 Follow too closely
44 Siouan tongue
47 Subject of a Will Ferrell "S.N.L." impersonation
48 Court edge
50 Porto-___, Benin
51 Cousin of a goldeneye
52 Mr. ___

by Julian Lim

147

ACROSS

1 Very harsh
7 Cash flow statement?
15 Ultra 93 vendor
16 Winner of the inaugural Václav Havel Prize for Creative Dissent (2012)
17 Two-dimensional
18 The Hub
19 Meander
20 "I say" sayer
21 Ferrari rival, informally
22 Wildly cheering
24 Real joker
25 First talking pet in American comics
26 Steel-eyed one?
28 Horse whisperer, e.g.
29 Moves uncertainly
30 Boorish member of King Arthur's Round Table
32 Like dungeons, typically
33 Footprint, maybe
34 Tough to figure out
36 Paraphrase
40 Coin with a hole in it
41 First substitute on a basketball bench
42 Van Gogh's "L'Église d'Auvers-sur-___"
43 Chop-chop
45 Willy Wonka Candy Company candy
46 Flint-to-Kalamazoo dir.
47 "The X-Files" program, for short
48 Soft spot
49 Modern storage space
51 Flush
54 How Columbo often worked
55 Queued up

56 Be at the end of one's rope?
57 Principal part

DOWN

1 Ancient symbol of royalty
2 French bottom
3 Very succinctly
4 "No problem, I'm on it!"
5 "Been there"
6 One of a vocal pair
7 Hack
8 Sacred: Prefix
9 Anticipate
10 50 ___
11 Google unit
12 It means "sulfur island" in Japanese
13 Into crystals and energy fields, say
14 Redhead
22 Be part of the picture

23 Indian novelist Raja ___
24 Kind of business
25 Be a patsy
27 Hat-tipping sort
28 Catchphrase for the paranoid
30 Faux money
31 Holly
34 Deity with more than 16,000 wives
35 "Easy-peasy"
37 Rush home?
38 Soupçon
39 Nation's exterior?
40 Submit
41 Greeted someone
43 Time immemorial
44 Fast
47 "Dirtbag," e.g.
48 Remote
50 Revolutionary name
52 Kill
53 "The Partridge Family" actress

by Ashton Anderson and James Mulhern

148

ACROSS

1 Not too wimpy
10 Sensational effects
15 Begging, perhaps
16 David had him killed, in the Bible
17 Dish with crab meat and Béarnaise
18 Associate with
19 Allen in history
20 Many an event security guard
22 Say you'll make it, say
25 They wrap things up
26 Dangerous blanket
29 Craftsperson
32 Like a Big Brother society
34 Food order from a grill
38 K'ung Fu-___ (Confucius)
39 Charge at a state park
41 Zenith competitor
42 Hit the dirt hard?
44 Subject of the 2010 biography "Storyteller"
46 "Honest"
48 Regarded
49 Knowledge: Fr.
52 The very recent past: Abbr.
54 Sound reproducible with coconut shells
57 Left, on un mapa
61 Mall features
62 Portmanteau bird?
65 Shakespeare character who asks "To whose hands have you sent the lunatic king?"
66 Left part of a map?

67 Weather map feature
68 Smiley, e.g.

DOWN

1 Shake a leg
2 Operating without ___
3 Webster's first?
4 Swell
5 Electric shades
6 They're not forbidding
7 Perennial N.C.A.A. hoops powerhouse
8 Stick selection
9 "This is yours"
10 Completely bare
11 She came to Theseus' aid
12 ___-in-law
13 Bayou snapper, briefly
14 Mall features

21 Punch-Out!! platform, for short
23 Dance in triple time: Sp.
24 Snoopy sorts
26 They're often fried
27 Joanie's mom, to Fonzie
28 One in arrears
30 Alternative to tea leaves
31 Opprobrium
33 It helps get the wheels turning
35 Act like a jackass
36 Really long
37 Completely bare
40 Part of a C.S.A. signature
43 Perfect
45 Uncovers
47 It changes when you go to a new site
49 Bolt (down)
50 Let out, say

51 Labor Day arrival, e.g.
53 "Semper Fidelis" composer
55 Some parlors, for short
56 Trashy, in a way
58 It uses sevens through aces
59 First of many body parts in "Alouette"
60 Cabinet dept. since 1977
63 Chess's ___ Lopez opening
64 Frequent winner in a 66-Across: Abbr.

by Kristian House

ACROSS

1 "___ Style," first video with a billion YouTube views
8 Goes for enthusiastically
15 Home to "alabaster cities"
16 Like Saudi Arabia
17 "Hmmmmm . . ." [as hinted at by the three groups of black squares in the middle of the grid]
19 It may contain mercury
20 One of its flavors is Mud Pie
21 Starwork, e.g.
22 Sounds from some mall temps
23 Those south of the border?
25 ___ soup
26 Medical suffix
28 Bests
30 "___ am your father" (classic "Star Wars" line)
31 Things that ties never have
33 Last part
35 Mythical predator
36 Vietnam's ___ Dinh Diem
37 Excellent, in slang
41 Quintet comprising "Ode to the West Wind"
45 See 51-Across
46 "It was you," operatically
48 Dictator's beginning
49 ___ angle
51 With 45-Across, Thor's co-creator
52 Many a base player
53 Like 19-Across
55 No sophisticate
57 Ovid's others
58 Best Picture of 1954 [see 17-Across]

61 Hardly the assertive type
62 Gander
63 As part of a series
64 A wild card is unlikely to beat one

DOWN

1 Hybrid on the road?
2 Lovingly, on a music score
3 Greek goddess of vengeance
4 170 is its max score
5 Minute beef
6 Really long?
7 First
8 Closes a session
9 Rostock bar stock
10 "Bravo" preceder
11 Optical separator
12 Like some famous frescoes
13 Secretary of state before Dulles
14 Neighbor of the Adam's apple
18 Where Sotheby's is BID
24 "NCIS" actor Joe
27 Spanish muralist
28 They're clutched during some speeches
29 Sharp or flat
32 Mies van der ___
34 Anderson of "Nurses"
37 Dessert preference
38 Told, as a secret
39 Rough housing
40 Test the strength of, in a way
41 Where snowbirds flock
42 Corral
43 Cadet, e.g.
44 Under
47 Like a guitar string
50 Indian chief, once
54 Prefix with john
56 Suffix with switch

57 Refuges
59 Southeast Asian temple
60 Metrosexual sort

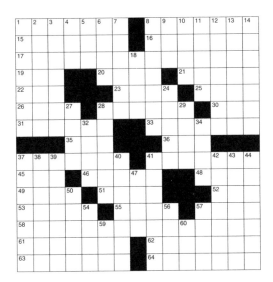

by Bruce Haight

150

ACROSS

1 Colonel's charge, once
4 Conventioneers: Abbr.
8 Washington, once, so they say
13 Creature that moves by jet propulsion
15 Loses one's shadow, say
16 Like John Belushi, ethnically
17 Spelunking supply
18 High level
19 Couscous ingredient
20 Ones working over the holidays?
21 Try to stop
22 Part of Austin Powers's attire
23 Big beat?
26 "Mad Men" award
27 One getting stuck in a horror movie
29 Powder holder
30 French locale of prehistoric cave paintings
31 Bellwether sound
32 Image on many an old map
34 ConocoPhillips competitor
35 Like top-shelf liquor
36 Place to walk to
37 Tired
38 "The Divine Comedy" has 100 of them
39 Ski lodge fixtures
42 Digression
43 Going in circles
44 Lear's youngest
45 British footballer Wayne ___
46 Inconvenience
47 Some modern fads
48 Reckon
49 Curtains

DOWN

1 Contents of some lockers
2 Drop off
3 Bolívar, Cohiba or Juan López
4 Patronize, in a way
5 Mount St. ___ (Alaska/Canada border peak)
6 Common dance theme
7 Fig. on some shredded documents
8 Case for a bootblack
9 Weak, with "down"
10 Drug dealer on "The Wire"
11 Many a flier under a door
12 Alternative to an elbow
14 Tomahawk for Andrew Jackson, surprisingly
15 Quickly produces in great quantity
19 One might have a cameo at the end
21 Bishop's place
23 Biblical quartet
24 Arlington House is his memorial
25 Monocle, in British slang
27 How Mount Etna erupts
28 The Battle of Thermopylae, for the Spartans
30 Some gatherings in halls
33 Raphael's "___ Madonna"
34 Swinging joints
36 Group of lovers, collectively
38 "___ mañana" (procrastinator's jokey motto)
39 "What's the ___?"
40 Shakespearean lament
41 Fashion designer Browne
42 A–F or G–K, maybe
44 Conqueror of Valencia, with "the"

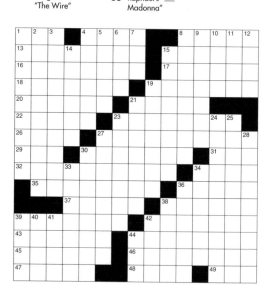

by Josh Knapp

ACROSS

1 "The Lion King" bird
5 Environmental pollutants, for short
9 Easter cake
14 Remote
15 Writer ___ Stanley Gardner
16 "Sounds like ___"
17 Staples of Americana
19 Iraqi P.M. ___ al-Maliki
20 One end of the [circled letters], which opened on 8/15/1914
22 Quanta
24 First female athlete on the front of a Wheaties box
26 Brew that gets its color from oxidation
27 Capillaceous
29 What a check might be delivered in
30 Tribal wear, for short
31 Part of the conjugation of "être"
32 Fiery eruptions
35 Features of many drive-thrus
39 Chicago market, with "the"
40 One with a once-in-a-lifetime experience?
45 Elation
47 ___ Wuornos, "Monster" role for which Charlize Theron won an Oscar
48 "Whew!" feeling
49 Was behind
50 The other end of the [circled letters]
53 Sonatas have four of them
54 What never lets go?
57 Hip place?
58 Second issue?
59 Prefix with zone
60 Gives it up, so to speak
61 N.B.A. coaching great George ___
62 Nobel pursuits?: Abbr.

DOWN

1 When doubled, onetime name in Hollywood
2 Pinnacle of "The Sound of Music"
3 Letter number
4 Deutsch marks?
5 Seed in Mexican cuisine
6 Homie's homes
7 Air bubble
8 Zaire's Mobutu ___ Seko
9 Ad form
10 Evangelist
11 Bird that, curiously, has a yellow breast
12 Bars in a bar?
13 Darth Vader's boyhood nickname
18 ___ Rutherford, the Father of Nuclear Physics
21 Result (from)
22 A pop-up has one
23 So-so
25 The Legend of Zelda platform, briefly
27 Trite
28 Electrical inits.
30 Stable role on TV?
33 "Ta-ta"
34 Boxing souvenir
35 Flight board abbr.
36 Medical product with no conceivable use?
37 Central American danger
38 Enliven
41 Family-friendly category
42 TV's Capt. Picard
43 Fountain feature
44 Suffix with opal
46 They'll rock your world
47 Remote power source
49 Rodeo performer
51 "Out of Africa" writer Dinesen
52 Island sometimes called El Cocodrilo
53 Peculiarity
55 Location of the William Tell legend
56 Lover of Orion, in Greek myth

by Jeff Chen

ACROSS

1 Genre for Django Reinhardt
10 Spaceship Earth setting
15 "Has the whole world gone mad?!"
16 Recipient of a major downgrade in 2006
17 Clicking point
18 Musical Hall of fame collaborator?
19 Stretch before giving birth
20 Islamic repub.
21 Not 100% sold
22 "The ___ true for . . ."
24 Winner of an annual "posedown"
26 One of saintdom's Fourteen Holy Helpers
28 Windbags beat them
29 Ones with low class standards?
32 Speaker connectors?
35 Thing pulled by a "hoss"
36 Her poison killed Creon
37 "The Next President" comedian
38 Boatload
39 Rude response to "Excuse me?"
41 Like some horror films, in modern lingo
42 Maternally related
43 What's round due to too many rounds?
48 2009 Grammy winner for "Crack a Bottle"
50 Giant in jets
51 "Pretty Little Liars" actor Harding
53 Give a powerful electric guitar performance
54 Convalesces
55 Hague Conventions topic
57 Shakespearean title role for Anthony Hopkins
58 Render unwell
59 Farm call
60 Spots for company cuisine

DOWN

1 Campers' annoyances
2 Cry that helps people pull together
3 Prey for an Arctic fox
4 Palindrome property
5 Start of an attention-getting cry
6 Sudden start
7 Starting lineup
8 Crashes, with "out"
9 "B.C." sound effect
10 Louis Braille and Les Paul
11 Cell interiors
12 Card
13 1995–2000 "S.N.L." cast member
14 Where captains go
21 Lament loudly
23 Not tolerate injustice, say
25 Gives elevator eyes
27 Phoenicians, e.g.
29 Sask. doesn't observe it
30 Cross you wouldn't mind bearing?
31 First name in tyranny
32 People's 2007 Sexiest Man Alive
33 Least dismal
34 Shooter's choice, briefly
37 Tacky television transition
39 He said "Music is the space between the notes"
40 Wiener link?
41 1959 #1 hit for the Fleetwoods
43 Southeast Asian coins
44 What goes after cows, ducks and pigs?
45 Close relative of Clio
46 Eric Cartman's mom on "South Park"
47 Packers' measurements
49 "Someone ___ Dream" (Faith Hill country hit)
52 It has a "Los Angeles" spinoff
55 Film director Wenders
56 Character string

by Peter Broda

ACROSS

1 Something that goes from a pit to your stomach?
12 Snarky sound
15 It has billions of barrels
16 Queen of Thebes, in myth
17 One may tell a conductor to slow down
18 Sound of a slug
19 Sashimi selection
20 Buckled
21 Dos little words?
23 Esther of "Good Times"
25 Large part of some herds
28 Brand of bait pellets
29 Fix
30 Walt Disney Concert Hall designer
32 Cop
34 Monarchial support
35 G squared?
37 Spotmatic, e.g., briefly
38 Unhelpful reply to "How did you do that?"
43 Screen entertainers with many gigs?
47 "All the President's Men" figure
49 Like many hipsters
51 Actress Blanchett
52 Pie hole
53 Parts of kingdoms
54 Juan's sweetheart
56 ___ rock (some George Harrison music)
58 & 59 Race that's not very competitive
60 Pill holder
64 Occasion to do a late shift?: Abbr.
65 Member of a "great" quintet
66 ___ Gonçalo, Rio de Janeiro
67 Mideast president who wrote "The Battle for Peace," 1981

DOWN

1 Regulus A and Bellatrix
2 Gets rounds around town?
3 Show fear of
4 Govt. project whose logo depicted a shield in space
5 Danny of the Celtics
6 Curiosity producer
7 First course selection
8 Do battle
9 Counterpart of "abu"
10 "Burn Notice" grp.
11 Freeze
12 Literally, "fire bowl"
13 Doesn't just attract
14 Cache for cash, say
22 1963 Pulitzer winner Leon
24 It's KOH, chemically
26 "The Killing" star Mireille ___
27 Like some lobbies
30 Trip up?
31 T. S. of literature
33 Member of a Latin trio
36 Line to Jamaica in N.Y.C.
38 Bar necessities
39 "Dream" group in Barcelona in 1992
40 Mounted below the surface of
41 Quick Time or RealPlayer format option
42 Like boors vis-à-vis gentlemen
44 Masseur gratifier
45 Raise crops on the Plains, maybe
46 So-called "Helen of the West Indies"
48 Director of the 2012 comedy "This Is 40"
50 Try to pull off, say
53 Epic start
55 Cutting it
57 Replicator, e.g.
61 ___-Boy
62 Old White House nickname
63 Guerra's opposite

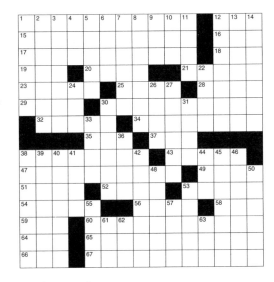

by Sam Ezersky

154

ACROSS
1 Rage
6 Hardly ice outside
10 Places for sprigs
14 Quiet parter?
15 Pie cutter's tool
16 Umber at the opera
17 First part of a hit for this crossword
19 Relative of "Hey, ma"
20 Arc's target, maybe
21 Plat pouch
22 Easter floor mat
24 Pog or Pogs, formerly
26 Lives
29 Bad member to pick?
30 Fly of film
32 Hit, part 2
34 Olympia with a watery realm
36 Perform peace
37 Fried with four legs
38 Covered with slug mud
40 Sorters' quarters
43 Dramatically scored sorceress
44 Ager
46 Hit, part 3
50 Cagey parts, e.g.
51 Early
52 Part of a euro
54 Tige, say
55 Adds a little toe to
57 Like a great bod
59 Bled for a social affair, perhaps
61 Dramatic cry from people who get subbed
62 Last part of the hit
66 Caker, for example

67 Car whose logo is liked?
68 Ever lost to
69 Starts of some chorus lies
70 Eve
71 Chia growth area?

DOWN
1 Crow
2 Vegas would love this type of world
3 Casio game
4 Kat's "I"
5 Slag for sleuths
6 Product made by Moe
7 Kid of poetic work
8 Arm from a Mideast lad
9 Did a baker's job
10 Covert, maybe
11 Margarine might be described thus
12 Grad's opposite

13 Gere of "Gulliver's Travels"
18 User's circuit
23 I pieces
25 You might board yours at the keel if you take a cruise
27 Wig of the old Greek army
28 Program that asks "Are we aloe?," for short
30 Metal worker's claim?
31 Abruptly becomes violet
33 Doe, e.g.
35 Bombs without bags
39 Sci-fi character remembered for her large bus
40 Strad part that becomes frayed
41 Wet like a seesaw

42 Spas that last 52 wks.
43 Bugled strokes
45 Deadly gag
46 Mesa prerequisite
47 Guy who may offer a girl a rig
48 Mystical chat
49 H.L. player
53 Refusal from a boy lass
56 "Ow!"
58 O
60 Murray who's highly raked
63 Be-___
64 Ed of some school addresses
65 Old rival of America

by Timothy Polin

155

ACROSS

1 Poll Internet users on, perhaps
12 Inn stock
15 Code often used for take-home tests
16 W. Coast airport one might think has poor security?
17 Summed up
18 Middle-earth baddie
19 Short order?
20 Kiwi's companion
21 Longtime N.F.L. coach whose name is French for "the handsome"
23 Ordinary person
25 Soprano Grist
27 Neighbor of St. Kitts
28 Symbol of sentimentality
30 Anti-Mafia measure, briefly
32 Eliot title surname
33 Budgetary concern
35 "Miss Julie" composer, 1965
37 Ray often seen over a range
41 As surplus
42 He played John Glenn in 1983 and John McCain in 2012
44 Bo Jackson was one in '89
45 Mideast's Gulf of ___
46 Department store chain founder
48 Like un bébé
52 Costa ___
54 Whaler's direction?
56 Angela Lansbury, e.g.
57 Group sharing a culture
59 Year Bush was re-elected
61 Kroger alternative
62 Mark, as a survey square
63 Singer known as "La Divina"

66 Natural rock climber
67 Words following an understatement
68 Leaves on a trolley, say
69 "Don't worry . . ."

DOWN

1 In-flight calls?
2 Doc Savage portrayer
3 Cousin of a donkey
4 Secured
5 One expected to get beaten
6 Cool red giant
7 The world, to a go-getter?
8 Mark the start of
9 Travel option: Abbr.
10 Word with wall or tower
11 Football Hall-of-Famer Tunnell
12 Juice source for a trendy drink

13 Bo Jackson was one in '89
14 Response to an insult
22 Played like Bird or Trane
24 Notable lifelong bachelor in U.S. history
26 Player of Fin Tutuola on TV
29 Host of 1950s TV's "Bank on the Stars"
31 Longtime Laker Lamar
34 Salon job
36 Answer, quickly
37 Means of furtive escape
38 12-Down, often
39 Neighbor of Georgia
40 "South Pacific" girl
43 Political theorist Carl
47 Steinway competitor
49 Suitable job?
50 "Count me in"
51 Like big hair, often

53 ESPN analyst Garciaparra
55 Sieves, in a way
58 Not unhinged
60 Relocation transportation
64 Travel options: Abbr.
65 Fighting Tigers' sch.

1	2	3	4	5	6	7	8	9	10	11		12	13	14
15												16		
17												18		
19					20					21	22			
23			24		25		26		27					
28				29		30			31		32			
		33		34		35			36					
37	38	39				40		41						
42						43		44						
45				46			47		48		49	50	51	
52			53		54		55		56					
57				58		59			60		61			
62				63	64					65				
66				67										
68				69										

by Daniel Raymon

ACROSS

1 ___ Street, London's onetime equivalent to New York's Wall Street
8 Lurid nightspot
15 Synthetic purplish colorant
16 Took too many courses?
17 Vicks product
18 Rap type
19 Assn. with a "100 Years . . . 100 Movies" list
20 Bygone Acura
22 Non-Roman Caesar
23 Have a dependency
25 "Would you look at that!"
26 Musical title character who "made us feel alive again"
27 What the Sup. Court interprets
29 " ___ in '56" (old campaign button)
30 Plantation machine
31 Hid
33 Sybill Trelawney, in the Harry Potter books
35 Gorp, e.g.
36 Like some projects, for short
37 Mesh with
41 Piece of trash?
45 Slightly ahead
46 "___ man can tether time or tide": Burns
48 Tim Tebow, in college football
49 "Sweet" girl of song
50 Ones with issues?
52 Person holding many positions
53 Ox- tail?
54 Trattoria specification
56 Key holder?
57 Mercury's winged sandals

59 Outlook alternative
61 Parasite
62 Cash in a country bar
63 Parallel bars?
64 Onetime "Lifts and separates" sloganeer

DOWN

1 "The Raising of ___" (Rembrandt painting)
2 Annual heavy metal tour
3 Big name in browsers
4 Popular chip flavor
5 Parisian possessive
6 Kicking oneself for
7 Trapezius neighbor
8 Welders' wear
9 Egg maker
10 Rowlands of "A Woman Under the Influence"
11 Assn.
12 Beverage with a triangular logo
13 Occasionally
14 Kindles, e.g.

21 Pride : lion :: gang : ___
24 Bleeth of "Baywatch"
26 Avon competitor
28 "Do I have to?," for one
30 Extraterrestrial, e.g.
32 Abbr. on a business card
34 URL ender
37 Japanese electronics giant
38 Download from Apple
39 "Funky Cold Medina" rapper
40 Not entirely of one's own volition, say
41 "Cloud Shepherd" sculptor
42 Ferocious Flea fighter, in cartoons
43 Producer of a hair-raising experience?
44 Certain movie house

47 Aldous Huxley's "___ and Essence"
50 Worked with
51 Common comedian's prop
54 Best Picture before "12 Years a Slave"
55 Wife of Albert Einstein
58 Party concerned with civil rights, briefly
60 "If I ___ . . ."

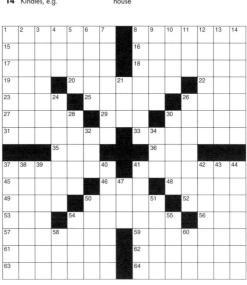

by David Steinberg

157

ACROSS

1 Elderly person on a fixed income
16 Propagandists' detention site
17 Deterioration of standards by competitive forces
18 1957 Patrick White novel adapted into a 1986 opera
19 Comprehends
20 Didn't clash (with)
21 What a chicken feels
24 G.P. grp.
27 Diversified investment strategy
32 Corp. whose name is also its stock symbol
33 L. Frank Baum princess
34 Title heroine of a Wagner opera
35 Ford from the past
37 It's easy to swallow
38 "Beats me"
39 Go outside the calling area, say
41 Dawg
42 Charging for every little thing
45 With 11-Down, become a part of
46 With 53-Down, many Marcel Duchamp works
47 Ray of old pictures
48 It's a mouthful
51 Silents actress Negri
52 Political machine practice
59 Eugenia Washington (co-founder of the Daughters of the American Revolution), to George Washington
60 Tumblers

DOWN

1 Bruin legend
2 Heartlessly abandons
3 Break down
4 Hymn opener
5 Courage
6 Friendly start?
7 Word that is its own synonym when spelled backward
8 Biblical ending
9 Baseball Hall-of-Famer Phil
10 PepsiCo brand
11 See 45-Across
12 Fall mos.
13 D.C. player
14 Like some broody teens
15 Dash letters
20 On hold . . . or what the seven rows of black squares in this puzzle's grid spell in Morse code
21 Pasta ___ (Italian dish, informally)

22 Smooth-leaved ___
23 Much like
24 Some backwoods folks
25 Alvin Ailey's field
26 "Just about done"
28 Metric weight
29 One coming out of its shell?
30 "Me too"
31 Best
36 Contents of a well
39 It's stranded, for short
40 Head-scratching
43 Televised fights?
44 Native New Zealanders
48 Pack (in)
49 Lanford Wilson's "The ___ Baltimore"
50 Messenger de Dieu
51 ___ colada
52 "War and Peace" has a lot of them: Abbr.
53 See 46-Across

54 Silkscreen target
55 Oomph
56 Lang. class
57 Blood test letters
58 Some appliances, for short

by Joe Krozel

158

ACROSS

1 Big chain closed on Sundays
10 Person lacking foresight?
15 Version of a song that's shorter or cleaner than the original
16 Point of origin for some flights
17 Nobody's opposite
18 Overly talkative
19 Cause of many unwelcome lines
20 "Uh-huh"
21 Ratso's given name
22 First name at the U.N., once
24 Predigital beeper?
27 Display
29 Seem forthcoming
30 Malt finisher?
31 Hit Showtime show
32 Nasdaq member?: Abbr.
34 An early Disney cartoon had one
35 BBC World Service std.
36 Contact briefly electronically
39 Like throwbacks
41 You might strain to produce them
43 Chief Chono Ca Pe, e.g.
46 Harmonica piece
47 Part of a funeral procession
48 Use a two-digit confirmation code?
51 Neighbor resort of Snowbird
52 Undergo induction
53 Silver Buffalo Award org.
55 "___ shall live your epitaph to make": Shak.
56 Type of white wine
57 One may soak a competitor
60 "Panic 911" airer
61 Tables or shelves
62 Position
63 Zippy

DOWN

1 Was hoarse
2 It can be a headache
3 Preoccupation
4 "Profiles in Leadership" publisher, briefly
5 "___ 2012" (viral video)
6 Completer of a career Grand Slam in 2009
7 Snake River Plain locale
8 Much-used epithet in hip-hop
9 P.R. setting
10 Prime piece
11 Jones
12 Duke of Illyria, in Shakespeare
13 Final sign
14 Kid-lit character with a long face, in more ways than one
21 Libido
23 National leader?
25 Stylish
26 "___ not thou fear God . . .": Luke 23:40
28 Ingredient in many salad dressings
33 Near
35 Opposite of contracted
37 Linguistically adventurous
38 "Most seeming-virtuous queen," in Shakespeare
40 Try
41 Go on
42 Like some teeth and glass
43 Leitmotif settings
44 Stereotypical wear for the paranoid
45 Connected
49 "Ish"
50 Meets
54 Give ___ (have any interest)
57 Burn prevention stat
58 As
59 Grp. with rules about carrying on?

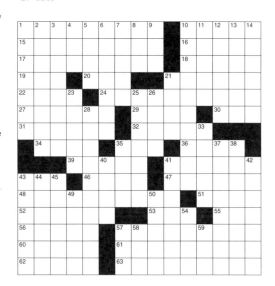

by James Mulhern

ACROSS

1 Queen's music
12 Film developer?: Abbr.
15 "Hasta la vista!"
16 Musician with the 2012 album "Lux"
17 Allows someone to walk, say
18 Big gun on a ship: Abbr.
19 Oxford, e.g., to its students
20 Michael of "Juno"
21 Oxide used in picture tubes
23 "A person who talks when you wish him to listen," per Ambrose Bierce
24 Lead
25 Shots
28 Coddle, e.g.
29 Shack
30 Artistic friend of Zola
31 Sharpshooter's skill
32 Poet Wilfred ___
33 Out of gear?
34 Buchanan in a bookstore
35 Word of logic
36 Moving day multitude
37 Governor or senator follower
38 Caught in a web
40 Certain book, sizewise
41 Makes out
42 Secure neatly, as an umbrella
43 Pioneer in the Nevada gaming industry
44 One of its categories is Agency of the Year
45 With 46-Down, two-in-one movie players
48 It's often an oxide

49 Something avoided in a factory outlet
52 Washington and McKinley: Abbr.
53 Commute, in a way
54 Replies of confusion
55 Stick here and there

DOWN

1 Archaeologists often find what they're looking for in this
2 Counterfeiter fighter, informally
3 Isao of golf
4 At full term
5 "No worries"
6 Comes out with
7 Skiing twins' surname
8 Sister of Phoebe, in myth
9 "Or softly lightens ___ her face": Byron
10 Like many kids' self-made greeting cards
11 Didn't let oneself go, say
12 Lead-in to some written advice
13 Blurred
14 Option for a marinara base
22 Not too big a jerk
23 Old bomber
24 A lot of what makes you you
25 Checked in with loved ones, say
26 Exclamation that might be punctuated "??!?"
27 Put too much weight on
28 Like some potato chips
30 Ceilings
33 From the Union
34 Hebrew for "to the skies"
36 Rival of Captain Morgan
37 ABBA's music

39 ___ Tamid (ever-burning synagogue lamp)
40 Thick spreads
42 Ace on a base
44 Give up
45 One of its fragrances is Poison
46 See 45-Across
47 Rink fooler
50 Small warbler
51 Inits. of Thoreau's mentor

1	2	3	4	5	6	7	8	9	10	11		12	13	14
15												16		
17												18		
19				20					21		22			
			23					24						
25	26	27					28							
29					30							31		
32				33							34			
35				36						37				
38			39					40						
41							42							
43					44						45	46	47	
48				49	50					51				
52				53										
54				55										

by Michael Wiesenberg

160

ACROSS

1 Pro
6 Paper job
15 Words repeated after "I shall no more," in "The Tempest"
16 Say
17 When bars close in Boston
18 TV screen format
19 Subject of a standing order?
21 ___ COIN
22 Super-corny
26 Pair
27 Font menu choice
28 It's between −1 and +1
29 Bag
30 Source of conflict, in antiquity
31 Film, e.g.
33 12/
34 Biker chick, perhaps
35 Dude
38 Invention that prompted NBC to adopt the peacock logo
39 ___ seeds, ingredients in some health drinks
40 "Gotcha," in old lingo
43 Star followers
44 Something that's fallen off a shelf?
45 What an article may refer to
46 Herb used in Thai food
48 Fair
50 Italian after-dinner drink
51 Party to a tryst
55 Toy company that introduced Rubik's Cube
56 Like bulldogs
57 Finely prepare
58 Something on either side of a bridge
59 One advised to take two tablets

DOWN

1 Beset
2 Call from the cellar
3 Like most philosophy dissertations
4 Ones involved in an elaborate courtship
5 Breaks
6 Radar's rank on "M*A*S*H": Abbr.
7 Bank deposit?
8 Universal area
9 Through
10 Kitchen brand
11 Like many new mothers
12 Still being tested
13 One running home, maybe
14 Modern-day "Let's stay in touch"
20 Agave product
23 Montreal eco-tourist attraction
24 Anemone, to name one
25 "Just relax, will you?!"
29 Chase scene producer, for short
32 Classic storyteller who wrote under the pseudonym Knickerbocker
34 Punch
35 Depreciates
36 Valuable commodity in New York City
37 What some homemade signs announce
38 Anchors of some malls
39 Box in a cab
40 Spark
41 Comedian Paul
42 Kind
46 Words that are rarely spoken
47 Teller of many tales
49 Unscrewed
52 [Thumbs up]
53 End of many a long race: Abbr.
54 P.E.I. setting

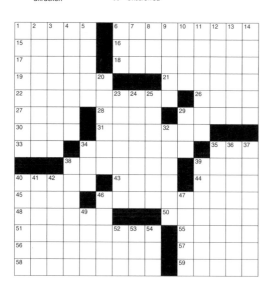

by Josh Knapp

161

ACROSS

1 Self-praise couched in self-deprecation, in modern lingo
11 Story lines
15 Wanting
16 What marketers might follow
17 2013 Golden Globe winner for "Girls"
18 Colony in ancient Magna Graecia
19 "Downton Abbey" title
20 Four-star figs.
21 Risotto relative
22 Refrain syllable
23 Going green?
24 South American cowboy
26 Animal that may swim on its back
28 It's often checked on a cell
30 ___-soul (style of Erykah Badu and Lauryn Hill)
31 Talent scout's find, informally
33 Public
35 Beginning of a process of elimination
37 One who gets numbers by calling numbers
40 Bathes
44 Coach Parseghian
45 44-Across's "Fighting" team
47 Between, to Balzac
48 One living in urban poverty, pejoratively
50 Baby docs
52 ___ pop
53 Contemporary and compatriot of Debussy
54 You may drop a big one
56 Toon toned down for the 1930s Hays Code
57 Resort options

58 A nerd may not have one
60 Some tributes
61 Alcopop relative
62 Christie novel title that, without spaces, is a man's name
63 New lease on life

DOWN

1 There's no place to go but down from here
2 Make public
3 Obamacare obligation
4 Fourth of July, for Calvin Coolidge, informally
5 Was up
6 Level
7 Unit of energy?
8 First name in Chicago politics
9 Not level
10 Peach

11 Eschewed takeout, say
12 Stuffed chili pepper
13 How you may feel after taking allergy medication
14 Shore dinner
21 Spots where artists mix?
23 Nickname for Oliver Cromwell
25 Turkish dough
27 Unstable compound
29 Ties up in a slip
32 ___ desk (newsroom assignment)
34 Either director of "True Grit"
36 Negligee
37 Fire
38 Sentinel's place
39 Taylor of "Twilight"
41 Chef de cuisine's shout
42 Publishing house employee
43 Dr. Ruth, for one

46 Bros
49 "Divine" showbiz persona
51 Bad place for a whale
55 Spots annoying teens
56 Stain
58 Match.com abbr.
59 ___ Lonely Boys (2004 Grammy winners)

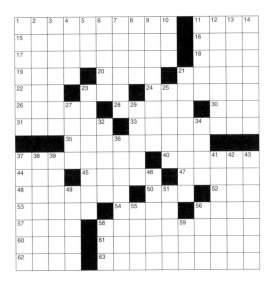

by Finn Vigeland

ACROSS

1 Goes quickly after takeoff?
8 Series of antecedents
14 Professor who tries to kill Harry Potter
16 ___ pectoris
17 One not favored
18 Randomly distributed
19 PBJ filling?
20 16:9, say
22 Muscles for some fraternity guys?
24 Shake
25 Mo. of National Grandparents' Day
26 Raft
27 Height
29 Viewfinder?
30 Some nerve!
32 Nobelist Frederick ___, pioneer in radiochemistry
33 Fashion series since 2004
37 Asner's "Elf" role
38 Browning, for one
39 It might be found in a café
40 Spanish interrogative
41 All-nighter, maybe
45 Writer Rand
46 Cold-shoulder
48 Mackenzie of "The Facts of Life"
49 Legerdemain
53 Cooperstown inst.
54 Words before and after "Am too!"
55 Longest continuous corporate partner of the Olympic Games
57 Get misty
58 Fall guy?
59 Galley slaves, e.g.
60 Least abundant

DOWN

1 Teams
2 Smuggling aid
3 Judges 14:14 has the only one in the Bible
4 "Maid of Athens, ___ we part": Byron
5 Hamlet takes a stab at it
6 Some gym shoes
7 Spill
8 Holds up
9 Word with deux or nous
10 Home of the Unesco World Heritage Site Fatehpur Sikri
11 Light refreshment
12 Hard to handle
13 Splendid array
15 "Life's Good" sloganeer
21 Sportsperson who may take a bow?
23 Situation that makes a double play impossible
27 Tucked away
28 Snap
29 Dungeons & Dragons attributes
31 Wear for the weary
32 TV inits. since 10/11/75
33 Feature of many a McDonald's
34 Macs and such
35 Part of a crater
36 Saucer, perhaps
37 Red juice hybrid
40 Contemptible sort
42 In
43 They take bows
44 Terrible one?
46 Comb
47 Certain address starter
48 Yoga pose
50 About
51 Some Red Cross supplies
52 Single-serving coffee holder
56 Abbr. found at the 56-Down of this puzzle's four longest answers

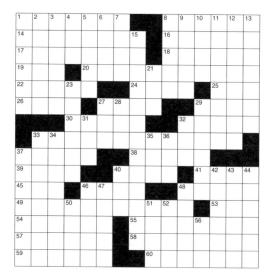

by Erik Agard

ACROSS

1 "Ninotchka" setting
6 Fad dance of the 1930s
10 Swedish Air Force supplier
14 Hollywood job
15 Water bearer
16 Lady Antebellum, e.g.
17 Someone might call your number this evening
19 Asian tourist magnet
20 Delayed sensation?
21 1920s–'30s debate opponent of Einstein
22 15-Across shape
23 "The road of excess leads to the palace of ___": William Blake
25 Succumb to drowsiness
26 Exceed 21 in twenty-one
28 Orchard Field, today
30 Spending time unprofitably
34 Little homewreckers?
35 Some carved Victorian toys
36 Strong and durable, in a way
37 Maid
38 Deli offering
39 Gin cocktail
43 They're on during the wee hours, briefly
46 Arab League member
48 Lengthened unnecessarily
51 Roofing material
52 1963 song investigated by the F.B.I. for supposedly obscene lyrics
53 Cartridge fillers
54 Forever, basically

55 In the intervening time
56 Cole Porter's "___ Magnifique"
57 Three-player card game
58 Wound up

DOWN

1 Brewer of Schlitz, nowadays
2 Catlike, in a way
3 Soprano Fleming
4 "Splendor in the Grass" screenwriter
5 Telegraphy word
6 Secretly carrying (off)
7 Weathercast numbers
8 Fruit grower's bane
9 Reach
10 Uninformed guess
11 Ancient mariners
12 Banned items at Wimbledon
13 Left the gate, say
18 Post office workers?
24 Hard-to-escape situation
26 Philosopher who wrote "Superstition is the religion of feeble minds"
27 Working while others play?
29 Improves
30 Answers wrongly?
31 Ultimate degree
32 Fault finder?
33 Systematize
34 Where firedamp can form
35 Like Tik-Tok in the Land of Oz
40 Runs without moving
41 Small tributary
42 Ritzy gym feature
43 Egyptian monetary unit
44 Power, slangily
45 Jousting need
47 First flight locale
49 "Somethin' ___" (Eddie Cochran song)
50 Dispatch

by Patrick Berry

164

ACROSS

1 Start of a weird infraction?
9 Sushi offering
14 First Indian tribe to sign a treaty with the U.S. government
15 Hand in hand
16 Eskimo wear
17 Hike, e.g.
18 Mideast pops?
19 Smoke without fire?
21 Naval petty off.
22 What was once cool?
23 Gray figures?
27 One-man Broadway hit of 1989
29 Only one U.S. prez has had one
32 Straight talker's slangy phrase
37 Country standard
38 Words from a good buddy
39 On the side
40 X or Y preceder
41 Site of class struggles?: Abbr.
42 Floor
43 One N.B.A. All-Star Game team
46 One telling you where to get off, for short?
49 High ranking?
55 Introductory ballet instruction
56 Whence the word "alcohol"
57 Listen here!
59 Words of support from an organization
60 Reacts to, as a nagging request
61 Game keeper?
62 Tiramisu ingredient

DOWN

1 Guesstimate opening
2 Deep-sea explorer William
3 Explain
4 Beginning of a seasonal refrain
5 Hurtful outbursts?
6 Playboy
7 Shortstop Aybar who was a 2011 Gold Glove winner
8 Start of an elimination
9 Time that little Susie is woken in the 1957 hit "Wake Up Little Susie"
10 Lo-cal
11 Military group
12 Canterbury's home
13 Beat by a whisker
15 Who said "I have a wonderful psychiatrist that I see maybe once a year, because I don't need it. It all comes out onstage"
20 Easily passes
24 Name in 2000 headlines
25 Mates
26 Old age
28 Early online forum
29 Inane
30 Spangle, say
31 "___ trifle!"
32 Having much at stake
33 ___ asada
34 Parade V.I.P.
35 Cockeyed
36 Song that ends "O dolcezze perdute! O speranze d'amor, d'amor, d'amor!"
44 Challenge for defenders
45 Bygone royalty
47 Measures of one's writing?
48 Mind
49 Shooters
50 Israeli conductor Daniel
51 Rain forest rodent
52 Aid in an uphill climb
53 Country name pronounced by natives in two syllables
54 Atlantic City resort, informally, with "the"
55 Common cleaning scent
58 Hole number

by Martin Ashwood-Smith and George Barany

ACROSS

1 Ones who get lighter sentences?
10 1983 action comedy with the tagline "When these guys hit the streets, guess what hits the fan"
15 "Hold on one cotton-pickin' minute!"
16 Band-Aid inventor Dickson
17 Situation that's gone absurdly out of control
18 Car or cellphone feature
19 Relative of Cie.
20 Exchange words
22 Land of the poet Máirtín Ó Direáin
24 Doctors' orders
25 Order (around)
26 City on the Seine
28 Ill-tempered
30 Victor at Gaines's Mill and Cold Harbor
31 One whose word is gospel?
33 Steadiness in leadership
35 ___ scale
37 Corn bread
38 Pfizer cold and flu medicine
42 Result of equal opposing forces
46 Number of African countries with español as an official language
47 Mild cigar
49 Pioneer of Dadaism
50 Auto parts giant
52 Pope Francis and others
54 "There!"
55 Leading lady?
58 Country with a red, white and blue flag: Abbr.
59 Dianne of "Parenthood," 1989

60 Musical "Mr."
62 Like much slapstick
63 Either way
64 Choice words?
65 Combined Latin/Jamaican/hip-hop genre

DOWN

1 Casting directors?
2 Horticultural problem caused by overwatering
3 Kind of rock
4 Direction from Luxembourg to Nürnberg
5 "Me neither," formally
6 Response to a lousy deal
7 Pitiful group
8 Sub-Saharan tormentors
9 Amasses
10 No longer working
11 Carr who wrote "The Alienist"
12 Company that makes Silly Putty
13 The Hebrew Hammer of Major League Baseball
14 Puzzled
21 Minute Maid Park team
23 Ronald who directed "The Poseidon Adventure"
27 College org. for sailors-to-be
29 Musical matchmaker
32 Muslim name that means "successor to Muhammad"
34 Sympathy
36 Thumb key
38 "Chinatown" co-star
39 Queued
40 Children
41 Talk up
43 Menace, in a way
44 Results from

45 Onetime Minnesota governor who ran for the G.O.P. presidential nomination nine times
48 Continuing obsessively
51 Bret Harte/Mark Twain collaboration
53 Urban Dictionary fodder
56 Record label for Cream and the Bee Gees
57 "And Winter Came . . ." singer, 2008
61 M.A. hopeful's hurdle

by Tracy Bennett

166

ACROSS

1. Two-man band?
9. Blush-inducing
15. Anti-spill, say
16. Green machine
17. Exponential unknown
18. "Anticipate the difficult by managing the easy" philosopher
19. Cause of a stinging breakup?
20. Less significant
21. Sonnet extender?
22. Enjoyed muchly
23. Mount ___, Charley Weaver's hometown
24. See 41-Across
27. Partner of many
30. Lambs, to Lucius
31. One being strung along?
35. Decline dramatically
37. 180s
38. Title subject of a search in a 2003 film
39. "Twilight," e.g.
40. Gets a clue, with "up"
41. With 24-Across, barbecue finger stainer
44. "___ really help"
45. Storm designation
46. To whom Charles Darwin dedicated "Different Forms of Flowers"
49. Bartending tool
53. In-flight
54. Mixer for losers?
55. Pioneer in literary realism
56. "Servant of the Bones" author
57. "Really?"
58. Ditch

DOWN

1. Like some straws
2. Have prestige
3. Org. that, when spelled backward, is an old-timey exclamation
4. What Gollum calls the Ring in "The Lord of the Rings"
5. Nadir's opposite
6. Dove's dream
7. Aids after blanking out
8. Slip
9. Service providers?
10. Statement of confidence
11. Musical component
12. Last part of "Waiting for Godot"
13. Was a slug
14. ___ Lane, London theater locale
20. Southeast Asian fruits with large, thick spines
22. Burgundy or claret
24. "Twilight," e.g.
25. Oodles
26. "Adventure most ___ itself": Emily Dickinson
27. Empty-headedness
28. Word with deep or dead
29. Newest fashion
31. Mother superior?
32. It's named for a Scand. god of battle
33. "Pencils down!"
34. Nonhuman Earth orbiter of 1961
36. Trip planner's option: Abbr.
40. More like a sheet?
41. Fanatically militant sort
42. "Veep" actor ___ Whitlock Jr.
43. Very much
45. Widening agent in medicine
47. Goggle
48. Gold-certifying grp.
49. 0.5, for 30°
50. ___ rage (result of juicing)
51. Sister brand of CorningWare
52. Shipping hazard
54. The U.N.'s ___ Hammarskjöld

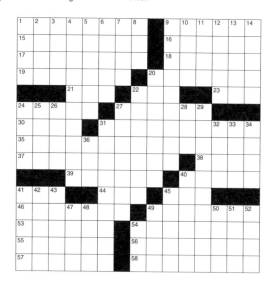

by Julian Lim

ACROSS

1 Major artery
8 No longer under consideration
12 "Absolutely!"
13 Raid target
14 Something a bride brings to a marriage
15 Originate
16 Like some nuts
17 Black-and-white
19 Sunroof, maybe
20 Count at the breakfast table
21 Golden Gophers' sch.
22 Woman's shift
23 Guilty sensation
24 Italian red
25 Bath site: Abbr.
26 Number 10-Down
27 Routes: Abbr.
30 Indian condiment
31 Sugar source
32 Was a hit, say
33 Ballerina descriptor
34 Blackened
35 Showed unhappiness, in a way
36 Mars, notably
37 1949 show tune with the lyric "Here am I, your special island!"
38 Olympian's first name that sounds like another Olympian's name
39 Site of the largest sports arena in Europe
41 Cupid's teammate
42 Ranch dressing?
43 Small change
44 Quickly reproduced

DOWN

1 Suggesting, as an idea
2 Extending the life of
3 City where the Lehigh and Delaware Rivers meet
4 Scene of W.W. II airstrikes
5 Do some yard work
6 Org. concerned with bridges and canals
7 "Unfair!"
8 Persian ruler dubbed "the Great"
9 Strand, in a way
10 See 26-Across
11 One changing locks?
12 Stage assistant
13 Dearth
14 Play group
18 Presidential candidate who wrote "No Apology"
20 Pulled up to a bar
22 Yakker
24 Spanish/Mexican pastry
26 Transportation for Helios
27 Judge of movies
28 Slights
29 Large bowls
30 River that flows past four universities
31 Touch-type?
32 2014 Kentucky Derby winner California ___
33 Low-tech hacker?
34 Dinner chicken
35 Certain shortcut
36 Only major U.S. city with a radio station whose call letters spell the city's name
37 Title in children's literature
40 Hail and farewell

by David Steinberg

168

ACROSS

1 Quite cheaply
12 Green piece
15 Guinness record-setter for "highest-rated TV series" (scoring 99 out of 100 on Metacritic.com)
16 Org. with a radon hotline
17 Ones in praise of angels?
18 Burmese greeting
19 Times in classifieds
20 Looking up to
22 Tom Petty's "___ So Bad"
23 Game of pure chance
25 Group of very small stars?
26 Third party label: Abbr.
27 Green piece?
29 Aid for collecting some samples
31 It's shown in much storm reportage
35 Biblical land in what is now Yemen
36 Get rid of jerks?
38 Mess (around)
39 Ripens
40 Tourist city on the Yamuna
41 Common scale topper
42 Spanish 101 verb
43 Country that includes the islands of Gozo and Comino
45 Bit of censure
46 Laotian money
49 Manhattan architect?
52 Spread of book and film
53 N.L. West team, on scoreboards
54 Far from scarce
57 Place for a monitor, for short
58 2014 N.B.A. M.V.P.
59 Omega, in physics
60 Millions of people swipe them

DOWN

1 Austen's "Northanger ___"
2 Architectural crossbeam
3 100,000,000 maxwells
4 Makes bale?
5 Clears
6 Year before the emperor Trajan was born
7 Key key?
8 They may be in a mess: Abbr.
9 Help complete a job
10 City in old westerns
11 Villager station wagon, e.g.
12 Like some chocolate
13 Restaurant availability
14 Bud, slangily
21 Catch badly?
23 Having gone south
24 Cartoon supplier
26 It's relatively lacking in iodine
27 "Benson" actor Phillips
28 Baker with a trumpet
30 Deep end?
31 Eastern leader
32 Force to walk with the arms pinned behind
33 Turtle locale, maybe
34 "Look ___!"
35 Animated hero of 2001
37 Big chicken
41 One after another?
44 Some desk materials
45 16th-century council site
46 Best Director of 1947 and 1954
47 Memorable hurricane of 2011
48 Gauchos, e.g.
49 "Soap" actor Jimmy
50 Many an exploding star
51 Eastern leader
52 Ring combatant
55 Big payroll service co.
56 "Of course!"

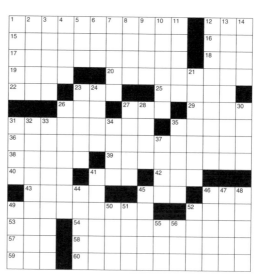

by Evans Clinchy

169

ACROSS

1 Something running on a cell
10 "The Waltons" co-star Ralph
15 Starting to succeed
16 Opera title boy
17 Been exposed to an awful lot
18 Like Royal Albert Hall
19 Roofing option
20 "Palindromania!" writer Jon
21 Male duck
22 Be up
24 Ones hanging around delis?
26 Flashers at a rock concert
30 Let up
31 Superslim
34 Some QB protectors
35 Out of service?: Abbr.
36 Gouge, e.g.
37 Dog tag?
38 Thespian Thurman
39 One who's often 31-Across
43 Orbiting Galaxy, e.g.
45 Hulu offerings
46 Like a cat-o'-nine-tails' nine tails
48 Spitfire org.
49 Paul who pioneered in quantum mechanics
50 Means to deep spiritual insight
53 Malaria-fighting compound during W.W. II
56 Development sites?
57 "V for Vendetta" writer
60 "Le Bassin aux Nymphéas" painter
61 Tabs, e.g.
62 Lead character in seasons 1–3 of "Homeland"
63 One-run homers

DOWN

1 Start of many records
2 Prime draft pick
3 Two-time belligerent against the British Empire
4 Country ___
5 "Magnum, P.I." wear
6 Things dealt with in passing?
7 Like many dogs' tails
8 Faint
9 TV's Goober and others
10 Was ducky?
11 Lacking scruples
12 2007 satirical best seller
13 2007 Jamie Foxx film set in Saudi Arabia
14 Many future monarchs
22 What atoms may have
23 Oakland Oaks' org.
25 Consist of
26 Overawed
27 Church-owned newsweekly, for short
28 Only Hispanic performer with an Emmy, Grammy, Oscar and Tony
29 ___ Club
32 Player motivator
33 Olympian troublemaker
37 Person's sphere of operation
39 Easy street's location?
40 Had
41 Town at the tip of Italy's "heel"
42 Carrying people, for short?
44 Didn't just peek
47 Couples
51 Potpourri
52 Fine ___ (Irish political party)
53 Dummy
54 "Consarn it all!"
55 Danny Ocean's ex-wife in "Ocean's Eleven"
58 Some mail for a mag
59 "Will ya look at that!"

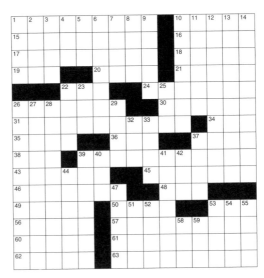

by Michael Ashley

ACROSS

1 Some military settings?
9 Pants part
15 Part of a bar code?
16 "Annie ___," old Scottish love song
17 Atlantis section
18 Sharp
19 Car radio button
20 Droids have them
22 When repeated, aerobics class cry
23 The Joker, e.g.
26 Certain punch
29 One in a one-on-one session
30 With 14-Down, literary yes-man
33 Connecting word
34 "Wait ___!" ("Hold on there!")
35 Strong ale, in British lingo
36 One who didn't make it to the office?
38 Classic British cars that pioneered in rear engines
39 They may be picked up by dogs
40 Integral course of study, briefly?
41 "The thing is . . ."
42 Bakery purchase
43 Competition where the last one standing wins
44 Current setting
45 Scorpio hunter of film
48 Noted avoider of the color red
50 Be full
51 Court star Nadal, informally
54 Really move
56 Oner
59 Parts of the Navy's full dress blues
60 Actor with Adam Sandler in "Funny People"
61 Leave one's company?
62 Like some business letters

DOWN

1 "Sheesh!"
2 Big things on Capitol Hill
3 Former Zairian leader Mobutu ___ Seko
4 "A hint of lovely oblivion," per D. H. Lawrence
5 Modern kind of campaign
6 Letters with a view
7 Brand once plugged by John Madden
8 First Christian martyr
9 Grip
10 "Batman" villain ___ al Ghul
11 Exceed
12 Subject of "The Word" on the first episode of "The Colbert Report"
13 Recognize
14 See 30-Across
21 Literary figure whose name is a letter short of something he wrote
24 Native Arizonans
25 Aid for clumsy thumbs
26 "Stop" at 44-Across
27 "Consider it done"
28 Abandoned storage units?
31 Say "amen," say
32 Gomer's biblical husband
35 Cobbler, at times
37 Walking very quietly, say
38 Dish whose name comes from the Latin for "ink pot"
40 Stuck
43 Kvass component
46 Statistical method for comparing the means of two groups
47 Start of a cartoon cry
48 Waste of a vote?
49 Wile
52 Order
53 Egg chair designer Jacobsen
55 Xerox option: Abbr.
57 Wrestler Flair
58 Pap

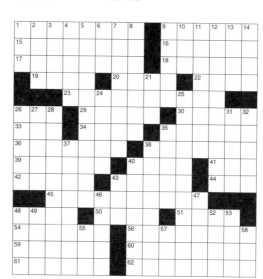

by Evan Birnholz

ACROSS

1 Times for speaking one's mind?
10 Coarse
15 Spot for shooting stars
16 Finish putting on pants, say
17 Became a bachelor, maybe
18 Onetime Coleco competitor
19 Rom-___ (some films)
20 Up to the present time
21 Beyond blue
22 Trivial Pursuit board location
23 Agreements
25 Richard March ___ (inventor of the rotary printing press)
26 Remotely monitored event, informally
28 Plum or pear
29 "Sharknado" channel
30 Save
32 Sleep on it
34 "Ash Wednesday" poet
36 Groups with play dates?
40 "Brokeback Mountain" role
42 "Hurry up!," en español
43 Henchman first seen in "The Spy Who Loved Me"
46 Stationery store stock
48 Pusillanimous
49 ___ Aduba of "Orange Is the New Black"
50 Stop obsessing
52 Not just a pop group, for short?
53 Tilting poles
55 Triton's domain, in myth
56 Dart
57 Two-time N.B.A. All-Star Brand
58 Free
60 Flowering plant named for a Greek god
61 Saloons
62 Onetime sponsor of "I Love Lucy"
63 "Boy, am I having fun!"

DOWN

1 Diagram showing company positions, briefly
2 Detours
3 Title carpenter of an 1859 novel
4 Watch things, for short
5 Condensed vapour
6 Patient looks?
7 Most fitting
8 People with signs at airports, e.g.
9 Part of E.S.T.: Abbr.
10 Bygone emperors
11 "Lovely" one of song
12 It may elicit a shrug
13 Not doubting
14 ___ sense
21 Nissan offering
23 Took courses at home
24 "Faster than shaving" brand
27 Yugoslavian-born winner of nine Grand Slam tournaments
29 One with a short hajj
31 $, € and £
33 Johnny Depp role of 2013
35 Formatting palette choice
37 Site of an annual encierro
38 They think they're special
39 Least excited
41 Outfit worn with goggles
43 Things downed at Churchill Downs
44 Rhododendron relative
45 Chinese appetizer
47 Rear ends
50 Actress/singer Lotte
51 Pot
54 Bop
56 Thwart
58 ___ Friday's
59 Start of an alley-oop

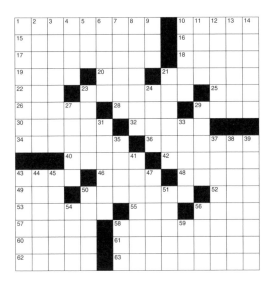

by Patrick Blindauer

172

ACROSS

1 Sting, e.g.
5 100th anniversary of Disney's "Fantasia"
9 Singer Aguilera's nickname
14 Not well, say
15 Second
16 Conventions
17 Coming or going
19 Shows of appreciation for services provided?
20 Characters from Sophocles
21 Prideful?
22 "Born again" woman
23 Figureheads?
24 Most laggardly
26 Pabst product
29 Some Arabian food
30 ___ Lumpur
31 Needles
36 "Huh?!"
38 How Marilyn Monroe sang "Happy Birthday" to President Kennedy
39 Blank
40 City near Arches National Park
41 Queen's "We Will Rock You" and others
42 Requiem Mass part
46 Musical partner of DJ Spinderella and Salt
47 Bit of writing that's slashed?
48 Household brand that's an anagram of 47-Across
50 Homophone of 55-Down
53 Minute hands, in a way
54 Sci-fi disturbances
56 Early Trinity College affiliation: Abbr.
57 It's hair-raising
58 When Hamlet says "The rest is silence"
59 Leaves in
60 Actor Bean of "Troy"
61 Grate

DOWN

1 Colorful breakfast option
2 Mysore Palace resident
3 Focus of some philanthropy
4 So says
5 They come and go
6 Sushi bar servings
7 Double-crossed?
8 Fraternity house cry
9 Map phrase
10 Rourke's co-star in "The Wrestler"
11 Greek goddess of peace
12 Leche drinkers
13 What you will?
18 Certain character set
23 They're easily caught
25 Ear-related
26 Lift things?
27 Sassiness, slangily
28 Spring fall
29 Bathroom brand
31 1977 PBS sensation
32 Pair of hearts?
33 Trumpeter Jones
34 What a soldier may be at?
35 Heads of some towns in Quebec?: Abbr.
37 ___ Pueblo (Unesco World Heritage site)
41 Half of a cigarette?
42 Cuts down
43 A little off
44 Fast ___
45 Ceiling support
46 Black-and-white creature
49 Skip it
50 Black-and-white creature
51 Some N.F.L. workers
52 Do something polite
55 Thrust provider

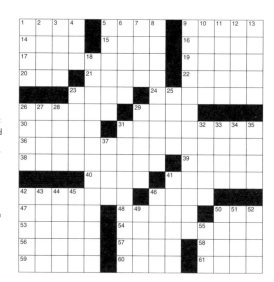

by Patrick Blindauer

ACROSS

1. Boston and Chicago, but not Seattle
10. Diddly-squat
14. Inuit's transport
15. Oscar nominee for "Fiddler on the Roof"
16. Recommended
17. Photoshop effect
18. Bright lights
19. What naturals have
21. With 24-Across, witchcraft, e.g.
22. Up
23. Sea-___
24. See 21-Across
25. Ring of islands?
26. Barely clear, in a way
29. Expert
32. Like Fortunato, in Poe's "The Cask of Amontillado"
33. "The Cask of Amontillado," e.g.
34. Ease
35. Predators in the "Predator" films, for short
36. Some I.R.A.'s
39. "Be on the lookout" signal, in brief
40. ___ country (rustic locale)
43. Gallows ___
44. Anthrax cousin
47. Prey for a dingo
48. Helpful
49. Get ready to click, maybe
51. Ora pro ___
52. Having human form
53. ___ chic
54. Didn't kill each other

DOWN

1. Where primatologist Dian Fossey worked
2. "We're in trouble now!"
3. Gambol
4. TV colonel
5. 20th-century first lady
6. Grp. with suits and cases
7. Easy decision
8. Start of an Eastern title
9. Fusses
10. Book after Hosea
11. Desire
12. Introduction to English?
13. Social gathering
15. Grp. with a lot of baggage
20. British kitchen accessory
22. Like the words "hoagie" and "kitty-corner"
25. Actor with the line "Rick! Rick, help me!"
27. Small dams
28. "___, like lightning, seeks the highest places": Livy
29. Base men?
30. Some E.R. cases
31. Topping for skewered meat
32. Idiot box
33. Desire
34. The son on "Sanford and Son"
36. Adam's apple coverer
37. X
38. Blackened
41. Parrot
42. Prefix with -graphic
43. Betty Boop and Bugs Bunny
45. "The way things are . . ."
46. Tous ___ jours (daily: Fr.)
47. Actress Russell of "Felicity"
50. Adolphe with an instrument named after him

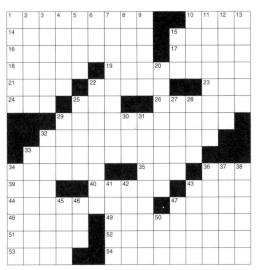

by Mary Lou Guizzo and Jeff Chen

174

ACROSS

1 Send
6 Future works?
11 Apricot or eggplant
16 Reveal
17 Husband of Elisheba
18 Laughable
19 81 + 27
21 Lists for
22 Bee relative
23 Kind of sleep
24 Get out of the line
26 Supertrendy
27 It's conducted in a theater
28 Old Memorial Coliseum player, for short
30 Utter
32 Staff with notes
34 61 + 86
39 He is one
41 National Junior Tennis League co-founder
42 Supervising
43 The Apostle of Cuban Independence
46 Checkout line?
48 Upgrade, as a shower
50 Explicatory words
51 Powerful guy
53 Digs near the ocean, perhaps
54 Miss dismissal
56 ___ a time
57 Ends of scissors?
58 Like illegal charades clues
59 1977 law school memoir
61 Flip
63 56 × 42
66 European Parliament locale
70 Blanket material
71 Crude
73 Wicked
74 Block number?: Abbr.
77 1989 AP Female Athlete of the Year
79 Sans le ___ (broke: Fr.)

80 "Go ask your mother" elicitor
81 Cul-de-sac, in some addresses
83 33 − 21
86 Match
87 Like some coincidences
88 Wind stopper?
89 Sentence units
90 Cans
91 Lay low?

DOWN

1 Jabbers, at times
2 Unhesitatingly go for
3 Threads
4 Word with bag or board
5 Developing option: Abbr.
6 Comparatively trouble-free
7 South American reptile
8 Eruption cause
9 Turn down a raise?
10 Comprehensive
11 "Academica" author
12 Subject of the tribute album "Every Man Has a Woman"
13 Eye liner?
14 Well aware of
15 Hinge (upon)
20 Cut from a log, maybe
25 Lorelei, notably
28 Novel about Dolores Haze
29 1979 comedy set at Camp North Star
31 #1 fans
33 Take after all?
35 Bolt with gold
36 Utopias lack them
37 ___ Porter, "Ally McBeal" role
38 Belts
40 "Newhart" production co.
43 No big deal
44 Be crazy about
45 Change the plot of
47 Carrying
49 Pop's ___ Brothers
52 Fleece

55 Tool along
60 John Tesh fan, maybe
62 Be crazy about
64 Team once owned by Gene Autry
65 & 67 Signer of the Oslo Accords
68 Like boxers
69 Paper cutter?
72 Shakes off
74 Not at all creaky
75 Ballet move
76 ___ bean
78 Not taken
80 Either "Inside Llewyn Davis" director
82 Tilt-A-Whirl part
84 "Che ___ è?" ("What time is it?": It.)
85 Abbr. on a Topps card

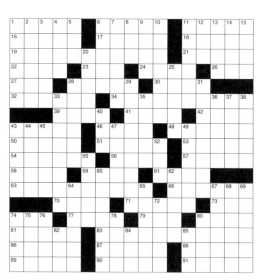

by Trip Payne

ACROSS

1 Kierkegaardian concept
6 Discharge from the R.A.F.
11 Org. that regulates tobacco products
14 Archibald ___, birth name of Cary Grant
15 Commercial blockers?
17 Title film character whose last name is Patel
18 Observances of the law
19 Car door feature
21 Rancho ___ (famed fossil site)
22 Very flexible
25 Like some humor
26 Place to stay
27 Into very small pieces
28 Essence
29 Horn of Africa native
30 Was bossy?
31 It might be beneath your notice
34 Really tired
35 Put right on paper
36 "That was unexpected!"
37 So far
38 1970s fad items
41 English channel
42 Two-person matchup on ice
44 University dubbed "The Country Club of the South"
46 Talking-to
47 California city whose name describes its location
50 TV producer Michaels
51 "Will do!"
52 Word with city or circle
53 Brief reproach
54 Regions
55 Mariachi's earnings

DOWN

1 Basic thing
2 Electrical cell
3 Decisive board game victory
4 Warrior's collection
5 Again and again?
6 Ticket info
7 Stretcher carrier, for short
8 Wharton deg.
9 Buffalo Bill's Wild West Show performer
10 Gluten-rich food
11 Typical sedan
12 Checked
13 Put to trial
16 Mouth, slangily
20 Viscous stuff
23 Girl's name that begins the lyrics of Neil Diamond's "Solitary Man"
24 Lines of reasoning that go nowhere
28 Mackinaw or Norfolk
29 Malamute's burden
30 Green keeper
31 Amount in six figures, say
32 In dire straits
33 Davis of "Of Human Bondage"
34 Penguin part
37 Muscle type
38 Rustic agitators
39 World's third-largest island
40 Changes directions, say
42 The San Diego Zoo's Gao Gao or Zhen Zhen
43 Hearth material
45 Are allowed to
48 "Alibi ___" (Ring Lardner story)
49 D.O.J. division

by Patrick Berry

176

ACROSS

1 Up-coming world phenomenon?
10 Material for a float
15 Anthrax, potentially
16 Big name in old strings
17 Notable switcher from Democrat to Republican to Independent
18 Not ripped
19 Offensive observance?
20 Binder?
21 Really into something
22 See 4-Down
24 It's turned before bolting
26 Like emissions from some 40-Down
27 Put out
29 Life preserver?
31 Puts in
33 Some notes
34 Adversaire's opposite
35 Aid in creating a part
37 Phils' rivals
39 Settings for donors, briefly
42 Pick, say
44 Allama Iqbal International Airport locale
48 Searchlight in comics
51 Searchlight element
52 Number line
53 1914 Belgian battle line
55 Searchlight element
56 Eisner's successor at Disney
57 Cause of temporary blindness
59 "Die Fledermaus" soprano
60 A tiny bit strange?
62 Banking facilities?
64 Still to be attained
65 First-and-second track options
66 "Sleepless in Seattle" quartet
67 Bureaucratic environmental regulations

DOWN

1 Cyclic recession
2 Banking facilitator
3 Get rid of
4 With 22-Across, obsolescent club
5 Eco-chic clothing option
6 Capital across the river from its sister city Salé
7 Drug used in aversion therapy
8 Assaults
9 Like Spender and Spenser: Abbr.
10 Relief may follow it
11 Libertine
12 Song whose title follows "Para bailar"
13 Harry and Wills acquired one in 2005
14 Puddle-jumper
23 Minute minute part: Abbr.
25 Author Hubbard
26 Pump add-on
28 Hot
30 Literally, "skyward"
32 Blanket produced in Mexico City
36 Too thin
38 Wooley of "Rawhide"
39 Like some references
40 Futuristic fryers
41 Goes with the flow?
43 One pulling a calf, say
45 A tiny bit
46 Detailed plan
47 How bands move
49 Bob may follow it
50 "Sainted maiden" of literature
54 Jamestown colonist
58 Cousin of a gnatcatcher
61 Some chessmen: Abbr.
62 N.B.A. scoring stat
63 Alternative to 10

by Barry C. Silk

ACROSS

1. ___ Store (debut of 2008)
4. Space on a bookshelf?
9. Bush found in Florida
12. "___ funny!"
13. Stray away
15. Short coming?
16. Boring thing
17. Part of a bridge truss
18. Apology opener
19. 10th-century pope
21. War room topic
23. "The Alphabet" artist
24. ___ itself
26. Sponges, say
27. Fly in the face of someone?
29. Mau ___ (forever, in Hawaii)
30. It may have a high grain content
31. B, for one
34. Bb, for one
35. Bb6, for one
36. Score at the half?
38. "You've got mail!" and such
41. Cry of innocence
42. Caesar's force
44. Notable 1979 exile
46. Invisible thing that's inflatable
47. They often succeed
51. States on a game board, e.g.: Abbr.
52. Soap of a medical nature
55. Fancy invitation feature
56. They might catch some rays

57. Some 24/7 facilities
58. Spanish for "basket"

DOWN

1. "Ben-Hur: ___ of the Christ"
2. Basis of the Nintendo Wii's processor
3. It has four mounted players
4. Gandhi who heads the Indian National Congress
5. Longtime luxury sedan
6. Sitter hitter, maybe
7. Pat Patriot and Billy Buffalo
8. Hypothetical example opener
9. Curtis of the screen

10. Player with Legos, for example
11. Authority figures
13. Big outdoor gear retailer
14. What might break people's trust?: Abbr.
20. Discoverer of the Amazon's mouth
22. Giggles
25. "Copacabana" showgirl and others
28. ___ b'Av (annual Jewish fast day)
30. Place for a glowing element
32. 20-20, e.g.
33. Hydroxyl-bearing compound
36. Turned-over part of a leaf
37. Alternative to Avia
39. See 49-Down
40. Wise one

41. Opposite of blanco
43. "___ Shoes" (2005 Cameron Diaz film)
45. Frequent Wyeth model
47. One aboard Marine One: Abbr.
48. "Wicked!"
49. Id ___ (39-Down)
50. Provide technical details for
53. Spanish demonstrative
54. Burning feeling

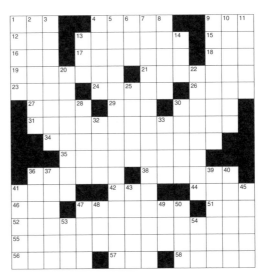

by Joe Krozel

178

ACROSS

1 "Eureka!"
10 Home tech product discontinued in 1987
15 Pants extender?
16 Request for a hero
17 Source of inspiration for Sir Isaac Newton, famously
18 Locked up
19 Drudges
20 "Illness" affecting the wealthy
22 What a gate change might affect: Abbr.
23 Join in the attack
24 Washed out
25 Nereus, Proteus, Glaucus and Phorcys, to the ancient Greeks
27 A little night music
28 "Can this be?!"
30 "Y" athlete
31 Speeding
32 Hit
34 "The Painter of Sunflowers" setting
35 "That's terrible!"
36 Classic Jaguars
37 Who said "Genuine poetry can communicate before it is understood"
39 Life force, in meditation
40 Chops meat
41 Terrain maker
44 Animal with a sweet tooth
46 First video game character to be honored with a figure in the Hollywood Wax Museum
48 Make a bank withdrawal?
49 Author who was the title subject of the Best Picture of 1937
51 Grant presenter?

52 Endgame
53 Freezing temps
54 Social butterfly, e.g.

DOWN

1 Emulate a King or Senator
2 High, in a way
3 Muted
4 "A half-filled auditorium," to Frost
5 Some early astronauts
6 Gang symbol, for short
7 Plain-spoken
8 Something fallen off a shelf?
9 Market leader
10 Not seriously
11 Hollow out
12 Excursions for some rock collectors?
13 Certain party deliveries
14 Did a week-long juice diet, say

21 ___ Pollos Hermanos ("Breaking Bad" restaurant)
23 Some dog rewards
25 Good ones are never cracked
26 HHH
27 Silent
28 Tireless sort
29 Ace
30 High-seas cry
31 Al Capone, famously
32 One doing the highlights?
33 Cut off the back
35 Loser in a 1970s–'80s "war"
37 Sight in an ice cream shop
38 Literary contemporary of Addison
40 Bristol's partner in pharmaceuticals
41 Place for a 17-Across
42 Meet someone?
43 Put in minimal effort

45 Locale painted in the Sistine Chapel
46 Note
47 Eastern Europe's Sea of ___
50 Printer setting: Abbr.

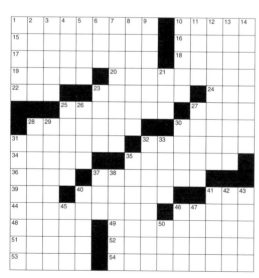

by Peter Wentz

179

ACROSS

1 Having a big itch
9 Giant jet
15 Sideways look?
16 "Swann's Way" novelist
17 Marinara, e.g.
18 When to put all your eggs in one basket?
19 Late legend in countdowns
20 Bell part
22 Fertiliser ingredient
23 Neighbor of 10-Down
24 Underlying
26 "Country Girl" memoirist O'Brien
27 Capital player, briefly
28 Fire
30 Soy, north of Mexico
31 Elves, in poetry
32 Heat loss, maybe?
34 Home of minor-league baseball's Brewers
37 Like lizards and lizardfish
38 Tennis since 1968
40 "Give this ___"
41 It can be dry or sparkling
42 Title woman of a 1977 Neil Diamond hit
44 Org. of sisters
47 Bit of design info
49 Not still
50 Where a ducktail tapers
51 Paroxysm
53 Looney Tunes devil, for short
54 Ceilings, informally
55 Refuse to leave alone
57 Farmers' market frequenter, maybe
59 Novelist Shreve and others
60 Hoosier
61 Key figure?
62 Spark

DOWN

1 Close-fitting, sleeveless jacket
2 1998 Masters champ Mark
3 Acknowledges without a sound
4 Footnote abbr.
5 Neighbor of India and China in Risk
6 Post-O.R. stop, maybe
7 What a boor has
8 Rock with colored bands
9 Boor
10 Neighbor of 23-Across
11 Good name for an optimist?
12 Call from the rear?
13 Avatar accompanier
14 Like music on Pandora Radio
21 Hassle
24 Giants' environs

25 Source of the delicacy tomalley
28 Like many mirrors
29 Nautilus shell feature
31 Home for a sedge wren
33 Like the out crowd?
34 "Come again?"
35 Moment when the fog lifts
36 "Go for it!"
39 Second: Abbr.
40 Major copper exporter
43 Slanted
44 State bordering Poland
45 Unlikely fare for philistines
46 Mind a lot
48 Kinkajou's kin
50 Like some forces
52 Those, in Toledo
54 Hermes' mother

56 Boomer for nearly 35 yrs.
58 Setting for many Card games

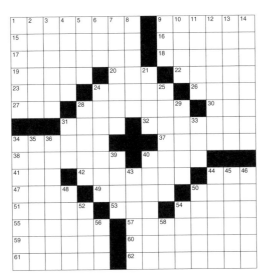

by Kevin Christian

180

ACROSS

1 Dated agreement?
10 Cognizes
15 Comment to an unapologetic burper, say
16 Cosmetics dye
17 Hawk
18 Q preceder
19 Fashion designer Saab
20 Mexican couple
21 Something locked in a cell?
22 Neuralgia : nerve :: costalgia : ___
23 Lightly towels off
25 Dickens pseudonym
26 Woman's name that sounds like a repeated letter
28 First name in design
29 Turn off, maybe
30 School basics, facetiously
32 Succeeded
34 Donnybrook
37 Moon named after the Greek personification of terror
38 SALT signer
40 Adèle, for one: Abbr.
41 Page, e.g.
42 Juice name starter
44 Letters at the top of a page
47 Brick, for example
48 Fictional locale of a John Wayne western
50 Eagle's place: Abbr.
52 Attacked verbally
54 Something most Americans won't take, for short
55 Destiny's Child, e.g.
56 Olympian Moses
57 iPhone competitor
59 Uniform
60 Where El Nuevo Herald is read
61 Classic sea adventure of 1846
62 Straight man of old comedy

DOWN

1 "The ___ the words, the better the prayer": Martin Luther
2 ___ acid (bleach ingredient)
3 Old record keeper
4 "An Enquiry Concerning Human Understanding" philosopher
5 Film speed letters
6 Castle town in a 1937 film
7 Start of something big?
8 "Hoop-Dee-Doo" lyricist
9 USD alternative
10 Writer in "The Electric Kool-Aid Acid Test"
11 A follower?
12 Slow-cooked Italian dish
13 Handy things in the game world?
14 Exhibited sternutation
21 Feels (for)
23 Lake catch
24 Stowe antislavery novel
27 It's temporarily hot
29 David who wrote the screenplay for "The Verdict"
31 Bad, and then some
33 Art purchase
34 Warm
35 Grocery product with a multiply misspelled name
36 Hematology prefix
38 Stool, typically
39 Jarrett of the Obama White House
43 "Ain't happening!"
45 "Boom" preceder
46 Lipitor maker
48 Taylor of "The Nanny"
49 String bean's opposite
51 Product once pitched by Ronald Reagan
53 Lake catch
55 Disneyland sight
57 Part of a certain cease-fire agreement, for short
58 Roman divinity

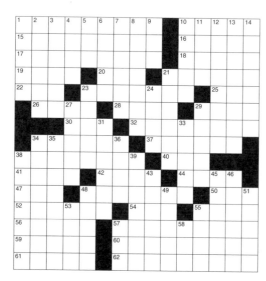

by David Steinberg

The New York Times

SMART PUZZLES

Presented with Style

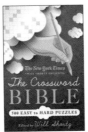
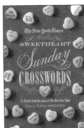

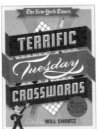

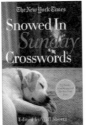

Available at your local bookstore or online at www.nytimes.com/nytstore

ST. MARTIN'S GRIFFIN

f fbmacmillan.com/smp/willshortz

Answers

1

```
U S B     A P P S     W A F T S
A Q U A   P E R U     O L L I E
W U R L I T Z E R O R G A N S
  I R A N   O G R E   G M T
T R I N I L O P E Z   A M I E
A M T   T U X   D O R M A N T
B Y O B   S E E     P I N E S
    J O H N A D A M S
O R S O N   U R N   H I L T
L I P R E A D   A K A   M A P
E C O N   L A U G H T R A C K
M O N   I S N T   I A G O
I T S A B O U T N O T H I N G
S T O R M   B E A N   S N I T
S A R I S   E R G O   E C O
```

2

```
N E S   N I P A T     P L O Y
O L E   E M I N E M   R O W E
T I L   A R C I N G   E O N S
I C E C R E A M T R U C K
M I N U S   Y A H   S A L O N
E T A L   C U T S I N L I N E
    T B O N E   L A C K E D
P S I   I R E   C L V   E S S
U P T A K E   B A B Y S
T R I V I A G A M E   A P I A
T Y S O N   I L E   S K I N S
    S W I Z Z L E S T I C K S
T H A I   I M P A L A   K I T
A D I N   P O I S O N   U N D
B L D G   S T Y E S   P D A
```

3

```
C A C H E   J A M B   A Q U A
A I R E S   O P E R   L U G S
S M A R T P H O N E   L I L I
T E N   I N P U T   N C I S
S E E T H E   S H R E K
    H O R S E   R A W B A R
A S S E T   U N D E R   U S E
H A H   F A S T O N E   C H A
A G A   O L S E N   B A K E R
B A R H O P   R E L I C
    P A T H S   A T T A C K
O P T S   A T L A S   G A L
P L U S   B R I G H T S I D E
E A R L   E A S E   W I L D E
D Y N E   T W A S   O B E Y S
```

4

```
B A S H   L A S S   L E F T Y
A M I R   A R C O   I L I A D
H O T H O T H O T   V I B E S
I N K   M E A T   S E C
A G A I N S T T H E W I N D
    N I T   E D I T O U T
A F T S   B A L E R   F R A
W E A T H E R F O R E C A S T
E L K   E R U C T   A T T A
S L E E P I N   O A S
A I N T N O S U N S H I N E
    G A S   K N E E   D A P
S P R I G   C O L D A S I C E
P I A N O   O R I G   T O R E
A X M E N   E T T E   U T E S
```

5

```
T H A T S   R A V E N   I C K
R I T Z Y   A L O N E   C O Y
I N S U M   R I N G A B E L L
A D E   B Y E   L O B O
D I A L I T D O W N   O R S K
    S O D   N A Y   R I S E
A C T A S   E G A D   D E E
W H A T I S T H E H A N G U P
F I T   S A G A   P O E M S
U N E S   G I L   C P A
L A R K   O F F T H E H O O K
  S T I R   E A R   H I E
P H O N E I T I N   D A W N S
R O T   E V A D E   A W O K E
O P S   D E P O T   N E W S Y
```

6

```
W A D E D   B M O C   U S D A
A M U S E   L I R E   S H U T
T A C O S T A N D S   H A S H
T S K   P O N E   T E N T O
    B R O N C O S T A D I U M
I D I O T S   Y E R   A P E
N O L A   H A N S O N
D E L M O N I C O S T E A K S
    S N O R E D   A M E R
A P O   I L E   O T T A W A
T E X A C O S T A T I O N
B O Y L E   I R O N   D I E
A R G O   H I D D E N C O S T
T I E S   A G E E   E R W I N
S A N S   B O S N   D O N N A
```

7

P	H	I	L	■	■	S	C	U	B	A	■	I	M	P
O	U	T	E	D	■	N	A	N	A	S	■	D	O	E
W	H	I	T	E	R	A	B	B	I	T	■	O	R	E
■	■	S	U	N	U	P	■	■	R	O	O	S	T	E	R
G	A	S	P	■	I	T	N	O	■	■	A	O	N	E
E	T	A	■	K	N	O	C	K	O	N	W	O	O	D
A	M	I	S	H	■	■	R	E	L	A	Y	■	■	■
R	E	D	C	A	P	S	■	N	A	N	E	T	T	E
■	■	O	K	I	E	S	■	■	C	R	E	E	D	■
A	M	E	R	I	C	A	N	P	I	E	■	L	A	D
N	A	V	E	■	W	O	O	L	■	■	A	L	L	Y
I	C	E	D	T	E	A	■	T	E	T	R	A	■	■
M	A	N	■	S	I	L	V	E	R	B	E	L	L	S
A	W	E	■	A	R	L	E	N	■	A	N	I	T	A
L	S	D	■	R	E	S	E	T	■	■	A	E	R	O

8

H	U	B	S	■	A	L	O	H	A	S	■	S	A	S
A	M	A	T	■	D	A	N	I	E	L	■	O	S	U
S	A	B	E	■	O	P	E	N	S	O	U	R	C	E
■	■	Y	E	G	G	■	I	D	O	■	S	T	E	M
A	M	B	L	E	■	F	L	I	P	P	H	O	N	E
T	Y	L	E	N	O	L	■	■	L	E	F	T	■	■
T	O	U	R	■	D	O	S	S	I	E	R	■	■	■
A	B	E	■	B	O	O	K	E	N	D	■	G	A	P
■	■	M	E	R	R	I	E	R	■	P	O	S	E	■
P	E	A	T	■	■	D	E	T	R	O	I	T	■	■
M	A	T	C	H	P	L	A	Y	■	S	O	D	A	S
A	R	C	H	■	O	O	N	■	S	P	R	Y	■	■
S	C	H	O	O	L	W	O	R	K	■	A	E	O	N
S	E	E	■	F	I	E	S	T	A	■	T	A	M	E
E	L	S	■	F	O	R	E	S	T	■	E	R	G	O

9

J	I	F	F	■	I	M	P	E	L	■	O	H	M	S
U	S	E	R	■	W	A	H	O	O	■	D	O	I	T
S	H	E	E	R	A	G	O	N	Y	■	O	S	L	O
■	■	D	O	N	O	T	■	■	Q	U	E	E	R	■
A	T	M	■	S	N	O	O	Z	E	A	L	A	R	M
N	O	I	D	E	A	■	■	O	A	T	S	■	■	■
I	N	N	O	■	■	S	O	S	A	■	A	T	T	■
S	Y	D	N	E	Y	A	U	S	T	R	A	L	I	A
E	S	S	■	P	E	R	M	■	■	S	T	A	B	■
■	■	H	E	L	I	■	■	S	U	P	E	R	B	■
S	A	M	U	E	L	A	D	A	M	S	■	R	A	Y
E	X	A	M	S	■	■	E	T	U	D	E	■	■	■
A	L	M	A	■	S	M	A	R	T	A	L	E	C	K
T	E	E	N	■	S	P	L	I	T	■	M	A	N	E
S	S	T	S	■	E	S	S	A	Y	■	S	U	N	G

10

N	C	R	■	T	R	A	N	S	■	S	C	R	E	W
A	H	A	■	V	I	X	E	N	■	H	Y	E	N	A
P	A	B	S	T	B	L	U	E	R	I	B	B	O	N
E	M	B	E	R	■	■	R	E	I	N	E	■	■	■
S	P	I	N	A	L	C	O	R	D	■	R	H	O	S
■	■	Y	E	A	■	S	E	R	P	E	N	T	■	■
A	B	E	■	S	L	O	■	B	U	L	K	Y	■	■
L	U	N	A	T	I	C	F	R	I	N	G	E	■	■
P	E	R	C	Y	■	T	U	E	■	K	A	Y	■	■
E	X	P	R	E	S	S	■	J	I	B	■	■	■	■
E	A	S	Y	■	A	L	P	I	N	E	L	A	C	E
■	■	P	O	B	O	Y	■	■	E	V	I	A	N	■
A	L	L	T	H	E	T	R	I	M	M	I	N	G	S
R	U	S	E	S	■	H	E	N	C	E	■	G	E	O
K	I	D	D	O	■	S	S	T	A	R	■	E	R	R

11

S	T	O	A	■	M	E	L	T	■	S	P	E	E	D
C	R	U	D	■	A	R	I	A	■	P	O	L	A	R
O	A	T	H	■	J	I	N	X	■	L	O	F	T	Y
W	I	D	E	R	E	C	E	I	V	E	R	■	■	■
S	N	O	R	E	S	■	■	E	E	N	■	A	S	H
■	■	E	X	T	E	N	D	E	D	S	T	A	Y	■
A	C	T	■	Y	E	A	■	P	I	E	R	R	E	■
P	R	O	M	O	■	L	O	W	■	D	E	I	G	N
P	O	W	E	L	L	■	M	A	R	■	P	E	A	■
L	O	N	G	D	I	V	I	S	I	O	N	■	■	■
E	N	S	■	S	A	N	■	C	R	U	M	B	S	■
■	■	S	T	R	E	T	C	H	E	D	O	U	T	■
I	T	A	L	Y	■	C	O	O	T	■	G	O	Y	A
M	O	R	A	L	■	K	A	L	E	■	E	D	I	T
P	E	E	V	E	■	S	T	A	R	■	D	Y	N	E

12

S	C	O	T	■	L	A	K	E	S	■	B	E	L	T
I	S	L	E	■	E	N	U	R	E	■	A	R	E	A
S	I	D	E	S	A	D	D	L	E	■	T	R	A	M
■	■	M	O	N	R	O	E	N	O	M	O	R	E	■
E	M	S	■	L	I	E	■	■	D	A	R	N	S	■
N	E	W	T	O	N	W	E	N	T	O	N	■	■	■
D	R	A	W	S	■	■	R	O	A	R	■	S	S	T
O	C	T	O	■	P	L	A	N	B	■	O	A	H	U
W	I	S	■	M	O	A	T	■	A	D	M	A	N	■
■	■	E	D	I	S	O	N	I	S	D	O	N	E	■
A	V	A	I	L	■	■	O	N	S	■	A	E	R	■
P	A	S	S	I	N	G	N	O	T	E	S	■	■	■
A	L	A	N	■	C	L	O	S	E	T	O	Y	O	U
R	U	D	E	■	A	U	D	E	N	■	D	A	M	S
T	E	A	R	■	A	T	E	S	T	■	A	P	S	E

13

B	U	L	B		A	S	A	P		B	A	B	A	S
I	G	O	R		B	A	B	E		U	L	T	R	A
B	L	U	E	B	E	A	R	D		G	E	E	K	Y
S	I	T	A	R		B	I	R	D	B	R	A	I	N
		K	I	M		M	O	U	E		M	N	O	
B	A	R	B	E	L	L			M	A	B			
A	M	O	R		B	A	N	K	B	R	A	N	C	H
R	I	L	E		H	E	N		C	I	A	O		
B	E	L	A	B	A	R	T	O	K		K	N	E	E
		D	U	G		B	I	G	B	A	N	D		
A	D	D		S	A	P	S		A	L	I			
B	E	E	F	B	R	O	T	H		I	T	S	O	N
I	G	L	O	O		B	E	E	R	B	E	L	L	Y
D	A	I	R	Y		O	V	I	D		R	A	G	E
E	S	S	E	S		X	E	R	S		S	W	A	T

14

S	A	P		P	R	E	Z		P	S	Y	C	H	O
C	F	O		R	E	D	O		I	H	E	A	R	D
H	O	W		E	M	I	R		L	O	A	T	H	E
W	R	E	C	K	I	T	R	A	L	P	H			
A	E	R	O		M	O	M	A			J	A	M	
	P	L	A	N	E		P	R	O	P	O	S	E	
E	E	L		L	E	N	S			M	E	H	T	A
D	J	A	N	G	O	U	N	C	H	A	I	N	E	D
G	E	N	O	A		L	O	A	N		G	R	E	
A	C	T	R	E	S	S		A	L	I	T	O		
R	T	S		P	A	S	T		E	O	N	S		
	K	N	I	G	H	T	A	N	D	D	A	Y		
A	M	B	I	E	N		A	R	N	O		M	I	R
B	O	O	T	I	E		R	E	N	O		A	L	I
S	I	L	E	N	T		K	E	E	N		N	S	A

15

M	A	J	O	R		F	A	D		Y	W	C	A	
A	M	I	N	O		E	R	R		F	O	A	L	S
S	O	F	T	C		Z	O	O		L	U	L	U	S
		O	K	D		U	P	M	Y		K	E	N	
E	G	Y	P	T	I	A	N		D	I	E	T	S	
L	O	O		H	A	N	D		I	N	C	H		
M	A	Y	B	E		E	T	C		G	R	E	T	A
S	T	O	I	C		W	H	O		T	U	D	O	R
	T	A	R	A		E	M	I	R		O	U	T	
O	R	S	A	Y		W	A	S	A	N	G	R	Y	
F	R	I		D	E	C	O		A	P	E			
L	O	C	A	L		I	R	K		E	P	S	O	M
A	N	K	L	E		A	L	I		Z	A	P	P	A
P	O	S	T			O	D	D		E	L	A	T	E

16

A	H	A		B	R	A	S	H		F	J	O	R	D
R	I	B		E	A	P	O	E		L	A	B	O	R
E	N	O		S	T	A	N	D	B	Y	M	O	D	E
A	D	M	I	T	S		A	D	O		S	E	E	D
S	U	B	C	O	N	T	R	A	C	T				
		E	W	E	R			A	U	S	T	I	N	
S	T	E	M		S	I	C	K		B	O	O	Z	E
C	O	V	E	R	O	P	E	R	A	T	I	O	N	
A	D	E	L	E		S	A	N	A		O	L	D	E
M	O	R	T	A	R		A	M	C	S				
	M	U	L	T	I	P	L	A	Y	E	R			
E	U	R	O		H	A	Y		E	E	Y	O	R	E
D	R	I	V	E	R	S	S	I	D	E		L	A	D
G	A	M	E	R		T	O	R	U	S		K	S	U
E	L	E	N	A		S	N	A	P	E		S	E	X

17

E	L	A	L		E	N	D	S		M	I	T	T	S
M	O	M	A		L	I	R	A		A	C	H	O	O
B	O	B	B	Y	F	L	A	Y		P	E	R	P	S
A	N	I	S	E			W	H	Y			I	S	P
L	I	E		S	P	A	N	I	S	H	F	L	E	A
M	E	N		T	E	N			L	U	L	L	E	D
S	S	T	S		L	I	M	P		R	O	A	D	S
		T	S	E	T	S	E	F	L	Y				
O	S	S	I	E		A	S	T	A		D	U	C	T
B	E	L	F	R	Y		A	R	K		S	O	I	
T	R	A	F	F	I	C	F	L	O	W		E	R	S
R	E	N		P	R	O			A	F	R	O	S	
U	N	D	I	D		Y	U	P	P	I	E	F	L	U
D	E	E	M	S		P	R	I	X		D	E	L	E
E	R	R	O	L		T	S	P	S		S	E	A	S

18

K	A	P	U	T		A	P	P	T	S		A	R	C	H
E	L	E	N	A		F	O	L	I	O		M	I	R	A
D	O	N	T	B	E	C	R	U	E	L		O	N	U	S
S	E	N	I	O	R			T	R	A	M		G	M	T
		D	O	N	T	W	O	R	R	Y	B	A	B	Y	
M	A	C	Y	S		H	A	N	A		L	I	L		
I	R	A			L	E	S			T	A	K	E	T	O
D	O	N	T	S	T	O	P	B	E	L	I	E	V	I	N
I	N	N	E	E	D		A	B	C			I	N	C	
	O	N	E		D	R	N	O		A	R	O	S	E	
D	O	N	T	Y	O	U	W	A	N	T	M	E			
E	B	B		A	L	M	A		H	O	S	T	E	L	
B	E	A	M		D	O	N	T	Y	O	U	C	A	R	E
I	S	L	E		I	N	D	I	E		N	U	R	S	E
T	E	L	L		E	T	A	T	S		T	E	S	T	S

19

```
B R A G . D A W G . . P O T S
M A L E . O K I E . L A T H E
W H I T E W A S H . O N I O N
. . . S S S . P R I C E C U T
B E L A T E D . I S I T . . .
E L I T E . E R G S . T R A P
A I M . E P E E . U S A U S A
U S B . M I N D S E T . N P R
T H E I S T . Y O D A . O I L
Y A R N . I C E D . T R U R O
. . F L E A . S W E A T E R .
E X T R A D R Y . E L S . . .
D R O O P . H O N E Y C O M B
E A R N S . O W E D . A R E A
N Y E T . P L O Y . L E W D .
```

20

```
A R K S . R U E D E . S P Y S
M E I R . A R R O Z . T O O T
I N K S . H I G H E N E R G Y
D O I . A R E . . R E A T A .
S I D E S A L A D . S K I M S
T R E N C H . I R A S . C A T
. S E R A . O R A L . R O T S
. . O P E N S P A C E . . . .
F E R N . A C H E . H U S K .
E D U . R U D I . G A P E R S
N I N J A . S P O R T S N U T
T O I T Y . G I S . H E R . .
C O F F E E R O L L . L O G E
G U F F . N A V E L . O R E S
I T S Y . S P A D E . B A R S
```

21

```
S N A P . E L M S . S T E I N
P E D I . M E A L . C O C O A
R A I L . P A G E L A Y O U T
A T E A S E . O P A L S . . .
Y O U F O R G O T M E . M P H
. . F O R . E N T I R E . . .
S U B A R U F O R E S T E R .
A L S O . B I C . A R G O . .
D O U B L E S T U F O R E O .
D O R S A L . L O A . . . . .
S P Y . U F O S I G H T I N G
. A D I M E . H U R R A H . .
C O N F I N E D T O . A I D E
I N C A N . G E A R . I S I N
G E O R G . A R O N . T H A T
```

22

```
L A B S . S C A M . B A J A .
E L I A . U N D O . O D E L L
T E D T U R N E R . R A F T S
B R E E Z E . O V E R F E D .
E O N . B C E . S I D E B . .
. D E A R . E D O . E T S . .
Y E S I K N O W . A M A Z O N
S T A R . S E A . S O F A . .
E N M E S H . B R E A K S U P
R A W . C A P . M V P S . . .
. A E R I E . S O P . A L E .
W A L M A R T . L L A M A S .
O N T O P . S T E V E J O B S
E N O T E . I O N E . A R E A
. O N E S . T O T S . R E L Y
```

23

```
M A D A M S . D O A . R A T E
A V E N U E . E I N . U S S R
C R E O L E . C L A M B A K E
H I D D E N V A L L E Y . . .
E L S E . I D I O T . E R G .
. S E C R E T G A R D E N . .
E T D . R I A S . A U R A . .
J O U R N A L . C R E W C U T
E I R E . P R O P . E N S . .
C L A S S I F I E D A D . . .
T E N . A S I C S . C A S E .
. P R I V A T E P A R T S . .
W E B S I T E S . B A R H O P
A S I S . M A S . B L E A R Y
S P O T . E M O . S L A T E S
```

24

```
T I B I A . L I G H T . O M G
I C A N T . A A R O N . M A N
S Y N C H . S M E L T . A D A
. D R O N E B E E . C R E W .
. C L O S E R . N U D E . . .
C H E W . E D T . P R O B S T
H E A D . D I E D . U S E T O
O E D . W I S H I N G . A R M
I S E R E . C E R A . S T O A
R E R O L L . E T D . P E N S
. A L O T . B A L I N G . . .
S C A M . R E F I L L E D . .
P A N . B R E A K . A D O L F
E K E . R I N S E . M O W E R
D E W . R E S T S . A N N O Y
```

25

```
W A S T E ■ T R E E D ■ ■ L G A
I D E A S ■ H O W I E ■ O A R
Z E R O P E R C E N T ■ S U M
A L A ■ ■ W U S S ■ O M E N ■
R I P S A W S ■ G U I L T Y
D E E P S ■ H E Y A R N O L D
■ ■ A T O ■ S O L ■ U S E S
■ S T R I N G Q U A R T E T ■
J E R K ■ E A U ■ S U E ■ ■
A N Y L O N G E R ■ B L A N D
B E H E L D ■ ■ A S S Y R I A
■ S A R I ■ A L M A ■ I C U
N C R ■ V O C A B L E S S O N
B E D ■ E R R O L ■ K N E L T
A D S ■ R E E S E ■ E L S E S
```

26

```
O R C A ■ B A T E D ■ B I K E
F E R N ■ A G R E E ■ A S I S
F L A G ■ S N A K E P L A N T
S O B E R S U P ■ P I L A T E
■ ■ G L A S S ■ M E N A C E S
V I R A G O ■ J E R K S ■ ■
A N A ■ E L I O T ■ ■ T W O S
M T S ■ D O G W O O D ■ O H M
P O S E ■ E L O P E ■ ■ ■
■ ■ S E X T S ■ I C E F O G
M E S T I Z A ■ L U C A S
A R M A N I ■ M A M A S B O Y
G O A T S B E A R D ■ Y A L E
I D L E ■ I S S U E ■ A N E W
C E L S ■ T O K E N ■ S E G S
```

27

```
R A C E ■ B R A G S ■ S H E S
I R A N ■ I O W A N ■ T A N K
M I L O ■ G O N Z O ■ O N C E
■ ■ C R A C K S A W I N D O W
A L U M N A ■ ■ S N E E R S
M E T I N T H E M I D D L E
M A T T ■ S A X O N Y ■ ■
O K A Y ■ D I N ■ E M M A
■ ■ B O O S T S ■ V I A L
G O D O W N T H E A I S L E
T U N E I N ■ ■ V A L U E S
A I R P L A N E S E A T S
S L I T ■ G O L A N ■ W A R M
E T C H ■ U P L I T ■ I G O R
D Y E S ■ N E E D Y ■ N E W S
```

28

```
C O B S ■ H O S T ■ M A R S H
A L O E ■ A B L E ■ A L O H A
P E T E R S O U T ■ C A M R Y
N O T S O ■ E R R S ■ D E E D
■ ■ L A M B ■ P A T S D O W N
B R E W P U B ■ A L I ■ ■
O A F S ■ G I S ■ T I N S E L
N N E ■ J A C K S U P ■ O X O
O D D J O B ■ Y E T ■ O R E O
■ ■ A G O ■ T E M P E S T
M A R K S O F F ■ S A U L
I D E A ■ S A L T ■ G L O S S
L I A R S ■ C A R R I E S O N
N O R T H ■ E R I E ■ N E H I
E S S A Y ■ T E M P ■ T R O T
```

29

```
C O M P ■ A F A R ■ A D L I B
A M I E ■ S A L E ■ F R A M E
T E N S ■ H A L L E L U J A H
C L O T H E ■ ■ A L A M O D E
H E L L E N I S T I C ■ L E A
O T T E R ■ D U E ■ S L I D
N S A ■ N E O N ■ S P L A T S
■ ■ H I L L B I L L Y ■ ■
O R D E A L ■ O K R A ■ M I T
L E W D ■ A W E ■ I N A N E
D R E ■ H O L L A N D A I S E
C O L B E R T ■ A S I D E S
H U L L A B A L O O ■ L E C H
A T E I T ■ R E A M ■ U N T O
P E R P S ■ S I R I ■ P S S T
```

30

```
A H A ■ E N D ■ ■ R A T T L E
D E M P S E Y ■ S E Y M O U R
A R I E T T A ■ I M E A N I T
M O N T E ■ D I D I ■ N Y S E
S N O R E D ■ N E N E ■ ■
■ ■ I M N O T A D O C T O R
A D Z ■ ■ A R R ■ S N O O P Y
C R E A M ■ B U T ■ S W O R E
T I A R A S ■ D O G ■ ■ L Y S
I P L A Y O N E O N T V ■ ■
■ ■ O N O R ■ P R I M P S
A F A R ■ A L S O ■ I D I O T
R E G A T T A ■ N U T E L L A
K L U G M A N ■ C L O O N E Y
S T A S I S ■ D E N ■ E D S
```

31

```
C A D   .   S C O W   .   S T I F F
O P E N   .   I O N E   .   P O O L E
O S C A R B A I T   .   A U T O S
P E K O E   .   C O L O R C A S T
.   C H E C H N Y A   .   A S S
A S H   .   D I E   .   T N N   .
T O A D   .   A S A P   .   A S S E T
A F I S H O U T O F W A T E R
D A R T S   .   P E L L   .   M A L E
.   U T E   .   I A M   .   T S K
.   S A D   .   B L A C K E Y E   .
U N D E R B I T E   .   T A S K S
S E I N E   .   M O V I E R E E L
M E E T S   .   O M A N   .   D A N E
C R U S T   .   S S N S   .   L O W
```

32

```
M E D A L S   .   C A P T U R E S
B I A L I K   .   G R O U P O N S
A R T I F I C I A L B R A I N
S E E   .   T H A   .   E N D S
.   Q U A S H   .   P D A   .
G E T U P T H E C O U R A G E
O R E O   .   R U S T   .   K I X
L A S   .   D O R O T H Y   .   I V E
A S L   .   A T O I   .   A V E R
N E A R T O O N E S H E A R T
.   U S E   .   E N T E R   .
S T A B   .   Z A C   .   D R E
Y E L L O W B R I C K R O A D
N A K E D E Y E   .   K L U T Z Y
C L A S S I S M   .   S E N S E S
```

33

```
S T E M   .   A S S T   .   P A B S T
T O T E   .   P O L O   .   R O U T E
A L T A   .   P R O F   .   E L M O S
B L U N D E R B U S S   .   B L T
.   T R A Y S   .   T E T L E Y
Z E S T E R   .   T E N S E   .
I N T O W   .   G A M E T A B L E
N Y U   .   M Y B A D   .   E A T
C A M E R A M A N   .   U P E N D
.   B E A M S   .   P H A S E S
A P L O M B   .   A K R O N   .
L I E   .   B O B B L E H E A D S
L A B E L   .   O N U S   .   L E A K
I N U S E   .   L E T T   .   E R I E
N O M A D   .   O R Z O   .   D O S E
```

34

```
P R I S M   .   D E B T   .   H A U L
S A N T A   .   A R E A   .   O G R E
A D A R K   .   M A R C O P O L O
L I L I E S   .   T O N E   .
M I L K P U N C H   .   A D L I B
.   E E L E R S   .   F I N E
T E T   .   A T N O   .   A M O E B A
O N E A C R E   .   I F O R G E T
P E N N E Y   .   A C R O   .   E D S
I M O N   .   S H E E T S   .
C Y R U S   .   M I S S P I G G Y
.   L A S E   .   H O N O R E
M E N L O P A R K   .   I N D I A
P A N E   .   C R E E   .   N E R D S
S U E D   .   A S S N   .   T R Y S T
```

35

```
G I Z A   .   J A P E S   .   E G A D
A C E D   .   I W O N T   .   M A L I
P E R L E M E S T A   .   M S G S
.   C O A L   .   S H I P M A T E S
S U S I E Q   .   T H E   .   A R E
A B U   .   M U S T Y   .   R U N I C
M E M O   .   A K A   .   P I C K A T
.   D E L I M E A T S   .
N A P A L M   .   E R R   .   B A S E
E T H Y L   .   S S G T S   .   P E W
T R A   .   I A N   .   Y U P P I E
L O S E S T E A M   .   I L E S
O P E L   .   L E G A L T E A M S
S H I M   .   A Z U R E   .   A S I A
S Y N S   .   S E A T S   .   D E C O
```

36

```
D A M N   .   P L A S M   .   N A S H
O D I E   .   R A S T A   .   U M N O
T E X T B O O K E X A M P L E
S N E L L   .   W I P E   .
.   R O O M T O I M P R O V E
.   S T R I V E   .   L A B E L
P I T S   .   M R E   .   M E L O N S
L G A   .   B E E R N U T   .   E O E
A L B E I T   .   D E S   .   I S M S
N O L A N   .   H U S T O N
B O A R D M E E T I N G S
.   F L A T   .   C E A S E
C O L L E G E E X P E N S E S
A R E A   .   I R K E D   .   U S E S
P E E P   .   C O E D S   .   E Y R E
```

37

```
S C O T S   O A T S   B L A B
W A H O O   B A I L   L E G O
A R B O R   A R E A C O D E S
B O O K O F M O R M O N
S L Y   R O A N   M A D A M E
    F I T   B E T   M O D
D O O R T O D O O R   R I B S
E L W A Y   I O N   H E N I E
T I N T   V O O D O O D O L L
E V E   A E R   L O O
R E D A C T   V E A L   A L P
    T H E B I G F I V E O H
W H I T E R I C E   G A R B O
W I F I   A L E S   A L I E N
I M A C   N E S T   N E E D Y
```

38

```
L O B   D A C H A S   C R A G
A M O   U P H O L D   H E L L
M A N N E R I S M S   U N I E
B R O I L   C E S   A B A B A
    N E M O   D U B L I N
A C C E D E   N A T T Y
S A L T   W A L L S O C K E T
A R E E D   S E A   S H A M U
P O W E R S T R I P   E R I N
    N A N A S   R C C O L A
P A S S G O   T O O K
A N T I S   T W O   S E P I A
S T Y X   F I E L D T R I P S
T I L T   U N S E A L   K O I
A C E Y   R A T T L Y   E D S
```

39

```
L E W I S   A C T S   A B S
A L A S K A   N O E L   L O U
B E L L Y D A N C E R   D Y E
O G L E   V R O O M   J A Z Z
R Y E   H I C   O E N O
    F I S H A N D C H I P S
E M M A P E E L   O N C U E
V I E T   D R E C K   D A R E
E L W A Y   P R I S O N E R
R O L L O F T H E D I E
    L U L U   S N L   G P S
Q U A Y   E V I T A   D R E I
U R L   B E A N S P R O U T S
I S E   U C L A   S A V E A S
T A X   D E U S   J E L L Y
```

40

```
G A T E   S P A T   W R I S T
O A R S   E R L E   H O R N E
T R A P   C O A X   Y U K O N
T O N Y T O N I T O N E
I N S   E N T   B I O   W A H
    L O N D O N O N T A R I O
E R U P T S   A O K   L I D S
L A C E S   P I K   V I T A E
E Y E D   G I L   R E T I N A
M O N S O O N S E A S O N
I N T   R Y E   R I P   G M A
    O N A N D O N A N D O N
B R A V E   U R I S   C E N T
E A G E R   T A C O   I S E E
E M E R Y   S W A N   S K Y S
```

41

```
B E A N   F A V O R   S C A M
E A V E   E R I C A   T O G A
S T I C K U P M E N   A M E X
T A L K E D   A G A T E
S T A T E   C A N E S U G A R
    I N L A W S   T R E V I
P I P E   O L E   T O E T A G
L S U   P O L E C A R   M I G
A L T E R S   B U N   G E L S
Y E S N O   S I E S T A
S T A F F C U T S   I N K E D
    S O S A D   A N G O L A
P A I R   R O D S T E W A R T
A C D C   A K I T A   A L O E
W H E E   T U N E D   R A Y S
```

42

```
S O B E   G A L A S   Y S E R
P L O W   A T O L L   A L D O
E D G E   M A G D A   Y O G A
N L E R S   R I A T A   A A R
D I Y   A K I N S   S U N R A
E N I G M A   H O N E S T
R E N O   S I M M E R S
    G O L D N U G G E T S
    S O A N D S O   O L A F
S T R E W N   A S W I R L
E R A S E   B L A T S   P L O
P U N   D R E A M   E A S E S
I D L E   O G D E N   L L D S
A G O N   C O L B Y   L O G E
S E W S   S T E A M   S P E D
```

43

```
M P H . A G H A S T . . S I B S
S E R . L O I T E R . J A M I E
N A H . I K N E W Y O U W H E N
B L A H . A D A . A L L T O L D
C E L E B R I T Y . D I O . .
. . D R A T . E S M E . N A B
S T E E L . A R G U E . M I R E
H U M B L E B E G I N N I N G S
E B A Y . L E A S T . O R E O S
P A N . I T L L . G U A M . .
. S R O . M A K E S G O O D
C L I P A R T . A N O . E N Z O
H O M E T O W N H E R O . T A P
A P A C E . I C E A G E . H R E
P E C K . N O D D E D . S K Y
```

44

```
B I L B O . A T A . N U K E S
A D O R E . D O W . B R A V O
R O V E R . D R E W C A R E Y
B L E W . P O I S E . N A N A
. B E G I N . A B U T S .
M I D A S . S A V E S . .
P O T U S . S P R E E . P S A
T H E P R I C E I S R I G H T
A S S . I N T E L . C D R O M
. O N D V D . S A L A D .
M A N G O . T E N E T .
T O B E . O O Z E S . W I L T
B O B B A R K E R . M I N E O
S L A I N . S A C . E L G I N
P A S T Y . O L E . I D S A Y
```

45

```
B S A . O B O E . I S A A C
O A S . N E T S . M O R P H S
L Y I N E Y E S . P R O P E L
T H A I . O R E S . B A L M Y
S I N G I N I N T H E R A I N
. . E T D . R O T . U S E
. H E R E . A P A R . D T S
R E X . M I S S I N G . E R S
A R C . W H I T . E D D Y
M C I . G O T . S R A . .
P U T T I N O N T H E R I T Z
A L A R M . N Y R O . I N R E
R E B E L S . M O V I N I N O U T
T A L K E R . E V E R . I M A
. N E S T S . T E D S . L P S
```

46

```
R I G . C L I M B . S A L U D
A A R . E E L E R . A T O N E
N C O . R A I S E . U T T E R
D O W N T H E H A T C H . .
A C T I . . K E Y E D U P
L C H A I M . S T A . T O F U
L A S . P E S C I . L O G O N
. B O T T O M S U P .
B R O O D . A R E A S . P E A
A E R O . C N N . C H E E R S
G O E S M A D . . S L I P
. T O Y O U R H E A L T H
A L I E N . U N I O N . E R A
G E N R E . T I P P I . T E L
T O A S T . S T E E D . S A T
```

47

```
P O R S C H E . S P A C E L Y
C R O Q U E T . C A N A S T A
S E C U R E D . O N E T E R M
. . A L L . G N A W S . .
P S A T S . L A C Y . C A R S
A N D S . C O M E . V A L E T
N O D . S A K E . G E N E V E
D O S . T W I S T E R . R E T
O K A P I S . E E L Y . T R I
R E L A X . T V A D . A L S O
A R T S . C H E R . K E Y I N
. . S A L O N . H E R . .
C H E A T E R . H E R O I C S
H A N G M A N . M A R B L E S
I N V E S T S . S P I E S O N
```

48

```
S C A B . C H E S T . G I V E
L A R A . L E V E R . A W A Y
O P E N . O H A R E . B O N E
T R A D E S E C R E T S . .
H A S S L E . A T A . B A A
. . T O U G H . O C H E R S
L A V A . P L O T P O I N T S
A M A N A . I R E . S T J O E
H A N D L E B A R S . T I O S
T I N S E L . S M U S H . .
I N A . R E S . B R E N D A
. . C O V E R S T O R I E S
A L V A . A D O P E . O T I S
D O W N . T E L E X . O R C A
E A S T . E R E C T . F E E D
```

49

```
G A D   B R O   M G M     T S P
A P E   L E T   O U I   A P U
S P L I T S E C O N D   X E R
    E N S U R E   L I T E S
T O G A   M I N U T E R I C E
H U A R T E     S E R A P H S
A C T O R   S P A N
T H E W I T C H I N G H O U R
      H A I R   L A P S E
O P T I C A L   C O R P S E
D A Y T R I P P E R   L O R D
E L R O Y     O R E G O N
S E A   P A S S I O N W E E K
S S N   T O P   C L U   N Y E
A T T   S K Y   H E S   T E N
```

50

```
R E M I X   D I G S   M A R X
E L I S A   I R O N   O P E R
H I G H C   N A N A   S A G A
M A R A T H O N E R S S T A T
    A L O U S   R E Q   O L E
N A T L   M A S S   U N W E D
A D O   O V U M   S E P
P A R T N E R O F W A R N E R
    O R E   T R E K   A V A
S I G M A   R E I D   S V E N
A P U   M P H   J E T T Y
W H A T P R I S O N E R S D O
Y O R E   A N A L   T I E U P
E N D S   D O L E   E V A D E
R E S T   A S K S   S E L E S
```

51

```
A C M E S   A N N A   J O T S
Q U O T A   P I E R   O K R A
U R B A N   A C R E   R A I L
A B S   D I C K V A N D Y K E
      T A L E S E   O A S E S
R E F I L L   C A I N
O V E N   P O E T S   S T P
D E A T H V A L L E Y D A Y S
E R R   I M P E L   A P P S
      A R I A   O U T S E T
M E A D E   J E A N N E
D V D R E C O R D E R   L O U
L A V A   O H I O   U M A S S
I N I T   O N K P   L A D L E
I S L E   P S A T   Y O Y O S
```

52

```
F A L C O   A M I S S     G S T
I L I A C   Z O W I E   L E I
A L L T H A T J A Z Z   I M A
T A T A R S   O S E   S T I R
    L E T       O U T T A
D A Y S O F T H U N D E R
S I N S   L O A N S   R O Y
P S S T   T O N Y A   T A P E
A C E   A E R I E   O T I S
  O L D B L A C K M A G I C
G U A V A     A T E
A N D I   N B A   S H T E T L
U T A   B E A T T H E H E A T
D E M   E X T R A   N E R D Y
Y D S   E T H A N   A R O A R
```

53

```
P I C T   S L A V   S L A T E
A D A Y   W A V E   A I L E D
Z I N C   A M E S   R E A R S
  C O M P A S S C O U R S E
S H E B A     E E N   M E L
C O L B Y C O L L E G E
A L L   S O D A   S K I M S
L E E R   D E B A R   G N A T
A D D E D   O R E O   D N A
    C O L O R C O P Y I N G
I W O   N T H     T O G A S
C O U N T R Y C O U S I N
I O N I A   E L L S   C A B S
N E C K S   A I D E   K N E E
G R E E K   H O E D   S T E W
```

54

```
H A L T S   H I G H     R A P
A L O H A   E G R E T   I S A
C A V E D   M O O N R O C K S
K N E W   P E R U   A T O M S
  B A R O N   P R I T H E E
S N I V E L   R H I N O
T O T E M   H O U S E   T O M
A P E   B L O G G E D   I V E
Y E S   R U L E S   E A M E S
    S A T Y R   T Y L E R S
I P H O N E S   H E E L S
N O E N D   Y O U D   D U F F
B I G S T I N K S   V O C A L
U S E   S T O R K   A N K L E
D E L   D D A Y   T E S L A
```

55

```
J A V A . Q U E S T . S T U B
A V E R . U N D U E . T A R O
D O N T M A K E M E L A U G H
E N D . A K I N . . U T T E R
. . E V E N . I D L E . . .
F U H G E D D A B O U D I T
O N I O N . . L E I S . C O G
R I P S . T W I X T . P I T A
A F T . G R A B . . H O N E Y
. Y O U R E K I D D I N G M E
. . N I K E . R A N G . . .
S T R I P . B A N D . F Y I
T H A T S R I D I C U L O U S
O O Z E . I N A N E . U R A L
P R E S . A B Y S S . G E N E
```

56

```
E T C . O K A Y . A T H E N S
S O O . I N C A . F I A S C O
C U P A S O U P . T R I T O N
A P P L E T V . B E A K . .
R E E L . S U P E R D U P E R
P E R C H . E L I D E . E R E
. . A O L . A N A . T R A P
. S U P P O R T G R O U P S .
T A R S . V I E . K E N . .
L S D . V E G A S . R A I M I
C H U P A C H U P S . O N A N
. . A C H T . L O U I S C K
M A I T A I . D O U B L E U P
S H T E T L . E S S E . A L A
G A S S E D . C H A R . M A D
```

57

```
S T R A P . E N J O Y . M A T
P O A C H . L O I R E . O B E
Y E N T A . K O F I A N N A N
. . . R I S K . . I S T O
P A C M A N . . S A U N T E R
A S H T O N K U T C H E R . .
T H I G H . I V A N S . O P S
T E C S . P L U M E . I S L E
I R K . E A R L E . P R I A M
. M A R I O A N D R E T T I
I M A G E R Y . Y E S Y E S
R A G E . . S P E C . . .
V I N D I E S E L . E M P T Y
I Z E . C R O N E . P O S E R
N E T . Y A L T A . T W I N S
```

58

```
A N A L . B L I P . S N A R K
D A L I . A E R O . C O C O A
S U P E R S T A R . R U T T Y
A S H . A S O N . W A G . .
L E A R N O F . C A P A B L E
E A S E L . F U L L S T E A M
. . P O P . N I N . D O T
. P O W E R C O U P L E . .
A W E . . L O A . T I E . .
H I G H H O R S E . S O C K S
I T S E A S Y . L E T S L I P
. . C S I . T Y P O . A G A
K O O K S . M U S C L E M A N
I D Y L L . O R E O . S U L K
M E L E E . W N E T . E P I S
```

59

```
F E E . S P R E E . M O U S E
L A X . P R I E D . C O Z E N
A G A . R O L L I N G P I N S
I L L F A M E . T A R S . .
L E T R I P . B E T A . O P T
. . O N T H E D O W N L O W
C M I . S L I D . . I D L E
R O F L . Y E S E S . P I K E
A O N E . . O R C A . E A T
F L O O R M I R R O R S . .
T A T . A A R E . T O U S L E
. . O S L O . A L U M N U S
L A U G H I N G G A S . O C T
A G R E E . I N A N E . O R E
B O N E S . C U R D S . P E R
```

60

```
M A S T S . B A D G E . S O S
I C O N S . E V I A N . U N H
C E N T E R F I E L D . S H O
A T A . . M O A T . A S P I C
H I T T I N G . . S T R E A K
. C A I N . S A L T . A N T E
. . F I T . L O A F . S U R
. F I F T Y S I X G A M E S .
L I C . S P A N . E R E . .
A N A T . E W E S . S U S S
Y A N K E E . . C L I P P E R
A L T O N . F I R E . . I M O
W I N . J O E D I M A G G I O
A Z O . O N T O P . R O O T S
Y E W . Y E A S T . M O T E T
```

61

A	L	I	E	N	■	A	B	D	U	C	T	I	O	N
V	I	O	L	A	■	M	I	D	P	O	I	N	T	S
G	E	N	I	I	■	A	N	T	A	R	C	T	I	C
■	■	C	L	O	S[ET]	■	■	O	S	O	S	■	■	■
P	R	I	S	M	S	■	■	I	N	N	■	■	■	■
W	R	O	T[ET]	O	■	■	T	E[ET]	O	T	A	L	■	■
[ET]	A	S	■	O	B	E	S	E	■	T	E	N	[ET]	■
T	I	[ET]	O	■	L	E	O	■	T	[ET]	E	S	■	■
E	S	T	A	■	[ET]	I	C	K	[ET]	■	H	M	O	■
R	E	E	K	I	N	G	■	H	O	M	E	I	N	■
■	N	A	H	■	■	T	E	R	E	S	A	■	■	■
F	A	H	D	■	[COW]	A	R	D	S	■	■	■	■	■
F	I	R	E	E	A	T	E	R	■	E	S	T	E	R
O	V	E	R	E	X	E	R	T	■	R	U	B	L	E
B	E	A	R	D	L	E	S	S	■	S	P	A	S	M

62

O	A	F	S	■	R	E	C	A	P	S	■	S	O	T
T	R	O	U	■	A	T	O	N	A	L	■	C	H	A
H	E	R	E	S	J	O	H	N	N	Y	■	O	W	N
E	N	T	R	E	■	O	U	I	■	M	O	O	G	■
R	A	Y	■	A	O	N	E	A	N	D	A	T	W	O
■	L	A	R	V	A	■	L	I	R	R	■	■	■	■
A	M	O	R	■	E	N	O	■	A	R	L	E	S	■
L	I	V	E	F	R	O	M	N	E	W	Y	O	R	K
S	T	E	A	L	■	S	U	M	■	M	O	N	Y	■
■	■	■	M	A	M	A	■	D	A	L	E	S	■	■
A	N	D	A	W	A	Y	W	E	G	O	■	E	D	T
P	O	O	P	■	N	E	A	■	E	E	L	E	R	■
A	M	T	■	I	T	S	S	H	O	W	T	I	M	E
R	A	T	■	C	R	I	T	I	C	■	U	P	O	N
T	R	Y	■	H	A	R	E	M	S	■	I	S	N	T

63

C	A	N	S	■	N	C	O	■	C	T	R	S
U	P	I	N	■	C	O	O	R	S	■	O	H	I	O
K	E	N	O	■	R	I	N	G	O	■	W	R	A	P
E	X	E	R	C	I	S	E	■	A	N	G	E	L	S
■	■	D	E	R	B	Y	■	A	N	N	I	E	■	■
A	Z	O	R	E	S	■	U	N	D	E	R	D	O	G
D	O	W	S	E	■	T	H	O	S	■	L	O	B	E
E	R	N	■	P	A	R	A	D	O	X	■	W	I	T
A	R	I	A	■	R	O	U	E	■	A	P	N	E	A
L	O	S	T	S	O	U	L	■	E	N	L	I	S	T
■	■	F	L	O	U	T	■	D	A	D	A	S	■	■
I	S	A	A	C	S	■	P	A	S	Y	S	T	E	M
K	O	L	N	■	E	E	R	I	E	■	T	R	I	O
E	A	S	T	■	S	M	E	L	L	■	E	U	R	O
A	R	E	A	■	■	S	P	Y	■	R	E	E	D

64

H	A	R	M	S	■	I	M	P	S	■	J	I	N	X
E	M	A	I	L	■	B	U	R	Y	■	A	D	A	M
W	I	N	S	O	M	E	L	O	S	E	S	O	M	E
S	E	T	H	■	A	G	E	N	T	S	■	L	E	N
■	■	A	P	B	■	■	T	E	S	S	■	■	■	■
■	E	S	P	R	E	S	S	O	M	A	K	E	R	S
P	T	L	■	O	L	E	O	■	Y	I	P	E	S	■
U	H	O	H	■	L	A	U	D	S	■	S	O	F	T
S	I	T	A	R	■	S	A	K	E	■	D	E	S	■
S	C	H	W	A	R	Z	E	N	E	G	G	E	R	■
■	■	K	I	W	I	■	■	W	O	O	■	■	■	■
Q	E	D	■	M	A	G	P	I	E	■	S	O	R	E
T	U	R	N	I	N	G	A	P	R	O	P	H	E	T
I	R	O	N	■	D	E	V	O	■	T	E	M	P	O
P	O	P	E	■	A	D	E	S	■	O	L	S	O	N

65

N	T	H	■	N	E	X	U	S	■	S	H	U	S	H
O	R	U	■	E	V	E	N	T	■	K	A	R	L	A
R	I	G	■	W	A	N	D	E	R	I	N	G	I	S
M	A	H	R	E	■	O	I	L	Y	■	D	E	P	P
A	L	L	I	S	A	N	D	E	A	R	S	■	■	■
■	A	T	T	N	■	■	■	N	E	U	R	O	N
C	R	U	Z	■	K	A	T	E	■	I	P	A	N	A
H	O	R	■	L	A	Y	I	S	O	N	■	Z	I	P
A	L	I	B	I	■	N	E	A	R	■	B	O	T	S
P	L	E	A	T	S	■	C	A	R	R	■	■	■	■
■	B	E	T	T	E	D	A	V	I	S	I	S
C	O	Z	Y	■	A	E	R	O	■	E	T	H	N	O
A	N	I	F	O	R	A	N	E	Y	E	■	A	K	A
M	E	T	A	L	■	R	I	S	E	N	■	R	E	P
P	A	S	T	E	■	S	E	T	T	O	■	P	R	Y

66

P	A	S	H	A	■	T	A	R	O	T	■	G	E	M
E	S	T	O	P	■	E	L	I	D	E	■	I	V	Y
P	L	A	N	E	R	A	P	P	E	R	■	R	I	M
S	A	N	E	■	O	U	S	T	■	R	A	L	L	Y
I	N	D	Y	C	A	R	■	I	P	A	D	S	■	■
■	■	B	A	N	N	E	D	L	I	E	D	E	R
D	O	T	E	D	■	A	E	O	N	■	O	R	E
R	A	V	E	■	A	R	T	S	Y	■	B	R	I	N
A	T	V	■	B	L	E	U	■	A	R	M	C	O
W	H	I	R	L	E	D	P	I	E	C	E	■	■	■
■	E	P	I	C	S	■	C	A	S	A	B	A	S
B	E	W	I	G	■	C	E	E	S	■	T	U	B	A
A	L	E	■	H	O	A	R	S	E	S	H	O	O	S
S	I	R	■	T	O	R	S	I	■	H	E	N	I	E
H	A	S	■	S	H	E	E	N	■	U	R	A	L	S

67

```
Q U I D ■ H I T M E ■ A H A B
E S S O ■ O N E A L ■ C A G E
I S A W ■ N A N N Y ■ E D I T
I R O N S ■ L A G ■ S H O N E
■ ■ ■ P I L L M O R N I N G ■
P A L A T E ■ ■ ■ A I G ■ ■
A N O T H E R O N E T H I N G
R T E ■ ■ U T E ■ ■ ■ T A U
C I B E F O R E E E X C E P T
■ ■ D A B ■ ■ ■ A T O N E S
R E A D I N G B U R N ■ ■ ■
H O R S E ■ O R E ■ A G O N Y
A X O N ■ N O I R E ■ A R E A
W I D E ■ I N F E R ■ M A I L
N E E R ■ B E T T E ■ E L L E
```

68

```
B A S S A L E ■ ■ E M B E R S
E D I T I O N ■ ■ N O I R O N
L O C A L P U B ■ C O G I T O
T S K ■ ■ F A T A S A C O W ■
■ A B L E ■ L A M E S ■ ■ ■
L E S L E Y ■ D I P ■ A B U
E L A I N E ■ A L S ■ W U S S
D I D N T ■ M S S ■ O H S A Y
S H O D ■ D O A ■ P L A Y I N
■ U G A ■ E T C ■ S A L A D E
■ ■ ■ S O C I O ■ Y V E S ■
S L Y A S A F O X ■ ■ A P E
T O O B A D ■ T R A S H B I N
O L D A G E ■ A R T D E C O
P L A T E S ■ Y E S L E T S
```

69

```
D A Z E ■ E P E E S ■ G W E N
U N I T ■ P A U L O ■ A H S O
E T N A ■ I N R E M ■ Y E T I
T I C T A C T O E B O A R D ■
■ ■ ■ S A N S ■ E R N E ■ ■
O R B ■ N E U E ■ R A T I O S
P O U N D S I G N ■ S H T U P
R U B E ■ S T Y E S ■ E S T O
A S B I G ■ S P A C E M A R K
H E L L N O ■ T R E N ■ T E E
■ ■ E S A U ■ S N O W ■ ■ ■
■ T W I T T E R H A S H T A G
F O R M ■ P R I O R ■ I O N A
I S A O ■ U T E R I ■ F O N Z
E S P N ■ T E L E O ■ F L E E
```

70

```
T H E E ■ I C B M ■ J A C K O
S A(W)S ■ R O O M ■ O R(G)A N
K E E P H O U S E ■ T R I T E
S C R A B B L E ■ A T A ■ ■
■ ■ R O O D ■ C H O I C E S
■ R O T ■ T A B O O ■ G(A)L A
R E M O P ■ E R R A N T L Y
U S E ■ H A N G M A N ■ D E O
S T A N D P A T ■ S P O R K
E U R(O)■ P R O B E ■ A M Y
S P A N G L Y ■ A N A T ■ ■
■ ■ ■ S H Y ■ A N A G R A M S
A P O L O ■ S H A M E O N M E
V A(D)I S ■ R E N O ■ N(E)V A
A D E P T ■ O M A R ■ S W I M
```

71

```
S H O ■ A F L A M E ■ G L E N
A O L ■ C O O G A N ■ L I D O
B R I G H[AMY]O U N G ■ O V E N
R A V E ■ K E Y S ■ (1)E R E
I C E D T E A ■ ■ B E R L E
N E O ■ E A T ■ S T R A Y E D
A S I D E S ■ P E R O T ■ ■
■ ■ L I T T L E W O M E N ■
■ R H E A S ■ W I R E U P
R A F T E R S ■ O E D ■ U N E
S P A Y S ■ ■ S L E P T I N
V I E[JO]O M I T ■ ■ O R C A
P A R K[MEG]E N E R A T I O N
E R I E ■ A L T A I R ■ N R C
D Y E S ■ S T O L A F ■ O N E
```

(1) BETH

72

```
D E F E R ■ A R A B ■ S W A N
A L O O F ■ D E L E ■ A R G O
F L U N K ■ M A P L E L E A F
(F)I R ■ ■ N I(L)■ F I E S T(A)
(Y)E A H M A N ■ B A D ■ T E T
■ L A R D ■ ■ A S E C ■ ■
S T A R S A N D S T R I P E S
H E R E ■ ■ E E E ■ ■ R O L E
H A M M E R A N D S I C K L E
■ ■ S P A R ■ ■ H O L E ■ ■
L A B ■ S I S ■ M I N E R V A
(A)M A Z O N ■(D)I P ■ ■ R I G
R I S I N G S U N ■ C R O O N
K N I T ■ O P E C ■ E C O L E
S O N S ■ D A T E ■ L A M A S
```

73

```
. S U E D . . L A R A . A P B
F E N N E L . O P E R A B L E
I N C O M E . M E G I L L A H
B A L L O F W A X . S L A T E
U T E . . T I N . S E I Z E S
L O N G E S T . D E S S E R T
A R C E D . . D O E . . . .
. S H O O T I N G M A T C H .
. . . R D A . . V I R U S
M A L A R I A . P R E S U M E
E L I T E S . S E E . . S I R
N O N O S . E N C H I L A D A
T H E W H O L E . A C I D I C
H A N N I B A L . B E S E T S
E S S . P I L L . S P R Y
```

74

```
T O M S . V E S T . S C A N S
O B I T . A R E A . H O B O S
W O R D F R E A K . R H E T T
N E O . A I S L E . I O T A S
. . A N E T . S E E R . . .
J U J I T S U . T S K T S K S
O P E R A . G E T S . I R A
A T T S . S P E N D . P O E T
D O T . A T O M . P L U M E
S P A Z Z E S . X E R O X E D
. . O A T S . A M I D . . .
S P O O L . I O N I C . L A P
E A T M E . B L A N K T I L E
A T R I A . L I D O . A M E R
M E A N S . Y O U R . M O S T
```

75

```
O P E C . T H E O C . S E M I
P O L O . T I A R A . P R O S
T W E N T Y Q U E S T I O N S
S E P T A L . . H O T T E A
. R H O S . G M C . G A I T
A L A R . T R I O S . N C I S
P I N T . H A D U P . D A Z E
E N T I C I N G L Y . P R E X
R E S O U N D E D . P O T S Y
. . N E A P S . A O L . .
M E L I S S A . D E L I R I A
O N E S T A R . O R I S O N S
T O O T I R E D T O T H I N K
E R N . C A N I T B E . L A S
T M I . K I T T I E S . E T O
S E A . S L S . E S T . D E F
```

76

```
L U N G . A M F M . B S I D E
O P E R . B O A R . U N D E R
F L U E . L E T S . S A B E R
T I R E L E S S W O R K E R S
S T O K E . . O H B O Y . .
. . M O T H . O S U . A B E
E B A Y . H A M . C T S C A N
L I S T L E S S F E E L I N G
M A S H E D . G I N . A D D S
O S T . G U N . T E R P . .
. . S O D O I . . E S T E E
R U T H L E S S T A C T I C S
O C H O A . A S I F . I P O S
A L I E N . L U N A . C I N E
R A N D D . T E A R . K N O X
```

77

```
A M B S . H A S . I S A B E L
L A L O . A H I . S T U R D Y
B R O A C H E D . S E R U M S
. S C R E A M E D . R I S E .
T A K E N . . B R A N C H E D
A L E R T E R . U S E L E S S
P A D S . D O R M S . E D E L
. . . G U E S T . . .
A B B Y . I N B E D . A B O O
P A R O L E D . T A B U L A R
B R O K E R E D . . I R A T E
. N O O N . R E C K L E S S
R A M O N A . B A L L O T E D
E R E N O W . I K E . L E E R
A D D O N S . T E E . E D D Y
```

78

```
S P A Y . R O B E . N O I S Y
A L B A . E L B A . O N C U E
P E A K S P I Q U E P E K E S
S A N . M A N S . A R T . .
. . D D A Y . . B R O W S E
. B O A R S B O R E B O E R S
L I N D T . A N O D . T R U
E S S A Y . D A N . A R S O N
A S H . O R I T . L I A R S
P A I R S P A R E P E A R S
. U P K E E P . A X L E . .
. . E L D . O G R E . C A T
I D Y L L S I D L E I D O L S
N E A L E . L I O N . U R S A
S A T Y R . K E P T . O D O R
```

79

[ASH]	A	M	E	D		A	R	C	S		M	S	G	S

Row 1: [ASH]AMED · ARCS · MSGS
Row 2: CRAVE · BOLT · OPEL
Row 3: RENEE · ON[ASH]ORTLE[ASH]
Row 4: OON · PDA · REH[ASH]
Row 5: FLIC · ERR · MOSDEF
Row 6: TEX[ASH]OLDEM · ORO
Row 7: OWE · PAR · TWIX
Row 8: MOUNTSTHELENS
Row 9: WEPT · EMI · LOL
Row 10: ETA · [ASH]LEYOLSEN
Row 11: THR[ASH]ES · ENO · SOSO
Row 12: TART · GN[ASH] · DSO
Row 13: W[ASH]ING[ASH]ORE · TR[ASH]ES
Row 14: VEST · EVEL · ONONE
Row 15: ANTI · DADS · NAPES

80

Row 1: DEPOT · RANGE · BAL
Row 2: RAJAH · USEIN · ETE
Row 3: JUSTARRIVED · EOS
Row 4: STEAD · EARNS
Row 5: MAD · SALESTARGET
Row 6: OBAMA · TORTUGA
Row 7: MADAGASCAR · TOR
Row 8: COSTARICA
Row 9: ADD · WISECRACKS
Row 10: SORORAL · EASEL
Row 11: TOURISTAREA · AGO
Row 12: ADMEN · COMET
Row 13: RLS · STARSTUDDED
Row 14: TEE · ESTEE · READY
Row 15: EST · SEEDS · ENSUE

81

Row 1: COUP · HILL · DAMNS
Row 2: ALKA · OBOE · PLAIT
Row 3: SMARTNESS · TANGY
Row 4: AESTHETES · KOHL
Row 5: SCENES · SEESINTO
Row 6: ENTS · ELON
Row 7: CZAR · WIT · LIGHTS
Row 8: DEW · PORKPIE · USE
Row 9: SELDOM · OYS · FEAT
Row 10: ELAL · MISO
Row 11: MNEMONIC · SPRING
Row 12: OOZE · SALLIEMAE
Row 13: VERSE · TREATMENT
Row 14: INANE · ELAN · ATOI
Row 15: EDSEL · NYPD · NAST

82

Row 1: A(T)AB · SCARS · OHTO
Row 2: NAME · PEROT · FERN
Row 3: TMEN · ERASE · A(R)IS
Row 4: WAR · SCALENE · OST
Row 5: ELITISM · ATLANTA
Row 6: (R)ECAP · IA(N) · SCRA(G)
Row 7: PSAS · SCENT · TYNE
Row 8: ISOSCELES
Row 9: ROMNEY · CRUTCH
Row 10: ADAGE · F(L)O · SPREE
Row 11: MEL · TIEUP · ALF
Row 12: EQUILATERAL
Row 13: RESURGE · ACETATE
Row 14: STEIGER · GAMELAW
Row 15: TEXT(E)RS · EN(S)NARE

83

Row 1: SUNS · CLAN · NOLTE
Row 2: ONEC · OGLE · ENORM
Row 3: PMUHWHALE · RECAP
Row 4: HEROIN · CDEF · ATT
Row 5: STOOL · OATS · ATTY
Row 6: LLAFPOSITION
Row 7: STN · TMS · ELMORE
Row 8: PROLIFE · INASNIT
Row 9: AURORA · UNC · SAS
Row 10: RETRAUQSNEAK
Row 11: ELHI · LUIS · PULPS
Row 12: TOE · STAN · NODEAL
Row 13: IVANA · YGGIPRIDE
Row 14: RESIN · LURK · OGRE
Row 15: ESTEE · EPEE · WHET

84

Row 1: BOAR · TALL · ZESTS
Row 2: ARTE · ALTA · IQUIT
Row 3: REOS · BODYDOUBLE
Row 4: TIMEOUT · MYNA
Row 5: ADIEU · RAE · TRIO
Row 6: BACKGROUNDSOUND
Row 7: SHORN · WRITE
Row 8: AVA · TOCCATA · NOS
Row 9: SITAT · OMEGA
Row 10: PERSONALBAGGAGE
Row 11: SWAK · AND · EATUP
Row 12: AIRY · DARKENS
Row 13: BLANKCHECK · HALO
Row 14: LANCE · OPIE · ASAN
Row 15: TOSEA · WAVY · NEWS

85

```
S L E W . E C A R T E . F D R
Y E A R . N O F E E S . L E E
N A V E . C A R P E T . I N N
C H E C K . . O U T . P N I N
. . . K A R T . T H E A T R E
S T A . R C A S E . V I S O R
A N A . O L I A . P A N T . .
S T A R . E L U D E . T O A D
. . B A N D . C U T S . N T O
O P A L S . S E L E C . E E S
G E T P A S T . C R I B . . .
R O T H . L E T . . S L I D E
I R E . S O L A N O . A K I N
S I R . D E L V E S . C E N T
H A Y . I S A I A H . K A O S
```

86

```
B L T . U N M A D E . . C B S
L I V . S E A S O N . S H E A
O T C . C O O K I E S H E E T
O H H I . . R I N S E O F F .
M E A S U R I N G C U P . . .
. . N A M E . . O S A G E S
C A N O P E N E R . S T E L A
A V E . F U M E D . . T E X .
M E L D S . M I C R O W A V E
P O S E A S . . A R O W . . .
. . . C U T T I N G B O A R D
G R A D E O N E . . D Y E R .
C H A F I N G D I S H . C P A
F I N S . T U R N I P . A R K
O A K . S P A S M S . R O E .
```

87

```
L O E B . C H I C A . A H A B
E A V E . H U N A N . L O C O
D R A G . O L O R D . B L E W
. C O M P U T E R K E Y . . .
U S U R E R . . E A R B O B
S T A R W A R S C A N T I N A
T O T A L . O O H . S A B I N
E V E . D A V I D . . L O G
D E S P A I R . L E S S E N S
. . R I S K . D E U S . . .
R E W O R K . P B A N D J
A X E . (1)(2)(3)(4)(5)(6)(7) . A R I
Z I N G S . J A B . S Q U I B
O L D E . A G A . . T R E E
R E S T . M E R . S U D S
```

(1) SPACE (2) SPACE (3) SPACE (4) SPACE (5) SPACE
(6) SPACE (7) SPACE

88

```
J U J U . B L O T . F R A S
E V A N . R O T H . C L O T H
T A X I . R I T A . A E T N A
. C O R N O N T H E C O Q .
A S H E N . . K A N T . . .
T H E F A Q F O U R . E S T A
M I A . T B A R . B R O I L
O F T . I S A D O R A . I N C
S T U M P . E R A S . T K O
T Y P O . J E R R Y Q U I L T
. . . D O R M . U P S E T
Q U E E N S I Z E Q E D . . .
U T I L E . N O N U . I C B M
I N N E R . E L O I . K O B E
D E E D . M A S K . E S Q S
```

89

```
L E N D S . M C A T . L U S H
A D O U T . A R C H . A S I A
D I T S Y . N O C O M M E N T
I S I T . J U S T M E O R . .
D O O M . O P S . . M U N I S
A N N I K A . . S T O R A G E
. . T A C K I E R . . M O W
. A R E T H E R E O T H E R .
F L U . . I N S P I R E . .
S A N R E M O . . K I S S E R
U N S E T . . C I A . G A Y E
. . A N A G R A M S . O F E M
K A T E S P A D E . I T I S I
F L A W . A G R A . V I R U S
C A B S . S E E N . S T E P S
```

90

```
S T E P P E . B U G J U I C E
M E N I A L . U N I O N R E P
A N G E R M A N A G E M E N T
. C A R T I N . S I L O S . .
H E R . B R I C . . . W I S P
A N D I . A L L A T I N G L E
S T E N T . U S E R . N O W .
. . S H O R T H A I R . . .
M O B . A N A T . . S E E Y A
T H E B R E W E R S . I C E D
G O Y A . . R O C K . L S D .
. O N C E A . B R O K A W . .
L A N G U A G E B A R R I E R
O C C U R R E D . W E I R D O
D E E P E N D S . L A S S O S
```

91

```
L T D S █ E R R █ █ P A L S
S H O P A █ L E A █ H O L I C
D E L I B █ E P I █ E R A T E
G E N T █ V A L █ L E B E N
T A O S █ A I R █ D A R E
E M U █ C I T R O E N █ M A R
L E T M E B E █ A N O M A L Y
█ R E E D █ D E M O █
D E L I L A H █ T R A I T O R
E M O █ O M I C R O N █ O B I
L E A R █ G R E █ H O E D
U N D E R █ H U S █ P A S S
I D I D N █ W I T █ T D O I T
S E N D S █ A S L █ A N O T E
E D G Y █ Y E E █ █ O N Y X
```

92

```
H A R D G █ L I L A C █ R A G
A B H O R █ A M I S H █ E S L
R R A T E D M O V I E █ D I A
M A P █ W E A K █ S S T A R
█ S E W E R █ U P S T A G E
T R O W E P R I C E █ E G O S
S I D E A █ F L A T S █
A M Y █ R E L E A S E █ C E O
█ S Y R I A █ A L L A H
O N T V █ L F R A N K B A U M
F O R E S E E █ L O E S S
N S Y N C █ F I S T █ S A E
O H S █ E S T R E E T B A N D
T E T █ N O M E N █ L U C K Y
E D S █ E S S E S █ E S T A S
```

93

```
T E M PO █ C L A S S █ R A P T
A L A W █ S A M O A █ A S H E
C A K E █ PO L E PO S I T I O N
I T E R █ T A R R E D █ A N A
T E A P O T █ L E I █ E PO N Y M
█ F L O R A █ F L A P █
S H I I T E █ W I I █ C E L S
P O S T O F F I C E B O X E S
Y E T I █ E O N █ G A R T E R
█ C A R L █ M E S N E █
D E I S M █ L O O █ S PO N G E
E L S █ I S O L D E █ P S A T
PO I S O N PO W D E R █ P I T H
S O U R █ K E I R A █ E V E N
E T E S █ E D E N S █ R E D O
```

94

```
A B J E C T █ S H I V █ F T C
R O A D E O █ C A L I █ O R E
C O N G E R L I N E S █ A I D
O K A Y █ E E O █ T A M P A
█ █ F R A N K Z A P P E R █
N E W M O O N █ O E S T E █
A C H O O █ I C K █ A L E
C H A R L I E T H E T U N E R
L O T █ R C A █ S A U D I
█ A L T A R █ S P A R T A N
S A L E S Q U O T E R █ █
E R A S E █ V A N █ E R S T
L I U █ T U B E R P L A Y E R
M E G █ S K I N █ A E R A T E
A S H █ E E G S █ L E N N I E
```

95

```
A D P A G E S █ A R B █ S I C
N E A R I S H █ M A E S T R O
N O T A S T E █ I N A T R A P
A R I B █ O L D N A V Y █
N O E L █ O U T E R A R M
█ N E P H E W S █ R E C U E
I T T █ R O A N █ I S N T I T
D I A R I S T █ M O D E R N E
E G R E S S █ W A W A █ E S S
S E E T O █ F A C A D E S █
T R A I N C A R █ R S V P
█ T W A D D L E █ A S I A
T A N L I N E █ O F F S E T S
S I S E N O R █ M O D E L A S
A R C █ G E S █ B R A S A L E
```

96

```
D E P P █ D E C O R █ M I C A
O V E R █ O C U L O █ A S A N
C A N O F W O R M S █ G A N G
S C H M O █ R E C R E A T E
█ P R I V Y C O U N C I L
D A K T A R I █ E N T S █
E T A S █ O C T A █ N A T T Y
L I Z █ W C H A N D Y █ E R A
I T A L O █ Y E T I █ P R O D
█ K A O S █ O C E A N I A
J O H N F K E N N E D Y █
E A S T S I D E █ I D O S O
S R T A █ H E A D S T A R T S
S E A N █ A M P E D █ Y E A H
E D N A █ T A S E S █ S O Y A
```

97

```
C L E A N ■ I N P E N ■ ■ F I B
T I L L S ■ T O R S O ■ ■ A D O
R E K L A T S R E E D ■ ■ R O D
L U S T ■ A M A S ■ E A R L Y
■ O N C E ■ S H A P E ■ ■ ■
T E M L E H ■ O R E R B M O S
A R I D E ■ T H O R ■ S O P H
S I X ■ D A Y B O O K ■ V I E
S C O T ■ F R O M ■ A R E N A
E K L U M R A Y ■ A R O D E F
■ ■ O N I O N ■ A S I P ■ ■
V E G A S ■ N U T S ■ E G G O
O U I ■ F L I P O N E S L I D
I R S ■ I L E U M ■ P I A N O
D O T ■ T B S P S ■ A N D O R
```

98

```
A P E M E N ■ S P A ■ U F O S
B O N A M I ■ H E M ■ N I C K
L U D W I G ■ A R M ■ A N T I
E T S ■ H O W Y O U B E E N
■ O C T A N E ■ K A R T S ■
S P A C E ■ T E A S E S ■ ■
P U T E R T H E R E ■ H A R P
E S T A T E ■ A S E V E R
C H A N ■ N O H A R M D O N E
■ B A D L O T ■ E L W E S
E C A R D ■ D O R S E Y ■ ■
G I V E M E T H A T ■ J A I
A L I E ■ L O A ■ A L B U M S
D I A Z ■ K W H ■ R E A D O N
S A N E ■ E N S ■ T S H I R T
```

99

```
M O O S E ■ A G O ■ P E A C H
A V A I L ■ L E A ■ C U R I E
T A K E S P A R T ■ P R I D E
■ V I E ■ A H S ■ S E L
G R E E T E R ■ A S N E R
F O E ■ C A D ■ G L O
L O T ■ B A R O N ■ A L O H A
A D A ■ A T T ■ O S S ■ F O X
B E G E T ■ H U N C H ■ A V E
■ D H L ■ P E R ■ G E D
T R Y S T ■ S T A T L E R
B E E ■ R A W ■ P O L
I N T E R ■ F I R E W A T E R
G O R M E ■ T N N ■ E M E R Y
D R O I D ■ A G A ■ R O X I E
```

100

```
T E R I ■ R E D O S E ■ S T P
B E E F ■ I M E A S Y ■ W E E
I R I S H C O F F E E ■ E N T
R I G ■ E E R O ■ B E E N E
D E N S E ■ Y E S M A S T E R
■ U P N ■ H E L O T S ■
E C C E ■ O R D E A L ■ A S H
L A O S ■ H O S E D ■ P L E A
M M M ■ S E L L T O ■ O K E D
■ B E E T L E ■ W A G ■
P R O S E P O E M ■ F O R A Y
R I F L E ■ L O S T ■ A T E
E D A ■ P O L L I N A T I O N
E G G ■ E L O I S E ■ I S N T
N E E ■ D E L E T E ■ P E E L
```

101

```
B I T E ■ A S I A N ■ M A M A S
L O O P ■ C A S E Y ■ A G A V E
O W N S ■ A L E R T ■ R A M O N
C A S I N C U E ■ A L I B I S
■ L A I T ■ A A S I N A R E
C O R O N A E ■ L I O N S ■
A R E N A ■ K I L N ■ T A G S
N Y U ■ S A S I N S E A ■ U N O
E X P O ■ R O M E ■ M U R A L
■ R A I N Y ■ I M I T A T E
E A S I N E Y E ■ N I C E ■
A L L E Y S ■ Y A S I N Y O U
S T A N D ■ I A M B S ■ S O B S
Y E N T A ■ Q R C I U ■ I L I E
A R T S Y ■ S C A T S ■ L O T S
```

102

```
L O A F S ■ N O R M A ■ U F O
A R G O T ■ O N E A M ■ N E W
M A R X A T T A C K S ■ F A N
P L A Y B O Y ■ T E T H E R S
■ F E Z ■ S E A M ■
A B E A U T I F U L M I N X
S L E E P ■ P A R ■ N I M
W E T C E L L ■ R E P L I C A
A P T ■ E Y E ■ R A N K S
T H E L O V E L Y B O X E S
■ D A L I ■ F E E ■
B R A N D T S ■ A L L O W E D
L A V ■ E A T X R A Y L O V E
U Z I ■ S T A E L ■ R A V E L
R E S ■ T E R R Y ■ E V E N T
```

103

```
G U M P _ S T E T _ O T O E S
I N R E _ O O Z E _ P E N A L
S A C A J A W E A _ P R E G O
_ _ C A P E K _ M O R A L E
R A C E R _ R I B O S O M E S
A E I O U _ S E I Z E R _ _
M O G U L S _ L G A _ A P P
O N A T E A R _ A R M E N I A
S S R _ D U B _ T A S T E R
_ _ A R I S E S _ S P O C K
S P A C E S H I P _ H O N E S
T A L C U M _ J A N U S _ _
A R L E S _ F I L I P I N O S
R E A D E _ O N K P _ T I D E
K E Y E D _ E G O S _ O L E G
```

104

```
A B O W _ P R O M _ S T U D
N E V A _ L I N U S _ T O N E
G R A N D O P E R A _ R I M S
E N T E R _ B R U C E L E E
L I I _ A V O C A D O P E A R
I N O R B I T _ Y I N _ T N T
C I N E _ C O O _ D U S T _
_ _ P R I E D O P E N _ _
_ I P S O _ D N A _ T B S P
O S A _ B A T _ U N C O U T H
W A L D O P E P P E R _ Y E A
L I M E T R E E _ E A S E S
I D O L _ I N S I D E D O P E
S N I T _ L E T M E _ A U E R
H O L A _ R O P E _ M T N S
```

105

```
S M U T _ F I S T _ N A S H
W I N O _ I N C A _ M O L T O
I N K S _ L U A U _ A B B A S
[EMC]I N S T [EMC]I N _ C O[EMC]A S T
A M O _ O A T _ R O I L _ _
P A T R O N _ B A D S P O R T
_ [EMC]L O V I N _ M R S U N
P A L L _ N A R C O _ I S N T
I L I A C _ S C H U L Z _ _
P L U T A R C H _ T O[EMC]A T S
_ I N T O _ A B C _ S H U
C A N V A S [EMC]Q U A T I O N
O N A I R _ A J A R _ H A R D
P A S T Y _ L O B S _ A G A R
S L A Y _ A B A T _ R O X Y
```

106

```
R A M _ I C E T _ S T A T S
U S A _ D A Z E _ O H T H A T
B A N _ E R I N _ T R U E T O
I D I O M _ N C O _ I N D E X
K A F K A _ E O N _ L E E _
_ E R N E _ M E A L _ S R I
A S S A D S _ M O N A _ C A B
J O T _ A S H A N T I _ E V E
A N D _ R E I N _ I N O N I T
R Y E _ E S T D _ S M U T _
_ S A C _ U M P _ A T O M S
T U T T O _ P E R _ N A F T A
S T I R U P _ N E H I _ M I X
P A N I N I _ T O I L _ A D E
_ H Y A T T _ S P C A _ N A S
```

107

```
C A S H _ J E A N _ C A P E
R A T E _ A M I E _ P O W E R
O B A M A C A R E _ L D O P A
P A R A S K I _ T R A _ K P S
_ C E L T _ O N E E Y E _
C A R R O T _ W Y A T T _ _
A B E E T _ F E E L _ Y O L K
K E N T _ B R E A D _ M P A A
E D D Y _ O E D S _ S O U T H
_ P I X E L _ B U N S E N
F R E E Z E _ E H U D _ _
R O B _ O S U _ A R A P A H O
A V O I D _ S K I N N Y D I P
M E N D S _ P I K E _ R A K E
E D Y S _ S P U R _ O M E N
```

108

```
S T A B _ D O C K S _ D I L L
C O S I _ Y A H O O _ E L O I
H U C K L E F I N N _ C L O T
I C R I E D _ R E A L I S T
R H I N E _ M B A _ P A N E L
R U B I K _ E L D E R W I N E
A P E _ B O A _ T O E _ _
_ S T R A W B L O N D E _
_ Y U L _ B E N _ A B A
R A S P B E R E T _ A A R O N
A I M E E _ E D S _ H E L L O
P R E S S E D _ S A G G E D
I S L E _ C H U C K B E R R Y
D E L T _ H O K E Y _ A E O N
S A Y S _ O T R O S _ N Y S E
```

109

```
C A L A I S █ N U D E █ T R E
A L U M N A █ E P I C U R E S
M E N T A L █ W H O O P I E S
S C A R L E T T E R █ A P S E
█ █ A L M A █ L S D █ L E X
L I C K █ W M D █ E V E █ █
A D O █ C A N E █ F R A P P E
P E R C Y B Y S S H E L L E Y
D A N U B E █ S T A G █ A P E
█ U T E █ N Y E █ B Y E S █
Z A C █ R B I █ E S A U █ █
A W O L █ L A N D O N O V A N
P A P A L A C E █ L O Y O L A
P R I M E R I B █ A D U L T S
A D A █ D E N S █ R E P E A T
```

110

```
G I L █ T A D █ F A T █ O M S
O B E █ S P I N A C H █ X O O
P E E K A B O O I S E E Y O U
F R A U █ X E R █ A G I N █
F I N N S █ I L E R █ S E N D
T A N G O E D █ S A Y I N G S
█ F A C E █ T I M E █ █ █
U N C U R L █ █ S C R O L L
S E A █ S A N G R I A █ N A E
A W R Y █ T I M O N █ C E N T
█ S L U M █ P O T █ C A L C █
A R O M A S █ P O N I E S █
F O R Y O U R E Y E S O N L Y
T O F U █ M O N E T █ L E O N
A M F M █ O Z O N E █ A R T E
```

111

```
C H A R G E █ S A S H I M I S
O U T E A T █ E M P A N A D A
A L T I M A █ M O R T I M E R
X K E █ E L M █ R U E █ E S A
█ M I T █ O V E N M I T T S █
O H P L E A S E █ G A B █ █
R I T E █ M E R V █ I N B E D
C H E █ D A Y S A I L █ A V E
S O D O I █ S A N S █ I S E E
█ B A T █ C I T A D E L S █
I N T I M A T E S █ T I M █
D O E █ E O E █ H I E █ E E L
L I M I T I N G █ D M I T R I
E S P R E S S O █ O P I A T E
D E S E R T E D █ S O I L E D
```

112

```
S E L A █ S P I R E █ A Q U A
P A I R █ E L L E N █ N U L L
F R U I T S A L A D █ G I N A
█ █ O R A N █ T I B E T A N
█ A S S A M █ P A N E L S █
A L P O █ E G I S █ F A M E D
G I L █ P O E T █ K O S O V O
O B I █ H I T S O N G █ K E N
R I T U A L █ T R E S █ I R E
A S S N S █ C O R E █ A N T E
█ C H E W U P █ B O N G S █
P A R A D E S █ B E A D █
O P E N █ I T S I N T H E R E
D E E D █ R E S O D █ O L E O
S S N S █ D R E G S █ W I T S
```

113

```
█ F L U I D █ R O B E █ █
█ P E A R C E █ A S O N E █
█ S I N U S E S █ W H O A M I
(1)P E N D A L E S D A N C E R S
P Y R E S █ █ R C A █ T E A T
E C O L █ P O T A T O(5) █ R N A
W A G █ (3)I N █ R A P M U S I C
A R I Z O N I A N █ P U P █
█ E T E █ V E R O N I Q U E
A R(2)E L A G O █ A S K █ U N C
S I S █ E L O C U T E █ L I P O
E C H O █ K E N █ S O C A L
C H O C O L A T E(4)C O O K I E
█ E T C H E R █ S P O R T E D
█ S A I N T █ C E N T E R █
█ M O S S █ O R E A D █
```

(1) CHIP (2) CHIP (3) CHIP (4) CHIP (5) CHIP

114

```
R E E L █ B R E R █ M A S T S
A L L E V I A T E █ I N U I T
D O W A H D I D D Y D I D D Y
O P E N S █ █ H O R █ S E X
N E S T █ C I A L I S █ █
█ █ O B L A D I O B L A D A
S S N █ O A T E R █ █ A T O M
I K O I K O █ █ S H B O O M
A I R S █ A E R I E █ P R O
M M M M M M M M M M M M M █
█ S T I R I N █ █ O R A L
A B C █ C S A █ P R I M O
D O O D O O D O O D O O D O O
D U N N O █ I N T E R S E C T
S T E A K █ O T T O █ E R O S
```

115

```
S K I P O L E S   O B I W A N
H E D O N I S T   R E S A L E
I N A S E N S E   E E R I E R
M O S E S   E M I G R A T E D
      D E R N   M O P E
P E S A C H   H O N O L U L U
A V A S   E B A N   N I N E S
R E D   P A R T I N G   S E A
I N A P T   Y E T I   B E R G
S T T H O M A S   S P A R S E
    A M A N   T I E R
G U A R A N T O R   E G Y P T
O R D A I N   S A O P A U L O
O D D O N E   T I R E I R O N
P U S H E R   E T E R N I T Y
```

116

```
A D V   P S S T S   M O H E L
G A I   P U T U P   A B O N E
G R A N D M E R E   C O R D S
I N G E   A N N E E   E S O S
E I R E   C O R   D E S E R T
S T A D T   S E O U L   C S A
    T A D   D E C I   A E R
  B R O K E N   R E C O R D
S A O   E P I C   D I N
E T D   M O C H A   T E A M O
R A C I E R   E C O   R D A S
A N A L   T H E I R   U L N A
P E R E C   O R D A I N I N G
H Y E N A   W I L M A   B E E
S E W E D   L O Y A L   S R S
```

117

```
W O R K   C O L O R   A T O P
A L I I   H A I K U   C A R S
S E A S   A T E I T   C I T Y
P A S S E S   T E A S E L S
    C R E D O   B A D
B A C A R D I   A A H E D A T
A T O M   S U R G E   E D U
N O R   G E N E R A L   R O N
D N A   O X E Y E   S E R E
B E L T W A Y   S M A C K E R
    I N C   S T O M A
  M A E S T R I   H A R R I S
C O R D   I O N I A   F O R D
B L E U   N B C T V   E L I A
C L A P   G E E S E   D E S K
```

118

```
R A W   H O I S T   W A S T E
A L A   O C C U R   I D I O M
M E X   T H E R E S N O T W O
E R E C T     E M I G R A N T
N O R A E P H R O N   E R S E
    L A R A   R E V
T H A I   I M P   I S L E S
N O N P R E S C R I P T I O N
T I T H E   S E W   P E S O
    A S K   F I F E
D U E L   N O M I N A T I O N
O K L A H O M A   T E M P O
W A Y S A B O U T I T   P E T
E S S E N   D R O V E   E R E
L E E R S   O A T E R   L A D
```

119

```
F O N T   D A P   I M C O L D
U T A H   O L E   M E R R I E
D O Z E   N E Z   B R A Z E N
D E I C I D E   B U T T O U T
    U N I   B A E Z
S N O R K E L E R S   C A I N
N E W S A G E N T   A C M E
E R N E   O O Z E D   P I P E
A V E O   N I N E S I D E D
K E R F   M I N D L E S S L Y
    Z A N E   A R T
A N E M O N E   A V A R I C E
L I Z A R D   Z E E   A Z O V
O N E A R M   E R G   N O P E
T O R S O S   B O A   O D E S
```

120

```
I S L E   B S A   A L T A R S
S P I T B A L L   C A R N E Y
M A S H U N I T   A V A I L S
  T A B I T H A   A D M I T
A D E N   S H O R E L E A V E
R A N   S H Y   E L I   L E M
F R U I T   O S I E R
  P R E S E N T A R M S
  S P L A T   E N A C T
A B A   I O R   I T S   L A D
F I R I N G L I N E   S E T S
G R A D S   S O F T E N S
H E R O I C   W A R G A M E S
A M A N D A   A N A G R A M S
N E T T E D   S T S   K N O W
```

121

```
C L I C K B A I T · · A N G S T
H E N R I E T T A · N O R A H ·
I N S O M N I A C · D R I V E ·
R A P S · · M L K J R · N A B ·
A P O S T L E · L E A N N E · ·
C E T E R A · A G O · N I N A ·
· · D O T T I E · J O N A S · ·
F I V E T H I R T Y E I G H T ·
A D A Y S · R E S E W N · · · ·
C O R E · R E D · L E T S A T ·
E N D S I T · A L L E N D E · ·
S T A · K E L P S · D A V E · ·
O L L I E · O U T S P O K E N ·
F I O N A · S T R A I N E R S ·
F E S T S · S T O P P E D B Y ·
```

122

```
M A K E S A M E S S · A T A D
O P E R A M U S I C · B O B O
B O Y S O P R A N O · S P O T
I S E E · D I E T Z · H U H ·
L E D · M M E · W I I M O T E
· · T I A R A · A G E N T J ·
P S A L M I S T · C O H O · ·
A L A S K A N K I N G C R A B
L A Y S · C O M E L A S T · ·
P C H E L P · F E T U S · · ·
H E E L E R S · S H E · F C C
A N Y · G O T A T · K A R L ·
S A K E · B A B A O R I L E Y
I M I T · S L A M D A N C E D
G E D S · T E A P O T D O M E
```

123

```
L C H A I M · · K R U G M A N
L E A D T O · D I E T R I T E
A T M O S T · A B N O R M A L
M U M B O J U M B O · E N L ·
A S Y E · U T I L I Z E · · ·
· · S H E E R A G O N Y · · ·
U N B E A T E N · I G L O O ·
S C U L L E R · C A R E E N S
M A N E T · T U N E D O U T ·
C A T C H A C O L D · · · · ·
· T O W R O P E · A N I L · ·
H E S · N O H A R M D O N E ·
A L P A C I N O · S I Z E U P
C L A R I N E T · O R E L S E
K E Y T A G S · N A S S E R ·
```

124

```
B A N J O · M C M A N S I O N
O L E I C · C R A Z Y B O N E
T O W N S · D O N T P A N I C
C H E X · C U E D · I N T · ·
H A R E M · S H A K · M A Y A
· S E Q U E L · M I N E R · ·
D S O · R U N T · B O N S A I
R A R E G A S · L A N T E R N
E L A T E D · W O R K · A S E
A L L E S · H E B R E W · · ·
M I E S · B A B E · Y A L T A
L E X · H E R S · P O O R · ·
A M A R Y L L I S · Z I P P O
N A M E P L A T E · A T E A M
D E S M O I N E S · P I Z Z A
```

125

```
Z A C H · M A M A · A M A Z E
I L I E · O V I D · P U T O N
N O G S · L E T I T B L E E D
C O A S T T O C O A S T · · ·
· F R E R E · H S T · I R R ·
· A N S · · · · · S P E E · ·
H O S T I L E T A K E O V E R
A T E E N A G E R I N L O V E
W H A T E V E R I T T A K E S
G E N E R A L I N T E R E S T
· R C A S · · · · G E N · · ·
· S E T · S A G · N C A A S ·
· · · E N T R A N C E F E E S
L A S T H U R R A H · I S N T
A S N E R · O T T O · R O S Y
X H O S A · W H E W · E P E E
```

126

```
F A S T P A C E · · W E B B S
A U T O L O A N · S A T U R N
U P I N A R M S · P R A G U E
L A F I T T E · C R Y · B C E
T I L T · A L M A Y · D E E R
· R E E F · C O M · K O A L A
· · T R A D E S E C R E T · ·
· P A O L O V E R O N E S E ·
L U C K B E A L A D Y · · · ·
A R E A S · L E T · A D A M ·
W I R Y · D R D R E · O R E M
O T B · B A Y · I M P L O R E
M A I T A I · A P P L A U S E
A N T O N S · G O T U P S E T
N S Y N C · O D Y S S E Y S ·
```

127

```
C A R O U S E S . . . P E R F
O V E R S T A T E . . O V A L
L A T E A U T U M N . S E G A
A I R G U N S . B O D E R E K
N L E A S T . D E G A U S S .
D I A N A . P I Z A R R O . .
E N T O . G U Z Z L E S . . .
R G S . D A Z Z L E D . M P S
. . T I Z Z I E S . W E R E .
. F O O Z L E R . M I X E R .
H E N N A E D . V I S I N E .
M O N T E R O . S E N E C A N
O M N I . A U N T I E M A M E
P E E N . T O L D T A L E S .
E R L E . B O T A N I S T . .
```

128

```
R A M B L E O N . . L I E T O
A N A L O G U E . B A N Y A N
N I C E W O R K . U P N E X T
I S A A C . S O M M E . S F O
N E W T O Y . E S L . F R A .
. . M O T H S . . B R A S . .
. T H E W H O S E L L O U T .
. N O O D L E D A R O U N D .
J I M M Y S W A G G A R T . .
E C H O . . O D E O N . . . .
T K O . S A M . T S K T S K
S N O . C U B I C . H A I T I
K A P L A N . G O T A H E A D
I M E A N T . O V E R L O R D
S E R B S . R E C K O N S O
```

129

```
B E A T P O E T . . H I F I S
L A D I E S M A N . A M I N O
O V E R S H A R E . H I N D U
T E L E . K I P S . A T E I T
S S E . L O L I T A . P A H .
. . M I S S T E P . G R A B .
J U D I T H . S A P P H I R E
A N I S E . . . R A N I N .
M U S T R E A D . M I N T E D
E S P Y . G R E N A D A . . .
S U E . G A L O R E . A C U
D A R L A . F I J I . A L E S
E L S I E . A L O N G S I D E
A L A M O . T A K E A S T A B
N Y L O N . H E R S T O R Y
```

130

```
S T R E E T F A I R . C O G S
P O O L N O O D L E . A N O N
R O U G H R I D E R . N E B O
E N T R A I L S . O U T L A W
E S S E N E S . S O L O I N G
. . C C S . P A T E R N A L
S T J O E . M E L E E . E N O
M I E S . L I K E D . G R A B
A G R . S O N E S . P O S S E
R E S E R V E S . D A S . . .
T R E A T E D . P A S S I N G
A M Y T A N . C O N T I N U E
L O I S . E M A N C I P A T E
E T T A . S E N T I M E N T S
C H E T . T R A I N E D E Y E
```

131

```
R I S K . F I V E K . A C S
A R C A D E F I R E . S N A P
M A R T I N A M I S . P I P E
S T U R M . . C H A I T E A
. E M I . A B S . A T T A C K
. N A R U T O . T A H O E .
J A V A S C R I P T . L I R A
A N A . H E I N I E S . L A S
C A P S . D A K A R R A L L Y
O B I T S . L E T S O N . .
B I D I N G . R E E . T S K
Z O N E O U T . . O N E A L
U S E R . T Y L E R P E R R Y
M I S S . S P E C I E S I S M
A S S . Y O Y O S . T A T E
```

132

```
S P A M B O T . W A L K O F F
M A N C A V E . A S A R U L E
I R A Q W A R . B E R A T E S
L A C . L L A M A . D U C A T
E D I T . S W I S H . T O B E
S E N O R . A S H O T . M A R
. . R E N T S . M A X E N E
F E A R N O T . D E B A S E D
O U T E A T . X E R O X . . .
O P T . L E G O S . R I F T S
S H E A . S E X E S . S A R I
B O S C O . T O R C H . K I N
A R T E M I S . T H E B E S T
L I T I N T O . E M E R I T A
L A O T I A N . R O L O D E X
```

133

```
M A D E M A N   N E T W O R K
C H O C O L A T E C O O K I E
I S H O T T H E S H E R I F F
      C L O S E T O   D E L I
A D R I E N       M I S E R
B R O D Y   O N E S I E
Z A N E   S K I N N E R B O X
U N C   C O A L G A S   L E D
G O O G O L P L E X   P A S O
      R A D I A L   B A N T U
R O G E T       R A C K E T
O D O M   S I E N E S E
S O U L J A B O Y T E L L E M
A U D I O V I S U A L A I D S
S L A N T E D   K R Y P T O N
```

134

```
J O A N B A E Z   P A C K O N
I N N U E N D O   E N H A L O
L E T S D O W N   N E A T E R
T I L   S T A K I N G   M A T
E D E R   E R O D E   G A S H
D A R E S   D U I   M O N T E
      P O I N T O F O R D E R
S C H E R Z O   S O J O U R N
C R A N B E R R Y B O G
H O S T S   T O N   S U E R S
A N T S   T O S C A   E L E C
E K E   D E N A R I I   I V O
F I N I A L   L A S T E X I T
E T E R N E   I S L A M I S T
R E D S O X   E Y E S O R E S
```

135

```
C L E A R O N E S T H R O A T
R E S T O R E T O H E A L T H
A T S O M E O T H E R T I M E
S T E P S O N O N E S T O E S
S S N     T R E     H E S
      A W G E E   J E D
R A I N H A T   D A Y   E L M
A M A T E U R   I N B O X E S
J O N   N S A   N I A L O N G
      H I S   S N E R D
    C A M   S T E     C A B
O R A N G E M A R M A L A D E
W I S D O M O F S O L O M O N
A S C E N T O F E V E R E S T
R E A L E S T A T E S A L E S
```

136

```
C A B O O S E   S H A S T A
A S S U R E D   C H E R O O T
S K I T E A M   P I N E N U T
T A D L I N C O L N   A G R A
S N E A D   B L U E S   C D C
      N A I A D S   K A Y A K
S H E D   R I S   S A N C T A
T O L E D A N   N E T T L E D
A V E R Y S   M A R   H E S S
L E A S E   R E D F I R
I R R   D I O N E   C A D I Z
N O N I   S O U R C E C O D E
E V I N C E D   I O D I Z E S
R E N D E R S   T A U T E S T
A R G Y L E   E X P E R T S
```

137

```
O N B A S E   B U M S   D R S
M O O R E D   A G E N C I E S
I R O N E D   R A N A L O N G
T A K E M Y W O R D F O R I T
      R T S   A N T E U P
M E E T   G I M E L   P S A T
A L T   E T T U   P E T R A
D O U B L E E N T E N D R E S
A R R A Y   C R O C   I N T
T O N S   I T H A S   O K A Y
    S A M O A N   O N E
H O T A S B L U E B L A Z E S
A P P L A U D S   I M P O R T
N A K E D E Y E   B E A N I E
S H E   A S A N   S C R E E N
```

138

```
A P R I C O T J A M   E X A M
G U I T A R S O L O   T R I O
A Z E R B A I J A N   C A R T
S O N Y A   N O M E   H Y P O
      N A G   O Y S   V A R
B A D S A N T A   E L V I S H
F R E E   T A B   D O E S S O
L E T G O   O C T   P R I A M
A Y E A Y E   T E E   D O G E
T O R R E Y   V A C C I N E S
M U M   Z E D   M O D
A S I F   M E O W   C H I L I
J U N E   A L L O S A U R U S
O R E S   S T A R T S M A L L
R E D S   K A F K A E S Q U E
```

139

T	A	K	E	S	T	O	■	B	O	A	T	E	R
O	N	A	L	E	A	S	H	■	I	M	B	U	S	Y
A	G	R	I	C	O	L	A	■	P	I	E	R	C	E
D	E	M	O	■	S	O	V	I	E	T	■	N	A	B
S	L	A	T	E	■	■	E	N	D	■	P	E	R	E
■	■	N	O	V	A	S	■	F	U	D	G	E
M	A	R	G	I	N	O	F	E	R	R	O	R
B	E	F	O	R	E	I	F	O	R	G	E	T
B	A	T	T	L	E	S	C	A	R	R	E	D
E	T	H	E	L	■	F	E	R	M	I
S	T	A	R	■	P	O	T	■	S	A	L	M	A
T	E	D	■	F	U	R	R	O	W	■	S	A	A	B
I	R	O	B	O	T	■	I	R	I	S	H	P	U	B
R	U	N	O	U	T	■	P	E	T	P	E	E	V	E
S	P	E	A	R	S	■	S	T	A	N	L	E	Y

140

S	C	A	R	F	R	I	N	G	■	B	O	M	B	E
T	O	L	E	R	A	N	C	E	■	A	V	A	I	L
R	O	L	L	I	N	G	O	N	■	D	I	N	K	S
A	L	S	A	T	I	A	■	D	R	A	F	T	E	E
P	H	O	T	O	N	■	G	E	A	R	O	I	L
P	E	R	E	S	■	B	A	R	T	E	R	S
E	A	T	S	■	J	I	M	B	E	A	M
D	D	S	■	F	A	K	E	I	D	S	■	B	A	H
■	D	I	V	E	B	A	R	■	M	I	R	O
■	B	O	L	E	R	O	S	■	C	A	N	S	T
■	N	O	M	E	R	C	Y	■	S	U	N	G	O	D
C	O	R	I	N	T	H	■	G	A	R	D	E	N	A
A	R	E	N	A	■	I	C	A	L	L	E	D	I	T
S	T	R	O	M	■	C	E	L	L	U	L	O	S	E
H	E	S	S	E	■	K	N	E	E	P	A	N	T	S

141

T	A	S	T	E	S	B	A	D	■	D	O	D	G	E
S	E	W	E	R	L	I	N	E	■	O	N	E	A	M
E	N	E	R	G	Y	B	A	R	■	G	U	M	U	P
T	E	A	M	O	■	K	I	N	G	S	I	Z	E
S	I	T	S	■	F	R	I	D	A	Y	■	J	E	R
E	D	Y	■	R	O	O	N	E	Y	■	P	O	P	O
■	B	U	T	T	S	■	L	E	H	A	R
F	A	C	E	B	O	O	K	F	R	I	E	N	D	S
L	I	O	N	S	■	Y	E	A	R	N
A	R	N	E	■	T	O	W	A	G	E	■	J	A	Y
P	F	C	■	C	E	D	A	R	S	■	M	E	R	E
J	O	E	C	A	M	E	L	■	B	A	R	C	A
A	R	D	O	R	■	S	K	I	P	A	R	K	A	S
C	C	E	L	L	■	S	E	V	E	N	C	E	N	T
K	E	S	E	Y	■	A	R	E	A	C	O	D	E	S

142

C	P	L	■	S	C	O	W	L	E	D	■	B	R	O
U	R	I	■	E	A	R	H	O	L	E	■	O	E	R
T	A	P	P	A	N	Z	E	E	B	R	I	D	G	E
L	I	B	A	T	I	O	N	B	E	A	R	E	R	S
E	R	A	T	O	■	■	T	U	G	A	T
T	I	L	T	■	S	N	O	O	P	■	L	A	D	E
S	E	M	I	S	O	F	T	C	H	E	E	S	E	S
■	A	L	L	H	A	I	L
I	D	O	N	T	F	E	E	L	L	I	K	E	I	T
N	E	V	A	■	A	R	R	A	S	■	E	L	M	O
S	P	A	N	G	■	C	R	A	I	G
E	A	R	T	H	S	H	A	T	T	E	R	I	N	G
A	R	I	Z	O	N	A	C	A	R	D	I	N	A	L
M	T	A	■	S	O	L	A	R	I	A	■	E	W	E
S	S	N	■	T	W	O	D	O	O	R	■	S	E	D

143

Y	A	H	E	A	R	D	■	F	R	A	I	D	S	O
O	P	E	N	B	A	R	■	T	E	R	R	E	L	L
G	E	L	C	A	P	S	■	C	A	C	K	L	E	D
I	S	L	A	■	G	E	O	■	C	O	S	T	A	S
■	S	C	R	U	N	C	H	■	A	Z	O
F	I	R	E	H	O	S	E	S	■	A	A	H	E	D
A	G	O	■	R	U	S	S	I	A	N	M	O	B
B	E	D	H	O	P	■	S	I	O	U	A	N
T	E	A	M	S	P	O	R	T	S	■	S	L	Y
D	I	O	D	E	■	T	H	E	R	E	B	E	L	S
E	T	D	■	S	A	N	J	O	S	E
B	O	R	A	G	E	■	O	O	N	■	N	A	P	E
A	K	I	H	I	T	O	■	I	A	S	I	M	O	V
S	A	V	A	L	A	S	■	N	U	T	C	A	S	E
E	Y	E	B	A	T	H	■	S	T	P	E	T	E	R

144

C	O	S	M	O	S	■	A	G	T	■	E	L	B	A
S	C	H	U	S	S	■	G	O	A	L	L	O	U	T
H	U	R	L	E	R	■	A	T	T	I	T	U	D	E
A	L	O	T	■	W	R	O	T	E	O	N
R	A	V	I	O	L	I	■	Y	O	U	N	G	E	R
P	R	E	T	Z	E	L	L	O	O	P	■	E	S	A
■	A	M	A	D	E	U	S	■	C	R	A	M
E	L	I	S	A	■	C	A	R	■	G	A	S	U	P
L	A	R	K	■	W	A	R	R	I	O	R
A	M	I	■	F	O	R	Y	O	U	R	L	O	V	E
L	A	S	S	O	E	D	■	O	D	E	S	S	A	N
■	H	O	T	I	T	E	M	■	A	M	I	D
I	M	A	L	O	S	E	R	■	B	E	G	O	N	E
T	A	L	I	S	M	A	N	■	E	R	A	S	E	R
S	P	E	D	■	E	M	O	■	D	I	N	E	R	S

145

M	A	Y	O	■	A	S	T	I	■	S	W	E	P	T
E	L	A	M	■	C	H	I	N	C	H	I	L	L	A
D	O	W	N	G	O	E	S	F	R	A	Z	I	E	R
S	E	N	I	O	R	S	■	A	U	G	■	Z	A	P
■	■	P	U	N	■	O	L	D	G	O	A	T	S	■
S	T	A	R	R	■	B	O	L	E	Y	N	■	■	■
T	O	L	E	D	O	O	H	I	O	■	C	O	S	A
D	I	S	S	E	N	T	■	B	I	A	L	I	E	S
S	L	O	E	■	A	T	A	L	L	C	O	S	T	S
■	■	■	N	E	L	L	I	E	■	C	U	E	I	N
A	S	H	T	R	E	E	S	■	T	O	D	■	■	■
T	E	A	■	O	A	S	■	T	U	R	N	S	T	O
B	R	I	T	I	S	H	S	O	L	D	I	E	R	S
A	R	T	I	C	H	O	K	E	S	■	N	A	I	L
R	A	I	T	A	■	P	A	S	A	■	E	L	M	O

146

G	E	T	S	R	E	A	L	■	■	M	O	V	I	E
A	L	I	T	A	L	I	A	■	W	I	N	O	N	A
S	T	M	O	R	I	T	Z	■	O	C	U	L	A	R
J	O	E	P	E	S	C	I	■	W	A	S	A	B	I
E	R	L	■	■	H	O	O	F	■	■	T	I	N	■
T	O	Y	O	T	A	■	P	A	U	S	I	N	G	■
■	■	■	P	O	S	T	E	R	C	H	I	L	D	■
■	■	S	E	A	C	R	E	A	T	U	R	E	■	■
■	J	E	R	S	E	Y	S	H	O	R	E	■	■	■
M	U	L	A	T	T	O	■	R	U	N	D	M	C	■
I	L	E	■	I	N	S	T	■	■	O	O	O	■	■
R	I	C	R	A	C	■	T	E	N	S	P	O	T	S
R	A	T	E	D	A	■	A	T	O	M	I	Z	E	S
O	N	E	N	I	L	■	L	O	V	E	B	I	T	E
R	A	D	O	N	■	■	K	N	O	W	B	E	S	T

147

A	C	I	D	I	C	■	C	H	A	C	H	I	N	G
S	U	N	O	C	O	■	A	I	W	E	I	W	E	I
P	L	A	N	A	R	■	B	E	A	N	T	O	W	N
■	■	W	E	N	D	■	B	R	I	T	■	J	A	G
A	R	O	A	R	■	R	I	O	T	■	T	I	G	E
C	A	R	N	E	G	I	E	■	T	A	M	E	R	■
T	O	D	D	L	E	S	■	S	I	R	K	A	Y	■
■	■	D	A	N	K	■	C	L	U	E	■	■	■	■
K	N	O	T	T	Y	■	R	E	S	T	A	T	E	■
K	R	O	N	E	■	S	I	X	T	H	M	A	N	■
O	I	S	E	■	A	S	A	P	■	N	E	R	D	S
W	S	W	■	S	E	T	I	■	S	O	F	A	■	■
T	H	E	C	L	O	U	D	■	L	O	A	D	E	D
O	N	A	H	U	N	C	H	■	I	N	L	I	N	E
W	A	T	E	R	S	K	I	■	M	E	L	O	D	Y

148

M	A	N	E	N	O	U	G	H	■	B	A	N	G	S
O	N	O	N	E	K	N	E	E	■	U	R	I	A	H
V	E	A	L	O	S	C	A	R	■	T	I	E	T	O
E	T	H	A	N	■	■	R	E	N	T	A	C	O	P
■	■	R	S	V	P	■	■	E	N	D	E	R	S	■
S	M	O	G	■	A	R	T	I	S	A	N	■	■	■
O	R	W	E	L	L	I	A	N	■	K	E	B	A	B
T	S	E	■	U	S	E	R	F	E	E	■	R	C	A
S	C	R	U	B	■	R	O	A	L	D	D	A	H	L
■	■	T	R	U	S	T	M	E	■	E	Y	E	D	■
S	A	V	O	I	R	■	■	Y	E	S	T	■	■	■
C	L	I	P	C	L	O	P	■	■	O	E	S	T	E
A	T	R	I	A	■	T	U	R	D	U	C	K	E	N
R	E	G	A	N	■	B	L	U	E	S	T	A	T	E
F	R	O	N	T	■	S	P	Y	M	A	S	T	E	R

149

G	A	N	G	N	A	M	■	L	E	A	P	S	A	T
A	M	E	R	I	C	A	■	O	I	L	R	I	C	H
S	O	M	E	T	H	I	N	G	S	F	I	S	H	Y
O	R	E	■	E	D	Y	S	■	A	S	T	E	R	■
H	O	S	■	■	E	S	O	S	■	M	I	S	O	■
O	S	I	S	■	O	N	E	U	P	S	■	N	O	I
L	O	S	E	R	S	■	T	A	I	L	E	N	D	■
■	■	R	O	C	■	N	G	O	■	■	■	■	■	■
A	L	L	T	H	A	T	■	S	O	N	N	E	T	S
L	E	E	■	E	R	I	T	U	■	I	N	R	E	■
A	T	A	N	■	S	T	A	N	■	C	A	D	■	■
M	I	N	E	D	■	R	U	B	E	■	A	L	I	A
O	N	T	H	E	W	A	T	E	R	F	R	O	N	T
D	O	O	R	M	A	T	■	L	O	O	K	S	E	E
E	N	S	U	I	T	E	■	T	O	P	S	E	E	D

150

K	F	C	■	D	E	L	S	■	■	S	W	A	M	P
N	A	U	T	I	L	U	S	■	S	H	A	V	E	S
A	L	B	A	N	I	A	N	■	P	I	T	O	N	S
P	L	A	T	E	A	U	■	P	I	N	E	N	U	T
S	A	N	T	A	S	■	D	E	T	E	R	■	■	■
A	S	C	O	T	■	G	I	N	S	B	E	R	G	■
C	L	I	O	■	V	O	O	D	O	O	D	O	L	L
K	E	G	■	L	A	S	C	A	U	X	■	B	A	A
S	E	A	S	E	R	P	E	N	T	■	H	E	S	S
■	P	R	I	C	I	E	S	T	■	F	I	R	S	T
■	■	S	T	A	L	E	■	C	A	N	T	O	S	■
H	O	T	T	U	B	S	■	T	A	N	G	E	N	T
A	W	H	I	R	L	■	C	O	R	D	E	L	I	A
R	O	O	N	E	Y	■	I	M	P	O	S	E	O	N
M	E	M	E	S	■	D	E	E	M	■	E	N	D	■

151

	Z	A	Z	U			P	C	B	S			B	A	B	K	A
	S	L	I	M			E	R	L	E			A	P	L	A	N
	A	P	P	L	E	P	I	E	S			N	O	U	R	I
		C	A	R	I	B	B	E	A	N	S	E	A
A	M	O	U	N	T	S			R	E	T	T	O	N
R	E	D	T	E	A		H	A	I	R	L	I	K	E
C	H	E	S	S		M	O	C	S		E	T	E	S
		T	I	R	A	D	E	S
A	T	M	S		M	E	R	C		H	A	J	J	I
R	H	A	P	S	O	D	Y		A	I	L	E	E	N
R	E	L	I	E	F		R	A	N	L	A	T	E
P	A	C	I	F	I	C	O	C	E	A	N
T	I	R	E	S		S	U	P	E	R	G	L	U	E
I	L	I	U	M		A	B	E	L		E	U	R	O
C	L	A	P	S		K	A	R	L		S	C	I	S

152

G	Y	P	S	Y	J	A	Z	Z		E	P	C	O	T
N	O	T	Y	O	U	T	O	O		P	L	U	T	O
A	H	A	M	O	M	E	N	T		O	A	T	E	S
T	E	R	M		P	A	K		U	N	S	U	R	E
S	A	M	E	S		M	S	O	L	Y	M	P	I	A
V	I	T	U	S			G	U	M	S
D	E	G	R	E	E	M	I	L	L	S		M	C	S
S	H	A	Y		M	E	D	E	A		S	A	H	L
T	O	N		D	I	D	I	S	T	U	T	T	E	R
		M	E	T	A			E	N	A	T	E
B	E	E	R	B	E	L	L	Y		D	R	D	R	E
A	I	R	B	U	S		I	A	N		W	A	I	L
H	E	A	L	S		W	A	R	C	R	I	M	E	S
T	I	T	U	S		I	N	D	I	S	P	O	S	E
S	O	O	E	Y		M	E	S	S	T	E	N	T	S

153

B	B	Q	S	A	N	D	W	I	C	H		H	E	H
S	A	U	D	I	A	R	A	B	I	A		I	N	O
T	R	A	I	N	S	I	G	N	A	L		B	A	M
A	H	I		G	A	V	E		T	E	A	M	O
R	O	L	L	E		E	W	E	S		D	C	O	N
S	P	A	Y		F	R	A	N	K	G	E	H	R	Y
	S	T	E	A	L		R	O	Y	A	L	I	S	M
			M	I	L			S	L	R
I	T	S	M	A	G	I	C		I	P	A	D	S
D	E	E	P	T	H	R	O	A	T		A	R	T	Y
C	A	T	E		T	R	A	P		P	H	Y	L	A
A	M	I	G	A		R	A	G	A		F	U	N
R	U	N		B	L	I	S	T	E	R	P	A	C	K
D	S	T		L	A	K	E	O	N	T	A	R	I	O
S	A	O		E	Z	E	R	W	E	I	Z	M	A	N

154

A	M	B	I	T		F	O	U	L		B	E	D	S
P	E	A	C	E		A	D	Z	E		A	R	I	A
E	A	C	H	C	L	U	E	I	N		P	S	S	T
X	T	C		S	A	C		T	A	T	A	M	I
	F	A	D		P	E	P	S		S	I	T	A	R
E	R	R	O	L		T	H	E	P	U	Z	Z	L	E
S	E	A	G	O	D		A	T	O	N	E
P	E	T		S	U	L	L	I	E	D		S	T	Y
			M	E	D	E	A		T	E	M	P	E	R
I	S	M	I	S	S	I	N	G		R	O	L	E	S
Q	U	A	S	I		A	X	O	N		B	I	T
T	I	N	C	T	S		A	A	A		T	E	A
E	T	T	U		T	H	E	L	E	T	T	E	R	N
S	O	R	E		A	U	D	I		O	W	N	E	D
T	R	A	S		T	R	U	E		P	A	D	D	Y

155

C	R	O	W	D	S	O	U	R	C	E		A	L	E
H	O	N	O	R	S	Y	S	T	E	M		L	A	X
I	N	A	N	U	T	S	H	E	L	L		O	R	C
R	E	G		M	A	T	E		L	E	B	E	A	U
P	L	E	B		R	E	R	I		N	E	V	I	S
S	Y	R	U	P		R	I	C	O		B	E	D	E
			C	A	P		N	E	D	R	O	R	E	M
R	A	C	H	A	E	L		T	O	S	P	A	R	E
E	D	H	A	R	R	I	S		M	V	P
A	D	E	N		M	A	C	Y		P	E	T	I	T
R	I	C	A	N		T	H	A	R		D	A	M	E
E	T	H	N	O	S		M	M	I	V		I	G	A
X	I	N		M	A	R	I	A	C	A	L	L	A	S
I	V	Y		A	N	D	T	H	E	N	S	O	M	E
T	E	A		R	E	S	T	A	S	S	U	R	E	D

156

L	O	M	B	A	R	D		G	O	G	O	B	A	R
A	Z	O	B	L	U	E		O	V	E	R	A	T	E
Z	Z	Z	Q	U	I	L		G	A	N	G	S	T	A
A	F	I		I	N	T	E	G	R	A		S	I	D
R	E	L	Y		G	O	L	L	Y		M	A	M	E
U	S	L	A	W		I	K	E		B	A	L	E	R
S	T	A	S	H	E	D		S	E	E	R	E	S	S
			M	I	X				D	I	Y
F	I	T	I	N	T	O		J	U	N	K	A	R	T
U	P	O	N	E		N	A	E		G	A	T	O	R
J	A	N	E		P	A	P	A	S		Y	O	G	I
I	D	E		A	L	D	E	N	T	E		M	A	P
T	A	L	A	R	I	A		A	O	L	M	A	I	L
S	P	O	N	G	E	R		R	O	S	A	N	N	E
U	P	C	C	O	D	E		P	L	A	Y	T	E	X

157

```
O L D A G E P E N S I O N E R
R E E D U C A T I O N C A M P
R A C E T O T H E B O T T O M
■ V O S S ■ ■ ■ K E N S ■ ■ ■ ■
W E N T ■ F E A R ■ ■ ■ H M O
A S S E T A L L O C A T I O N
I T T ■ O Z M A ■ I S O L D E
T O R I N O ■ ■ C A P L E T
I D U N N O ■ R O A M ■ B R O
N I C K E L A N D D I M I N G
G E T ■ ■ D A D A ■ A L D O
■ ■ ■ C H A W ■ ■ ■ P O L A ■
P A T R O N A G E H I R I N G
G R E A T G R A N D N I E C E
S T E M L E S S G L A S S E S
```

158

```
C H I C K F I L A ■ M Y O P E
R A D I O E D I T ■ A E R I E
O N E A N D A L L ■ G A S S Y
A G E ■ Y E H ■ E N R I C O
K O F I ■ R O A D R U N N E R
E V I N C E ■ L O O M ■ O S E
D E X T E R ■ A S S O C ■ ■
■ R E E L ■ G M T ■ P I N G
■ ■ R E T R O ■ P U R E E S
O T O ■ R E E D ■ E S C O R T
P I N K Y S W E A R ■ A L T A
E N L I S T ■ B S A ■ O R I
R H I N E ■ S Q U I R T G U N
A A N D E ■ P U T S A S I D E
S T E A D ■ F A S T P A C E D
```

159

```
S T A D I U M R O C K ■ D I R
I M O U T T A H E R E ■ E N O
T A K E S T H E R A P ■ A D M
U N I ■ C E R A ■ Y T T R I A
■ ■ B O R E ■ G O F I R S T
P H O T O S ■ B E N I C E T O
H O V E L ■ M A N E T ■ A I M
O W E N ■ N A K E D ■ E D N A
N O R ■ B O X E S ■ E L E C T
E N S N A R E D ■ Q U A R T O
D E T E C T S ■ F U R L ■ ■
H A R R A H ■ C L I O ■ D V D
O R E ■ R E T A I L P R I C E
M T S ■ D R I V E T O W O R K
E H S ■ I N T E R S P E R S E
```

160

```
A D E P T ■ C O L U M N I S T
T O S E A ■ P R O N O U N C E
T W O A M ■ L E T T E R B O X
A N T H E M ■ ■ I N S E R T
C H E E S E B A L L ■ I T E M
K E R N ■ S I N E ■ S N A R E
E R I S ■ C O A T I N G ■ ■
D E C ■ B A D G I R L ■ C A T
■ ■ C O L O R T V ■ C H I A
I M H I P ■ M A G I ■ B E R G
N O U N ■ L E M O N G R A S S
C O M E L Y ■ ■ G R A P P A
I N A M O R A T A ■ I D E A L
T E N A C I O U S ■ M I N C E
E Y E S O C K E T ■ M O S E S
```

161

```
H U M B L E B R A G ■ A R C S
I N A D E Q U A T E ■ T E L E
L E N A D U N H A M ■ E L E A
L A D Y ■ A D M S ■ P I L A F
T R A ■ I L L ■ L L A N E R O
O T T E R ■ E M A I L ■ N E O
P H E N O M ■ O N R E C O R D
■ ■ O N E P O T A T O ■ ■
P O L L S T E R ■ S T E E P S
A R A ■ I R I S H ■ E N T R E
S L U M D O G ■ O B S ■ V O X
S A T I E ■ N A M E ■ B O O P
I N N S ■ S O C I A L L I F E
O D E S ■ W I N E C O O L E R
N O R M ■ F R E S H S T A R T
```

162

```
S T R E A K S ■ L E A D U P
Q U I R R E L L ■ A N G I N A
U N D E R D O G ■ S T R E W N
A N D ■ A S P E C T R A T I O
D E L T S ■ L O S E ■ S E P
S L E W ■ A P E X ■ P O L L
■ ■ O P T I C ■ S O D D Y
■ P R O J E C T R U N W A Y ■
C L A U S ■ R I F L E ■ ■
L A I T ■ C O M O ■ R A V E
A Y N ■ S H U N ■ A S T I N
M A G I C T R I C K S ■ H O F
A R E N O T ■ C O C A C O L A
T E A R U P ■ S T U N T M A N
O A R E R S ■ S P A R E S T
```

163

```
P A R I S ■ S H A G ■ S A A B
A G E N T ■ P I P E ■ T R I O
B I N G O N I G H T ■ A G R A
S L E E P E R H I T ■ B O H R
T E E ■ ■ W I S D O M ■ N O D
■ ■ ■ B U S T ■ ■ ■ O H A R E
■ B U M M I N G A R O U N D ■
■ C A R P E N T E R A N T S ■
■ R O C K I N G H O R S E S ■
O A K E N ■ ■ ■ L A S S ■ ■ ■
B L T ■ G I B S O N ■ P J S
O M A N ■ D R A G G E D O U T
T I L E ■ L O U I E L O U I E
I N K S ■ E O N S ■ S I N C E
C E S T ■ S K A T ■ E N D E D
```

164

```
I B E F O R E E ■ ■ F L U K E
D E L A W A R E ■ J O I N E D
S E A L S K I N ■ O U T I N G
A B B A ■ E C I G A R E T T E
Y E O ■ ■ K E E N ■ ■ ■ ■ ■
■ ■ R E B S ■ ■ T R U ■ M B A
I C A L L E M A S I S E E E M
N A T I O N A L A V E R A G E
B R E A K E R O N E N I N E R
I N O N E S S P A R E T I M E
G E N ■ S C H ■ ■ S T U N ■ ■
■ ■ ■ E A S T ■ ■ ■ G P S
T O P T E N L I S T ■ P L I E
A R A B I C ■ E A R P I E C E
W E C A R E ■ G R O A N S A T
S N A R E ■ ■ E S P R E S S O
```

165

```
A R S O N I S T S ■ D C C A B
N O T S O F A S T ■ E A R L E
G O A T R O D E O ■ A L A R M
L T D ■ I L L T R A D E Y O U
E R I N ■ D O S E S ■ B O S S
R O U E N ■ T E S T Y ■ L E E
S T M A R K ■ S U R E H A N D
■ ■ M O H S ■ P O N E ■ ■ ■
D I M E T A P P ■ S T A S I S
U N O ■ C L A R O ■ E R N S T
N A P A ■ I C O N S ■ T A D A
A L P H A F E M A L E ■ R U S
W I E S T ■ B O J A N G L E S
A N T I C ■ A T A N Y R A T E
Y E S N O ■ R E G G A E T O N
```

166

```
B R O M A N C E ■ R I B A L D
E A S Y P O U R ■ E C O C A R
N T H P O W E R ■ L A O T Z U
T E A R G A S ■ D I N K I E R
■ ■ ■ E E R ■ D U G ■ I D Y
S A U C E ■ V A R I E D ■ ■
A G N I ■ M A R I O N E T T E
G O T O R A C K A N D R U I N
A B O U T T U R N S ■ N E M O
■ ■ S E R I E S ■ W I S E S
R I B ■ I T D ■ S H E ■ ■ ■
A S A G R A Y ■ S T I R R E R
M I D A I R ■ D I E T C O K E
B A L Z A C ■ A N N E R I C E
O H Y E A H ■ G E T R I D O F
```

167

```
■ ■ F R E E W A Y ■ D E A D
■ P L E A S E D O ■ P A N T Y
T R O U S S E A U ■ A R I S E
R O A S T E D ■ C R U I S E R
O P T I O N ■ C H O C U L A
U M I N N ■ C H E M I S E ■
P A N G ■ C H I A N T I ■ ■
E N G ■ C H A N T E Y ■ R D S
■ ■ C H U T N E Y ■ B E E T
■ C H A R T E D ■ P R I M A
■ C H A R R E D ■ M O A N E D
W A R R I O R ■ B A L I H A I
A P O L O ■ B A R C E L O N A
C O M E T ■ O V E R A L L S
O N E S ■ ■ X E R O X E D
```

168

```
A T W H O L E S A L E ■ S O D
B R E A K I N G B A D ■ E P A
B A B Y S I T T E R S ■ M E W
E V E S ■ ■ E S T E E M I N G
Y E R ■ W A R ■ ■ D L I S T
■ ■ ■ S O C ■ E C O ■ S W A B
A F T E R M A T H ■ S H E B A
G R E A S E T H E W H E E L S
H O R S E ■ M A T U R A T E S
A G R A ■ T E N ■ S E R ■ ■
■ M A L T A ■ T S K ■ K I P
B A R T E N D E R ■ T A R A
A R I ■ A D I M E A D O Z E N
I C U ■ K E V I N D U R A N T
O H M ■ S M A R T P H O N E S
```

169

```
M O B I L E A P P . W A I T E
O N O N E S W A Y . A M A H L
S E E N I T A L L . D O M E D
T A R . A G E E . D R A K E .
. . B A T . S A L A M I S . .
S T R O B E S . R E L E N T .
T H I N A S A R E E D . R G S
R E T D . M A R . F I D O . .
U M A . F A S H I O N I C O N
C O M S A T . S T R E A M S .
K N O T T E D . R A F . . . .
D I R A C . Y O G A . D D T .
U T E R I . A L A N M O O R E
M O N E T . D I E T S O D A S
B R O D Y . S O L O S H O T S
```

170

```
M E S S K I T S . C R O T C H
A G E L I M I T . L A U R I E
N O S E C O N E . A S T U T E
S E E K . A P P S . S T E P .
. P S Y C H O P A T H . . . .
A W L . T U T E E . U R I A H
V I A . A M I N . S T I N G O
A L S O R A N . C O O P E R S
S C E N T S . C A L C . S E E
T O R T E . R O L E O . S E A
. D I R T Y H A R R Y . . . .
C R I P . T E E M . R A F A .
H U S T L E . R A R E B I R D
A S C O T S . E R I C B A N A
D E S E R T . D I C T A T E D
```

171

```
O R A L E X A M S . C R A S S
R E D C A R P E T . Z I P U P
G R A D U A T E D . A T A R I
C O M S . Y E T . X R A T E D
H U B . A S S E N T S . H O E
A T E S T . T R E E . S Y F Y
R E D E E M . S E R T A . . .
T S E L I O T . T R O U P E S
. . . E N N I S . A N D A L E
J A W S . I N K S . T I M I D
U Z O . L E T I T G O . P T A
L A N C E S . S E A . F L I T
E L T O N . T U R N L O O S E
P E O N Y . G I N J O I N T S
S A N K A . I T S A B L A S T
```

172

```
T R A P . M M X L . X T I N A
R A R E . A I D E . M O R E S
I N T R A N S I T . A M E N S
X I S . L I O N S . R E N E E
. C P A S . P O K I E S T . .
S T R O H S . O A T S . . . .
K U A L A . I R R I T A T E S
I D I D N T C A T C H T H A T
S E N S U A L L Y . E R A S E
. . . M O A B . B S I D E S .
P I E J E S U . P E P A . . .
A N D O R . D R A N O . O E R
R A D I I . I O N S T O R M S
E P I S C . U P D O . A C T V
S T E T S . S E A N . R A S P
```

173

```
R O C K B A N D S . . J A C K
W H A L E B O A T . T O P O L
A D V I S A B L E . S E P I A
N E O N S . R A W T A L E N T
D A R K . R A I S E . T A C .
A R T . L E I . A W E I G H .
. . C O G N O S C E N T E . .
. . B U R I E D A L I V E . .
. . H O R R O R S T O R Y . .
L O O S E N . E T S . C D S .
A P B . A M I S H . T R E E .
M E T A L L I C A . K O A L A
O F U S E . M O U S E O V E R
N O B I S . I N C A R N A T E
T R E S . C O E X I S T E D .
```

174

```
E L A T E . S C I F I . C O L O R
L E T O N . A A R O N . I N A N E
B A T T L E F I E L D . C O S T S
O P I E . R E M . D E L E . H O T
W A R . L A R A M . P U R E . . .
S T E N O S . N E U T R O G E N A
. E L E M . A S H E . O V E R . .
M A R T I . T A T A . R E T I L E
I D E S T . M R B I G . V I L L A
N O M A A M . M A N Y . E S S E S
O R A L . O N E L . P E R T . . .
R E P E A T E D L Y . A L S A C E
. S N O W . S A L T Y . R A D . .
S P F . G R A F . S O U . C A N I
P L A C E . G R O S S P R O F I T
R I V A L . E E R I E . B E A N O
Y E A R S . R E A R S . I N T E R
```

175

A	N	G	S	T			D	E	M	O	B			F	D	A
L	E	A	C	H			E	M	B	A	R	G	O	E	S
K	U	M	A	R			S	T	A	K	E	O	U	T	S
A	R	M	R	E	S	T				L	A	B	R	E	A
L	O	O	S	E	L	I	M	B	E	D			D	R	Y
I	N	N			F	I	N	E	L	Y			C	O	R	E
			S	O	M	A	L	I			M	O	O	E	D
	B	U	L	L	E	T	I	N	B	O	A	R	D
W	I	P	E	D			I	N	D	E	N	T
E	G	A	D			T	O	D	A	T	E			C	B	S
B	B	C			P	E	N	A	L	T	Y	S	H	O	T
F	U	R	M	A	N				L	E	C	T	U	R	E
O	C	E	A	N	S	I	D	E			L	O	R	N	E
O	K	E	Y	D	O	K	E	Y			I	N	N	E	R
T	S	K			A	R	E	A	S			P	E	S	O	S

176

E	A	R	T	H	R	I	S	E			B	A	L	S	A
B	I	O	W	E	A	P	O	N			A	M	A	T	I
B	L	O	O	M	B	E	R	G			S	O	B	E	R
T	E	T			P	A	C	T			R	A	P	T
I	R	O	N			T	A	I	L			G	A	M	M	A
D	O	U	S	E			C	E	R	E	A	L	B	O	X
E	N	T	E	R	S			S	O	L	S			A	M	I
			C	O	M	B			N	A	T	S
O	R	S			T	O	O	L			L	A	H	O	R	E
B	A	T	S	I	G	N	A	L			X	E	N	O	N
L	Y	R	I	C			Y	S	E	R			B	E	A	M
I	G	E	R			S	N	O	W			I	D	A
Q	U	A	R	K			P	O	O	L	R	O	O	M	S
U	N	M	E	T			P	E	R	F	E	C	T	A	S
E	S	S	E	S			G	R	E	E	N	T	A	P	E

177

A	P	P			S	C	I	F	I			J	E	B
T	O	O			R	O	A	M	O	F	F			A	R	R
A	W	L			E	N	D	P	O	S	T			M	E	A
L	E	O	V	I	I	I			T	A	C	T	I	C	S
E	R	T	E			A	L	L	B	Y			W	E	T	S
	P	E	S	T			L	O	A			S	I	L	O
C	A	P	I	T	A	L	L	E	T	T	E	R
	M	U	S	I	C	A	L	N	O	T	E
		C	H	E	S	S	M	O	V	E
D	E	C	A	D	E			A	L	E	R	T	S
N	O	T	I			V	I	S			S	H	A	H
E	G	O			P	R	I	N	C	E	S			A	V	E
G	E	N	E	R	A	L	H	O	S	P	I	T	A	L
R	A	I	S	E	D	L	E	T	T	E	R	I	N	G
O	R	C	A	S			E	R	S			C	E	S	T	A

178

S	O	T	H	A	T	S	I	T			I	B	M	P	C
K	N	E	E	P	A	T	C	H			N	O	O	I	L
A	P	P	L	E	T	R	E	E			F	R	O	Z	E
T	O	I	L	S			A	F	F	L	U	E	N	Z	A
E	T	D			P	I	L	E	O	N			W	A	N
			S	E	A	G	O	D	S			T	A	P	S
	W	H	A	T	T	H	E			Y	A	L	I	E
T	O	O	F	A	S	T			C	L	O	C	K	E	D
A	R	L	E	S			B	O	O	H	I	S	S
X	K	E	S			T	S	E	L	I	O	T
C	H	I			M	U	T	T	O	N			G	M	C
H	O	N	E	Y	B	E	A	R			M	A	R	I	O
E	R	O	D	E			E	M	I	L	E	Z	O	L	A
A	S	N	E	R			L	A	S	T	M	O	V	E	S
T	E	E	N	S			E	X	T	R	O	V	E	R	T

179

J	O	N	E	S	I	N	G			A	I	R	B	U	S
E	M	O	T	I	C	O	N			P	R	O	U	S	T
R	E	D	S	A	U	C	E			E	A	S	T	E	R
K	A	S	E	M			L	I	P			N	I	T	R	E
I	R	A	Q			B	A	S	A	L			E	D	N	A
N	A	T			P	A	S	S	I	O	N			I	A	M
			F	A	Y	S			N	B	A	G	A	M	E
H	E	L	E	N	A			S	C	A	L	E	D
O	P	E	N	E	R	A			A	T	R	Y
W	I	T			D	E	S	I	R	E	E			S	O	R
S	P	E	C			A	S	T	I	R			N	A	P	E
T	H	R	O	E			T	A	Z			M	A	X	E	S
H	A	R	A	S	S			L	O	C	A	V	O	R	E
A	N	I	T	A	S			I	N	D	I	A	N	A	N
T	Y	P	I	S	T			C	A	T	A	L	Y	S	T

180

F	O	S	H	I	Z	Z	L	E			K	N	O	W	S
E	X	C	U	S	E	Y	O	U			E	O	S	I	N
W	A	R	M	O	N	G	E	R			S	U	S	I	E
E	L	I	E			D	O	S			G	E	N	O	M	E
R	I	B			P	A	T	S	D	R	Y			B	O	Z
	C	E	C	E			E	E	R	O			M	U	T	E
		R	R	R			R	E	P	L	A	C	E	D
F	R	A	C	A	S			D	E	I	M	O	S
B	R	E	Z	H	N	E	V			S	T	E
A	I	D	E			C	R	A	N			H	T	T	P
R	E	D			R	I	O	L	O	B	O			A	F	B
S	N	I	P	E	D			E	S	L			T	R	I	O
E	D	W	I	N			D	R	O	I	D	R	A	Z	R
A	L	I	K	E			M	I	A	M	I	A	R	E	A
T	Y	P	E	E			Z	E	P	P	O	M	A	R	X